THE WO

ANWAR AL-SADAT

SERIES EDITOR: Bonnie G. Smith, Rutgers University

THE LIVES OF PEOPLE and the unfolding of earth-shaking events inspire us to love history. We live in a global age where big concepts such as "globalization" often tempt us to forget the "people" side of the past. The titles in *The World in a Life* series aim to revive these meaningful lives. Each one shows us what it felt like to live on a world historical stage and even to shape the world's destiny.

The lives of most individuals are full of activity and color and even passion and violence. The people examined in *The World in a Life* series often faced outsized challenges, but they usually met the great events of their day energetically. They lived amid enormous change, as we often do. Their lives show us how to navigate change and to find solutions. They made fateful decisions, often with much soul searching or—as often—on the spur of the moment and even intuitively. We have much to learn from these fateful past lives.

Their actions, however, were filled with complexity. Biographies in this series give a "nutshell" explanation of how important paradoxes and dilemmas have been in the stories of individuals operating on the world stage. Their lives become windows onto the complicated trends, events, and crises of their time, providing an entry point for a deeper understanding of a particular historical era. As such events and crises unfolded, these historical figures also faced crises in their personal lives. In the intertwined dramas of the personal and political, of the individual and the global, we come to understand the complexities of acting on the world stage and living in world history.

BONNIE G. SMITH

ANWAR AL-SADAT

TRANSFORMING THE MIDDLE EAST

ROBERT L. TIGNOR

New York   Oxford
OXFORD UNIVERSITY PRESS

Oxford University Press is a department of the University of Oxford.
It furthers the University's objective of excellence in research,
scholarship, and education by publishing worldwide.

Oxford   New York
Auckland   Cape Town   Dar es Salaam   Hong Kong   Karachi
Kuala Lumpur   Madrid   Melbourne   Mexico City   Nairobi
New Delhi   Shanghai   Taipei   Toronto

With offices in
Argentina   Austria   Brazil   Chile   Czech Republic   France   Greece
Guatemala   Hungary   Italy   Japan Poland   Portugal   Singapore
South Korea   Switzerland   Thailand   Turkey   Ukraine   Vietnam

For titles covered by Section 112 of the US Higher Education
Opportunity Act, please visit www.oup.com/us/he for the
latest information about pricing and alternate formats.

Published by Oxford University Press
198 Madison Avenue, New York, New York 10016
http://www.oup.com

Oxford is a registered trademark of Oxford University Press

Library of Congress Cataloging-in-Publication Data
Tignor, Robert L.
  Anwar al-Sadat : transforming the Middle East / Robert L. Tignor,
Princeton University, Emeritus.
     pages cm. -- (The World in a Life)
   Includes index.
   ISBN 978-0-19-024898-7 (pbk. : alk. paper) 1. Sadat, Anwar, 1918-1981.
2. Presidents--Egypt--Biography. 3. Egypt--Politics and
government--1970-1981. 4. Egypt--History--1970-1981. I. Title.
   DT107.85.T54 2015
   962.05'4092--dc23
   [B]
                                                          2015008410

Printing number: 9 8 7 6 5 4 3 2 1

Printed in the United States of America
on acid-free paper

CONTENTS

LIST OF ILLUSTRATIONS

LIST OF MAPS

ACKNOWLEDGMENTS

Although I never met Anwar al-Sadat or any other member of his family, I spent so much of my life in Egypt during his presidency that I almost felt that he was my president. My family and I lived in Cairo in 1974, 1975, and 1979, and I was in and out of the country during that decade and the early 1980s innumerable times. I heard all of the wry jokes that Egyptians love to make about their leaders, so Sadat's assassination did not come as a complete shock to me as it did to many Americans. Through my contacts with the Egyptian academic establishment I knew that Sadat had lost their favor, partly because of his peace treaty with Israel and partly because he had failed to deliver on the promise of making Egypt a free and open society. I was also fully aware that the president and his wife did many things to upset the more conservative, religious members of Egyptian society.

This book owes much to many people, who have read and commented on many of my writings on Egypt. I must single out for special thanks three individuals with whom I have conversed over many years. My earliest friends, the dynamic economist pair, Professors Karima Korayem and Gouda Abdel Khalek, I got to know in the 1970s, and they have remained comrades throughout, though we have not always agreed on many topics, including, I am sure, some of my views on President Sadat. The other colleague is Professor Abd al-Aziz Ezz al-Arab, whose dissertation I helped to supervise and who in turn became a powerful academic innovator at the American University of Cairo. Professors L. Carl Brown and Israel Gershoni read and made extensive comments on the chapter dealing with the 1973 war. Professor Gershoni, who was at Princeton's Institute of Advanced Study during the 2011–2012 academic year, shared his vast knowledge of Egyptian politics over the course of that year. Of course, it goes without saying that none of these individuals is responsible for the contents of this study.

Finally, I had an editor who truly outdid herself with sage advice. Not only did Priscilla McGeehon find energetic and obviously highly qualified outsider readers, who had numerous suggestions for ways to improve the manuscript (most of which I incorporated in one form or another), but she made extensive comments from the vantage point of an interested and careful reader. Although the outside reviews were written anonymously, four of these individuals have permitted me to thank them personally here. I am, of course, delighted to do so. They are Professors Laura Bier, Georgia Institute of Technology; John Calvert, Creighton University; E. Thomas Ewing, Virginia Polytechnic Institute; and Eve M. Troutt Powell, University of Pennsylvania. I hope that I have taken advantage of their extraordinary input. Let me also express my thanks to Professor Bonnie Smith for coming up with the idea for this series and putting forward my name as a potential author. Last but far from least are Lynn Luecken and Charles Cavaliere at Oxford University Press, the final resting place for this book. The two of them took up the challenge of bringing this series of biographies to light, and they did so with verve and energy.

ABOUT THE AUTHOR

Robert L. Tignor taught African and world history at Princeton University for forty-six years, was chairperson of the Princeton University History Department for fourteen years, and has published many books on Egypt. He is the Rosengarten Professor Emeritus of Modern and Contemporary History and has received mentoring awards for teaching from Princeton University and the Middle East Studies Association of the United States. He is a member of the African Historical Association, the Middle East Studies Association, and the Association of World Historians. His most recent book, *Egypt: A Short History,* provides one of the most readable and thorough introductions to Egyptian history.

INTRODUCTION

FROM THE MILITARY COUP D'ÉTAT of 1952 until the Arab Spring of 2011, three military men have ruled Egypt. The personality and policies of each were well suited for the roles that they chose to play. The secretive and disciplined plotter, Gamal Abdel Nasser, was the ideal coup planner. He galvanized the movement that toppled the decrepit regime of King Faruq and overthrew a political system dominated by wealthy landlords. In time, as president of Egypt, his policies and charisma gave him world prominence as a champion of Arab causes and an apostle of anticolonialism and neutralism in world affairs. His premature death in 1970 at the age of fifty-two saw his fellow conspirator, Anwar al-Sadat, the subject of this study, assume the mantle of power. Flamboyant, impulsive, and erratic, not expected to hold on to power, Sadat paid lip service to Nasser's legacy but transformed Egypt's place in the Arab world He sacrificed Nasser's pan-Arabism to Egypt's interests, becoming in the process America's chief ally in the Arab world. He ousted the Soviet Union from Egypt and signed a separate peace treaty with Israel. For this and other radical departures from the policies of his predecessor he paid with his life in 1981. His successor, Hosni Mubarak, a military man and methodical bureaucrat, maintained his predecessor's policies but less provocatively. His embrace of the Americans and the peace accord with Israel did not antagonize the other Arab states as Sadat's policies and personality had. Egypt was welcomed back into the community of Arab countries.

Important historical figures, especially those who acquire world renown in the political arena, as Sadat did, invariably provoke controversy. This was palpably true of Sadat, who was lionized in the West and vilified in the East. The Nobel Prize Committee awarded him and his Israeli counterpart, Prime Minister Menachem Begin, their coveted peace prize in 1978 following the Camp David framework for peace between Egypt and Israel. Not surprisingly, the two American political leaders with whom he dealt most closely—Henry Kissinger and Jimmy Carter—were unstinting in their praise of him. Kissinger regarded him as a "great man," who understood the essence of problems and could envision a future different from the present. According to Kissinger, he "was killed by the apostles of the ordinary, the fearful, the merchants of the ritualistic whom he shamed by being at once out of scale and impervious to their meanness of spirit."[1] In Kissinger's estimation, although Sadat was not an accomplished statesman, he had an uncanny knack for understanding the realities of global politics and knowing how to gain the favor of the four American presidents with whom he dealt (Nixon, Ford, Carter, and Reagan). The American president, with whom he worked most closely, Jimmy Carter, wrote that he was "a man who would change history and whom I would come to admire more than any other leader."[2] His funeral in 1981 witnessed the largest turnout of Western political leaders for decades. Three American presidents (Nixon, Ford, and Carter), two French prime ministers (Mitterrand and d'Estaing), a German chancellor (Schmidt), and many other celebrities made the journey to Cairo to pay their respects.

His detractors were as vehement in their criticisms as his proponents were lavish in praise. Not surprisingly, the longtime Soviet foreign minister, Andrei Gromyko, described him as a person "suffering from megalomania" and wrote that while his predecessor, Nasser, had been "a fighter for Egypt's security and for the Arabs' legitimate interests, Sadat demonstrated a truly astounding ability to ignore both factors."[3] David Hirst, an Arab-based journalist for *The Guardian* and an astute observer of the Middle East, whom Sadat banished from Egypt, had little good to say about the Egyptian president. Hirst used the Egyptian colloquial word "fahlawi" to describe Sadat's personality. "Happy go lucky, hail fellow well met, a blusterer who loves his pomp," Sadat did succeed, in Hirst's opinion, in putting his act over on the world.[4] He failed to convince his own people, however. His greatest sin was that for which the world gave him the highest marks—the peace treaty with Israel, which Hirst regarded as a cowardly act that immorally and selfishly sacrificed the cause of Palestinian Arabs to Egyptian interests.

In Egypt, though the criticism was less biting, a book published by the Egyptian journalist and important political figure Mohamed Heikal only two years after Sadat's death was savage and unsparing in its portrait of the man. Heikal, too, accused Sadat of selling out his country. In *Autumn of Fury: The Assassination of Sadat*, Heikal's longest and angriest chapter bears the title "organized loot." The man who had been Nasser's closest confidant and then had been instrumental in promoting Sadat as Nasser's successor went on to assert: "Not since the days of [nineteenth-century ruler] Khedive Ismail had Egypt been the scene of looting on such a massive and organized scale as it was during the last years of President Sadat."[5] Most of the Arab leadership shared Heikal's dislike of Sadat's policies and complained that Sadat had sacrificed his country's dignity in a quest for American approval. The only Arab statesman to join with the Western dignitaries at Sadat's funeral was Gaafar al-Nimeiry, president of Sudan, grateful for Egypt's support in keeping him in power. Nor did the Egyptians display the kind of emotion that they showered on Gamal Abdel Nasser at the time of his funeral in 1970 when scenes of wailing and grieving for a fallen hero filled the streets of Cairo and the other cities of Egypt. In contrast, those who witnessed the journey of Sadat's casket to its burial site opposite the grandstand where the president had been gunned down maintained a sullen silence.

Until the revolution of 2011 the underground stations of Cairo's relatively new metro system have borne the names of Egypt's most powerful native-born political leaders—Urabi, Zaghlul, Nasser,

Sadat, and Mubarak. The ousting of President Mubarak in February 2011 resulted in the removal of his name from a station. It is inconceivable that the names of Urabi, Zaghlul, and Nasser will disappear, for they are iconic figures of Egyptian nationalism. But will Sadat's name survive the Arab Spring? There will surely be those who demand its removal.

It is hard to imagine how the man who inherited the mantle of power in Egypt following the death of Nasser in 1970 could make such a decisive mark on Middle Eastern and world history as Sadat did. His education was modest, consisting of a mere nine months of military training beyond secondary schooling. He had no demonstrated administrative skills before he became president. Although he was an early advocate of a young officers movement to transform Egyptian society, his four years of imprisonment during and just after World War II forced him to the sidelines at a time when the Free Officers movement was gaining momentum and Nasser was assuming leadership. He was nearly absent during the coup of July 23, 1952, and after the coup, he was relegated to subordinate roles in the government of Egypt. Nasser's selection of him as his vice president in 1969, just one year before his death, came as a surprise to most. Few expected Sadat to last as Egypt's president. But he defied these odds and then went on to stun the world by carrying out the October War of 1973 against Israel and followed this development by signing a peace treaty with Israel in 1979. These are the focuses of this book.

Sadat's impact on Egypt, the region, and global politics was transformative. As president, he opened Egypt's state-dominated economy to foreign investment. He excited the populace about Egypt's future by proclaiming that free societies were more dynamic and creative than repressive regimes and that democracy was the wave of the future. His treaty with Israel brought peace to the country. Yet his efforts to implement these policies were inconsistent and deeply flawed. He backed off early efforts to promote free elections, and when a plethora of new political parties appeared, many in opposition to his policies, he severely curtailed

the number and autonomy of political parties. He tolerated corruption and funneled foreign aid to the military even after promising that his treaty with Israel would yield a peace dividend and
improve the standards of living of the people. When complaints
about his policies reached a groundswell following his peace
treaty with Israel, he announced that the country was not yet ready
for full-bore, Western democracy. Although his ambition, on display in his finest moments when he was not being challenged by
critics at home and abroad, was to fashion a peaceful, politically
stable, and democratic Middle East, he failed to convince his
countrymen and women that he could achieve these goals or was
truly committed to them.

While the October War and the peace treaty with Israel catapulted Sadat to world prominence, they could not have occurred
except for the unique place that Egypt has consistently occupied
in international affairs and global politics. Greatness is sometimes
thrust upon individuals not well prepared for this role by the exalted positions that they come to occupy and by the geopolitical
importance of the territory over which they rule. This was surely
the case with Anwar al-Sadat, who became the leader of one of the
most strategically placed territories in global politics at a time of
heightened international tensions.

Egypt has enjoyed geopolitical significance from the time of
the pharaohs right down to the present. At first, the territory was
a regional imperial center, notably during the New Kingdom era
(1550–1069 BCE) when pharaohs like Ramses II dominated the
Nile valley and the Fertile Crescent and were themselves ruthless
colonizers. But other aspirants to world empire did not lose sight
of Egypt's geopolitical significance, the territorial lynchpin link-
ing the African continent to Asia. First came the Greeks under
Alexander the Great, who were followed by the Romans. Arab-
Muslim warriors burst out of the Arabian Peninsula in the seventh
century CE, carrying the message of the Prophet Muhammad and
were in occupation of Egypt a mere nine years after Muhammad's
death. If we leap forward to modern times, in 1798 a young French

general, Napoleon Bonaparte, envisioned making Egypt an important French colonial possession, which would rival British India and would jeopardize Britain's connections with the Orient. Once the Suez Canal had been constructed and opened to traffic in 1869, the British, as the dominant commercial and imperial power of the late nineteenth century, could not draw back from seizing control of this vital possession. Although their statesmen promised a speedy withdrawal after invading the country in 1882, their forces did not leave the country for three-quarters of a century (1882–1956) and tried unsuccessfully to return militarily a mere four months after their last soldiers had departed.

In short, empire builders, even in the age of nationalism and decolonization that have dominated the world scene since the end of World War II, have endeavored to control Egypt's foreign policies and to influence its ruling elites. The Americans sought to replace the British as the predominant actor in the Middle East, seeking to draw the Egyptians into an anti-Soviet political alliance. Similarly, the Soviets, even when they realized that Egypt's ruling elites were determined to reject their Communist ideology, were eager to align Egypt with Soviet foreign policies. They found an ally in Sadat's predecessor, Gamal Abdel Nasser, who failed in his effort to pursue a policy of neutralism in the cold war era and allowed Egypt to slip into the Soviet orbit.

The Egypt into which Sadat was born on December 25, 1918, had been under foreign domination for more than 2,000 years. In the twentieth century, the age of nationalism, Egyptians had become even more frustrated at their political subordination and had launched a powerful movement in favor of political independence. The country's latest occupiers, the British had imposed even heavier burdens on the people than imperial powers usually do, the consequences of their needs during World War I and then again during World War II. Although the British promised the Egyptians in 1914 that they would be spared the travails of this global conflict, the people and the country were not. A large British army, numbering close to 100,000 men, decamped in the country in order to defend it from a Turkish assault across Sinai. As all large armies bivouacked on foreign populations do, the British forces extracted substantial financial, social, and economic resources from the country. The most reviled of the British military extractions were the large-scale levees of animals and manpower taken from villagers for military campaigns carried out against Ottoman forces based in Palestine and Syria. The loss of lives was enormous, and the resentments deep. After the war, when the British refused the demands of Egypt's leading nationalist spokesman, Saad Zaghlul, to present the country's petition for political independence to the Versailles peace conference, the country erupted in rebellion. Although Sadat was only an infant during this uprising, which lasted for three full years (1919–1922), during which Britain lost control over many parts of the country, this anticolonial and nationalist rebellion became for him as for most Egyptians of his generation, a foundational event—the coming to full flowering of a long simmering anticolonial desire to end foreign domination and to restore Egyptian rule to its own people.

Zaghlul and his new nationalist political party (the Wafd) argued at the time of the Versailles peace conference that their country was as deserving of nationhood as any of the new eastern and central European nation-states that were coming into being at that time. Egyptian nationalists were quick to point out that Egypt possessed all of the prerequisites of a nation-state. The country had natural borders, a national language (Arabic), a dominant religion (Islam), and a well-defined sense of national identity—an Egyptianness—forged over countless millennia.

Egypt's British critics countered these claims by arguing that for centuries foreigners, at first the Turks and from the late nineteenth century onward Europeans, had ruled the country and were the only effective guarantors of political stability and economic progress. Lord Cromer, who was Britain's Consul-General in Egypt and virtual ruler of the country from 1883 until 1907, was the chief proponent of this claim. He asserted it with vigor in his widely read, two-volume study of the country, entitled *Modern Egypt*, published in 1908. In it he depicted Egypt as a mélange of nationalities, religions, and regions, held together only by benevolent British overlords. Nor was Cromer's patently self-serving view wholly wrong, for, in reality, Egypt's economy was dominated by foreign investment and foreign business leaders; its polity by British officials, and its high society by European tastes and sensibilities. Even Egyptian nationalists understood these realities but attributed Egypt's subordination to the presence of a large British army of occupation and the unwillingness of British officials to cede authority to well-deserving and well-educated Egyptian elites. In underscoring Egypt's backwardness and need for British tutelage, British officials noted the country's educational deficiencies, its mono-export, cotton-based agricultural economy, and a population that was exploding beyond the limited territorial space and resources of the country—without, however, recognizing how their own policies had contributed to these drawbacks.

By 1918, when Sadat was born, disparities in the country's income and wealth were shocking and prospects for economic progress dismaying. Although the country had experienced significant economic progress during the nineteenth century, the prospects of further growth, based on additional Nile hydraulic reforms and an expanding cotton cultivation, were unsatisfactory. Egypt had seen its cultivable land expand rapidly throughout the nineteenth century and had used a lucrative, high-quality, long-staple cotton export crop to fill state coffers and line the pockets of rich landlords and foreign investors. But by the end of the century, even the most optimistic projections for increasing the area of cultivable lands would not enable the country to keep pace with its expanding population. The only way forward was through economic diversification and industrialization. Whether Egypt was likely to become an industrial powerhouse in the Middle East was dubious, however, given the opposition that British officials had already demonstrated to industrial initiatives and the heavy concentration of wealth and technical expertise in agriculture.

According to the census of 1917, the total Egyptian population was 12,718,255, of whom 91 percent were Muslims and 7 percent Coptic Christians. Although, then, the foreign populations residing in Egypt numbered less than 200,000, constituting a mere 1.5 percent of the total, their wealth and power were so substantial that many Egyptians complained that they lived as second-class citizens in their own country. Foreign capital dominated the joint-stock companies, most of which had been established to provide financing for Egypt's foreign trade and loans to its mostly native-born large landowners and foreign-born merchants. At the outbreak of World War I foreigners owned over 90 percent of the shares of joint-stock companies operating in Egypt. Perhaps the company that best represented the overwhelming influence of foreign business firms over the country's affairs was the Suez Canal Company. Although chartered as an Egyptian joint-stock company in 1854, virtually all of its increasingly lucrative shares, which made it the most heavily capitalized joint-stock company functioning in Egypt at a valuation of £33 million in 1919, were in foreign hands. The largest individual shareholder was, ironically, the British government, which had adamantly opposed the digging of the canal and had counseled British investors against purchasing shares when they were first being sold. But in 1875, as Egypt descended into bankruptcy, Khedive Ismail (r. 1863–1879) approached the British government with an offer to sell the Egyptian government's shares of the company, and the British Prime Minister, Benjamin Disraeli, leaped at the opportunity to purchase what amounted to a 44 percent interest of the company's holdings at a price of L4 million.

The one arena in which Egyptians predominated was land-holding, and it was here that income and wealth disparities were the most pronounced, visible, and resented. Muhammad Ali, who ruled Egypt from 1805 until his death in 1849, brought most of Egyptian landholdings under the control of the state. Later in his reign he began a trend of doling out estates to powerful and wealthy supporters, a practice that his family's successors as rulers of Egypt and the British after conquering the country in 1882 continued. By 1920, 41 percent of the approximately 5.5 million acres of cultivable land was owned by families possessing 50 acres or more. Most of the large estates were in the hands of a small number of well-connected families. The largest estate owners, not surprisingly, were members of the royal family, who owned no less than 180,000 acres before the military came to power in 1952 and enacted its land reform legislation. Although a 50-acre estate was capable of generating a handsome income, the vast majority of Egypt's population was small landowners, holding less than 5 acres, or landless peasants forced to eke out a desperate existence.

CHAPTER 1

MAKING A REVOLUTION, 1918–1952

ALTHOUGH ANWAR AL-SADAT LIVED for only six years in the village of Mit Abul-Kum in the province of Minufiyya in the Egyptian delta, the experience gave him an unshakeable identity. He believed that growing up in this village and coming from peasant stock equipped him to deal with the many deprivations that he faced in later life. His long years in prison and his relatively minor political status during the Nasser years challenged him but did not undermine his belief that the future held out the promise of greatness. In his memoirs, *In Search of Identity*, he describes the childhood routines that gave him the greatest pleasure and connected him with the soil and his community: sowing seed, irrigating the family's two-and-a-half acre farmstead, harvesting cotton, taking the cattle to the canal for water, and looking after the oxen-drawn threshing machine. As a son of the Egyptian countryside, he returned over and over again to Mit Abul-Kum even while he was president, drawing sustenance from the people and his rural roots.

Individuals who transform history need inspiration in their early years. For the first six years of his life Sadat drew this sustenance from his grandmother. His father's absence in Sudan, where he served as a clerk with a British medical mission, left his mother, but especially his grandmother, with the task of rearing the youngster. The latter, a woman of wisdom and passion, did much more. She stoked his imagination with tales of heroism and derring-do and caused him to believe that fate would bring him fame and power. Many evenings, as he lay on top of the simple oven in the family's one-room, mud-walled homestead drifting off to sleep, he delighted in his grandmother's stories. Her heroes were men who defied colonial authority and fought for the people. They included Egypt's mightiest nationalists: Mustafa Kamel, who challenged the British before World War I, and Saad Zaghlul, at the center of Egypt's 1919 rebellion against the British. Yet the individuals who most inspired him were people of lesser historical reputation, men who came from the same peasant stock as he. He never tired of the ballad of Adham al-Sharqawi, a rural brigand and Robin Hood, who made life difficult for the British and their Egyptian collaborators. The rebel he admired even more and whose name he repeated over and over again as a youngster and even later in life was the peasant, Zahran, from the neighboring village of Dinshaway.

The Dinshaway tale is one well known in Egyptian history. It revolves around a contingent of British soldiers who were marching through Lower Egypt on their way to Alexandria in 1906, a time when Egypt was fully under the occupation of British forces. While camped near Tanta, a group of soldiers went on a hunting expedition near the village of Dinshaway, a popular pastime with the British, but much resented by the villagers, who raised the pigeons, often the target of the huntsmen. Zahran and other peasants resisted the soldiers in a clash that resulted in the death of a British soldier. Condemned to death, Zahran went to the gallows with head held high, proud that he had defended the honor of the village and thwarted the British, or so the story told by his grandmother had it. Sadat heard these stories over and over again. Although the details never varied, he loved them all the more for their familiarity. They instilled in him a powerful message: oppression must be resisted. Through them he came to view the British as "aliens to us . . . evil because they poisoned people."[1]

Sadat left Mit Abul-Kum when his father returned from Sudan following the assassination of the British Governor-General of Sudan in 1924 by Egyptian nationalists. The British used the event to solidify their control over Sudan and to clip the wings of Egypt's nationalist leader, Saad Zaghlul, and his Wafdist party. In addition to forcing Zaghlul to step down as prime minister in the Egyptian parliament, they expelled Egyptian officials working in Sudan.

By the time Sadat left Mit Abul-Kum at age six, he had already gained a modicum of education. His grandmother, though illiterate, wanted him to have the same educational opportunities that she had obtained for his father, a primary school education leading to the general certificate for primary education. First, however, perhaps because she valued religious training and was a devout Muslim, she sent him off to the local Quranic school, where he learned to read and write and memorized the Quran. She then enrolled him in a nearby Coptic school, apparently believing that it would better prepare him to advance to a government primary school.

In Cairo, Sadat completed primary schooling, obtained the general certificate for primary education, and moved on to the Fuad I Secondary School. Attended mainly by the sons of well-to-do families, Fuad I proved a financial stretch as well as a social challenge for Anwar and the family. For Sadat's father, responsible for the upbringing of thirteen children, school fees were a heavy burden. Sadat writes that he was never jealous of his wealthier classmates who came to school in chauffeur-driven automobiles and had many suits to his one. Although he made light of these youthful challenges, they were severe. His father had taken a third wife, who bore nine children, all crowded into a four-room flat in a poor Cairo neighborhood. His early confidant and later savage critic, Mohamed Heikal, claimed that Sadat's upbringing left him with deep scars and unresolved bitterness, asserting that Sadat was "the neglected second son of an inferior family watching every day the humiliation of a mother despised for her [Sudanese] color."[2]

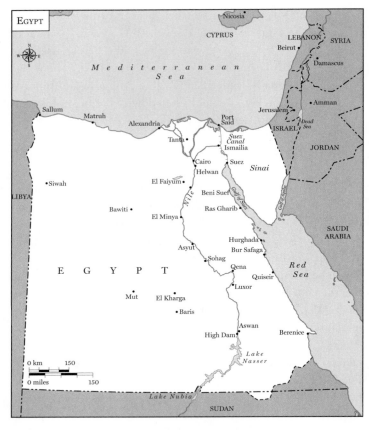

MAP 1. CONTEMPORARY EGYPT

In light of Heikal's and others' account of his upbringing, it is difficult to know how much credence to attach to Sadat's assertion that he was not like so many of the young officers who seized power in 1952—an angry poor boy. Yet, among the young officers who ruled Egypt, he was to gain little pleasure from lording it over the wealthy classes or bringing powerful individuals down. In contrast, future president Gamal Abdel Nasser had a burning resentment of Egypt's upper classes and enjoyed exacting revenge against those whom he regarded as having scorned him and his ilk and exploited the Egyptian poor. Later on, Sadat, also in contrast to Nasser, came to enjoy the trappings of wealth and moved easily among the rich, successful, and powerful.

Sadat experienced difficulties in advancing to the next stage on the educational ladder, acquiring the much coveted general certificate of secondary education. He had to attend three different schools before succeeding. In his memoirs, he attributes his difficulties to negligence and overconfidence, but it would not be out of the question to wonder if the family's financial limitations and his own penchant for attending nationalist rallies did not affect his classroom performance. He did, however, succeed in gaining the certificate, which opened the door to further training, but here, unlike many young men of his age, he elected to enter Egypt's Military Academy. Just why he chose the army as his career he does not make clear in his various writings. He does mention that his childhood tales caused him to idolize military men like Ahmad Urabi, the Egyptian army officer who had led a rebellion against the Egyptian Khedive; Mustafa Kemal Atatürk, the Young Turk officer who built modern Turkey; and, for that matter, Napoleon Bonaparte, who despite being the invader of Egypt was seen by many Egyptians as a military man who changed history.

Egypt's Military Academy was at the time that Sadat and other young Egyptians entered it undergoing fundamental changes. Historically, the Egyptian army itself had experienced many transformations. Under Muhammad Ali, who ruled Egypt in the first half of the nineteenth century, it had been a powerful, modernizing institution that had promoted the ruler's territorial ambitions. Defeated by British invading forces in 1882 and its leaders sent into exile, the British nonetheless turned the armed forces into an instrument of British overrule. Commanded by British officers, the Egyptian army facilitated the conquest of Sudan in 1898 and the creation of the Anglo-Egyptian Sudanese state. Because it was meant to buttress British authority, Egypt's colonial rulers tried to ensure that its higher ranks were filled with Egyptians drawn from upper classes and supportive of their policies. To this end, entrance into the Military Academy was limited to individuals who came from propertied families and who were able to obtain recommendations from persons of stature, connected to the Egyptian ruling elite.

In the late 1930s, as the storm clouds of World War II grew more ominous, the Egyptian political elite decided to enlarge the army and to open the officer corps to individuals less tied to the ruling class. Property and income qualifications were lowered so that individuals like Sadat, whose father was only a senior clerk in the Egyptian department of health, and Nasser, whose father was an officer in the post office, met those requirements. The reference qualification still existed, and Sadat used a connection that his father had with the head of the admissions committee to obtain an important endorsement. His father also coaxed the chief medical officer of the Egyptian army, under whom he had worked, to recommend his son. Sadat admits that his references were "the least impressive (at the time such 'references' ranged from the Crown Prince Muhammad Ali to highly influential pashas and beys)" and that his name "was at the bottom of the list" of the fifty-two men admitted.[3] In 1937 Sadat joined a group of young recruits, including Nasser, many of whom would form the inner corps of the Free Officers movement that engineered the July 23, 1952, seizure of power.

Under pressure to expand the officer corps rapidly, the academy placed these young men on an accelerated course of study. Many, like Sadat and Nasser, completed their formal training in less than a year and were rapidly commissioned as second lieutenants. Sadat and Nasser were known as good students. They were thought to have bright futures and were expected to move up the officer ranks quickly. Sadat, as we will see, spoiled his advancement opportunities because of his nationalist zeal and repeated challenges to the British during World War II, which included

Sadat as a young cadet.

conspiring with the Axis military forces as they advanced on Egypt. Nasser, far more cautious and secretive, did not run afoul of the authorities. Moreover, Nasser's abilities as an officer stood out, and he entered the Military Staff College for further military training during World War II and then served as an instructor at the Military Academy after the war. These experiences provided Nasser with a level of general education and military professionalism that Sadat failed to obtain.

In 1938 several of the recent graduates of the Military Academy found themselves posted to a small town in Upper Egypt, Manqabad, near the city of Asyut. They trained hard during the day and then met to talk about their lives and the politics of the country in the evenings. Because Sadat had been given the largest room, previously the officers' mess but made available to him because of a shortage of rooms, they often congregated in his room for their conversations. Within a year Nasser joined them. The Manqabad gatherings were pivotal for these young men; they discussed the turmoil that was confronting Egypt and the role that they and the army should play in the country's future.

The main accounts of Manqabad come from Sadat's own writings and are in some ways confusing and contradictory. In the accounts written before Nasser's death, Sadat portrays Nasser as the most forceful of the participants, constantly bringing the group back to "grave topics" and arguing that the country's backwardness and stagnation was the direct consequence of Britain's oppression of Egypt.[4] In his later memoirs, however, written after Nasser's death and at a time when Sadat was challenging many of Nasser's policies and attempting to present himself to Egyptians and a world audience as a worthy successor, Sadat presented a different Nasser. He described him as a quiet person who "listened to our conversations with interest but rarely opened his mouth. . . . He kept to himself so conspicuously, in fact, that our relationship at the time never went beyond mutual respect and even that was still from a distance."[5] In these later reckonings, Sadat asserts that he dominated the discussions and brought them back to the most serious matter, notably how Egypt was to be delivered from its present predicament.

The truth about the roles of Nasser and Sadat probably lies somewhere in between. No doubt, Sadat facilitated the conversations before Nasser arrived and may well have focused them on politics. He claims that the discussions eventually became so politicized that his room was nicknamed "The National Assembly." Nasser's appearance changed the dynamics. There can be little doubt of Nasser's seriousness of purpose and his ability through the force of his personality to command attention. Manqabad may well have been the first moment in a long route toward the formation of the Free Officers movement, but it was no more than a first step. Sadat's contention that the Free Officers actually came into existence at this time and that he was its founding figure is surely wrong.

The 1930s was a tempestuous time in the Egyptian polity. The enthusiasm that the 1919 uprising and the emergence of a charismatic political leader, Saad Zaghlul, and a populist nationalist party demanding independence, the Wafd, had dissipated. Zaghlul died in 1927, leaving his political legacy to a less dynamic political leader, Mustafa al-Nahhas, who headed up the country's major Egyptian party, the Wafd, and became prime minister on many occasions. But the British repeatedly intervened in the Egyptian political arena, using their influence with the Egyptian monarch to undermine the Wafd and to promote the power and agenda of conservative, pro-British politicians. Increasingly, as Egypt's parliament failed to achieve the nationalist aspirations of the people, left-wing and right-wing political groups emerged, criticizing Egypt's democracy as a sham and embracing violence and more autocratic forms of government. The antiparliamentary and state-run programs of Fascist Italy and Germany and Stalinist Russia seemed to offer many Egyptians, especially the young officers, impatient with Egypt's continuing colonial subjugation, hope for the future. The discussions that Sadat and his fellow officers had, for which, unfortunately, we have no record, must have revolved around the virtues and defects of parliamentary governance, the diminished appeal of the Wafd as a champion of Egyptian nationalism, the attractions of fascism, as articulated by the Young Egypt movement founded in 1933 by Ahmad Husayn, and the appeals of Soviet communism.

Far from the least of the extra-parliamentary groups whose messages appealed to the young officers was the Muslim Brotherhood, founded by Hassan al-Banna in 1928. Banna's organization was destined to play a powerful role in Egyptian politics from that moment onward. The attractions that Hassan al-Banna had to Egyptians and Muslims throughout the Arab world, including the young Egyptian officers, were immediate and dynamic, stemming in large measure from a shared upbringing, education, and sense of marginalization in colonized societies.

Educated at Dar al-Ulum, a teacher training school founded in Cairo in 1871 for the purpose of blending modern science and Islam, Banna took up his duties as a teacher of Arabic in a primary school in the canal city of Ismailia in 1927—a city dominated by the powerful foreign-run and foreign-financed Suez Canal Company, which to many Egyptians symbolized the exploitative nature of European capitalism. It is hardly surprising that in this environment and only one year after Banna began to teach he established the first branch of the Muslim Brotherhood, which grew by leaps and bounds, and he boasted that it had half a million Egyptian adherents by the end of World War II. Regarding himself as an heir to an Islamic reformist and nationalist tradition that dated back to Jamal al-Din al-Afghani, Muhammad Abduh, and Rashid Rida, Banna believed that the only way forward for Egypt was to return to the teachings of the Prophet Muhammad and the ideals of early Muslim leaders. Deeply influenced by the Muslim journal, *al-Manar*, which Rashid Rida edited and which helped to spread the radical Salafi movement across the entire Muslim world, he sought to make his own journal, *al-Shibab*, a worthy successor to *al-Manar*, and he supported the work of Muhibb al-Din al-Khatib, proprietor of the Salafiya book shop and editor of the newspaper *al-Fath*, in circulating the ideals of the Brotherhood.

In Banna's view, what distinguished early Islam from its later, less successful incarnations was the piety and learning of its original leaders and their commitment to the spirit and law of Islam. In contrast to later rulers—the Umayyads (661–750), the Abbasids (750–1258) and their many successor regimes, who, he claimed, introduced the false principle of kingship and ruled in order to enrich themselves—Muhammad and the first four "rightly guided" Caliphs placed their talents at the disposal of the people and attended to the needs of the community of believers. Even more destructive developments were to occur with the arrival of European imperialists and the seductions that European capitalism and imperial rule let loose in Muslim lands. By the twentieth century not only had Muslims lost their political independence and become subordinate to non-Muslim, mainly Christian rulers, but they had also found their faith under assault both from Christian missionaries, who preached the superiority of their faith and attempted to make conversions, and from a strong Western secularist and rationalist discourse that attacked all religions.

For Banna, the Brothers, and many others, who heard the message but did not become outright members, the solution to the colonial subjugation of Muslim lands was a return to this original, pure form of Islam. Muslims need not look to imported ideologies, not because they were utterly false, but because Islam itself contained the best features of the major world ideologies. Islam had enunciated freedom, equality, and brotherhood, the watchwords of the French Revolution, and the social equality of the Russian Revolution well before these revolutions took place. It did so, however, without sacrificing a belief in God.

As for Egypt itself, Banna's critique focused on the gross maldistribution of wealth, especially land holdings, and the power of foreign capital. He preached social justice and national unity, urged opposition to the activities of Christian missionaries, and alerted his followers to the designs of the Zionist movement on

Palestine. His message had enormous salience to individuals in their twenties, mainly young men, who like many of the young officers had been reared in village communities and had used their schooling to pursue careers in Egypt's rapidly expanding cities.

At first, Hassan al-Banna stressed the welfare functions of the Brotherhood, urging members to become deeply involved in education, public health, and care for the less fortunate. In addition to building mosques, Banna's organization constructed hospitals and opened health clinics. In the late 1930s, in an effort to expand the membership of the Society and make it a more effective vehicle in local communities, the Society organized its members into "battalions" of workers, students, and civil servants. Later when this system was judged to have failed, family units of five to ten members, headed by a chief, emerged. These groups stressed strong religious training, propagandizing, and service functions. They worked to improve the sanitary knowledge of the adherents and the conditions of public health. But they had another function that marked the emergence of the Brotherhood into the political area. A separate body, known as the special apparatus, became the militant wing of the Society. Founded in 1940, this para-military unit opposed Zionism in Palestine and British power in Egypt and enhanced the move of the Brotherhood into nationalist politics. The Society's ultimate goal was not merely to expel the British from Egypt and oppose the creation of a Zionist state in Palestine but also to establish Islamic communities throughout the Muslim world, governed by the tenets of Islamic law, the sharia. Although the Brotherhood's family cells and its secret apparatus engaged in acts of violence before the outbreak of World War II, it was after the war, during a period when nationalist fervor and anti-British protests were at a fever pitch, that the group became caught up in political demonstrations and political assassinations.

Because neither Sadat nor Nasser wished to while away their days in a remote part of Upper Egypt far removed from the center of political activity in Cairo, they both put in for a special two-and-a-half-month training course run by the Signal Corps of the Egyptian army in the Cairo suburb of Maadi. Both were accepted and were excited to return to the capital. For Nasser, whom superior officers had already identified as a man who might make trouble for them, that stay was temporary. He was posted to Sudan following his course in signaling so as to remove him from the political center. Sadat, however, stayed on and soon found himself in touch with two individuals who had a profound radicalizing influence on him and other young officers. These two individuals represented the violent and autocratic alternatives to Egypt's crippled parliamentary regime that was gaining many adherents in the 1930s.

The first of these individuals was Hassan al-Banna, whom Sadat met in 1940. At the urging of some of his military colleagues, Sadat asked Banna, by then the Supreme Guide of the Muslim Brotherhood organization, to speak to his unit. Expecting Banna to confine his remarks to religious matters, Sadat was surprised when Banna "spoke of worldly as well as 'other worldly' matters, using a style quite uncommon among religious preachers."[6] Sadat's surprise changed to admiration as his relationship with Banna and the Brothers deepened. He attended Banna's weekly sermons delivered every Tuesday and spoke privately with him in his office after the sermons. The organizing skills of the Brotherhood impressed him and made him realize that the Brothers were a force to be reckoned with politically. He let Banna know that there were many young men in the army who shared the Brotherhoods' religious sentiments and radical political ambitions and were prepared to work with the Brotherhood to transform Egypt.

Banna introduced Sadat to the second mentor in his early life, a man whom Sadat had wanted to engage with ever since he had encountered him at Manqabad in 1938, the retired Egyptian military Chief of Staff Aziz al-Masri. Masri had an exalted reputation among the young officers, having served with the Ottoman army before World War I, participated in the Arab revolt during

HASSAN AL-BANNA, FOUNDER OF THE MUSLIM BROTHERHOOD, BORN IN 1906 AND ASSASSINATED IN 1949. *He was close to many of the Free Officers, including Sadat, before they seized power.*

World War I, and then became chief of staff of the Egyptian army during the interwar years. He had been forced to retire from the military because of his anti-British and pro-German sympathies. Masri took Sadat and other young officers under his wing, encouraging them to see themselves and the army as the vanguard of a reformed Egypt.

The outbreak of World War II brought Italian and German armies close to Egypt and led several members of the Egyptian army, including Sadat, to see an opportunity to expel the British from the country and claim Egypt's complete political independence. Masri shared this view, and working with Sadat, he offered to provide information on British military plans and the names of important Egyptian political figures prepared to work with the Germans as their forces under the command of General Erwin Rommel advanced from Libya into Egypt. His effort to escape from Egypt and join Rommel's forces in Libya failed, however, and Masri was court-martialed and jailed. Sadat continued his plotting against the British, often in unconcealed ways that eventually exposed him to British intelligence. In 1942 he was arrested for working with German agents in Cairo, having in his possession a radio transmitter to communicate with Rommel's forces. He was sentenced to a two-year stint in jail.

Working with fellow officers, conspiring with Aziz al-Masri and Hassan al-Banna, and steeping himself in Egyptian politics did not, however, prevent Sadat from making important decisions in his personal life. In 1940, two years before he entered prison, at the age of twenty-two, he married a woman from his village of Mit Abul-Kum, Ekbal Madi, daughter of the village Umdah or mayor. By then, Sadat had already graduated from the Military Academy and must have seemed to local villagers a dashing young soldier. Nonetheless, not every member of the Madi household approved of the marriage. Ekbal's brothers did not approve, believing Sadat was far beneath the Madi family in prestige and life chances. Not only did Ekbal's father possess a large house and significant landholdings but as a minor government official he enjoyed the title of bey, an Ottoman honorific meaning chieftain. The brothers wondered what Sadat had to offer other than a fancy-looking military uniform and questioned the long-term security of a military career. Only the mother favored the marriage, inquiring of the daughter whether she liked Sadat, and when she learned that Ekbal did, she said that she did, too.

If we are to credit Sadat's later memoirs, his marriage was little more than a traditional, family-arranged alliance. He describes it as a necessity in rural life, "part of, if not the crowning of, the process of growing up. It was, in short, inevitable."[7] It was a decision that he would come to regret as he moved up in the world of politics and acquired national exposure. Before he finally divorced his wife in 1949, he had four children, three of whom survived, all daughters, whom, as we shall see, he treated more shabbily than he did his wife.

Sadat's prison sentence came to an end in 1944. He did not, however, remain a free man for long but returned to prison in 1946, implicated in the assassination of Amin Uthman, a well-known and much reviled Egyptian politician and minister who had declared that the British–Egyptian relationship was much like a traditional Catholic marriage. It could only be dissolved through death, no matter how disliked. His second imprisonment, described in a separate chapter in his memoirs, was an altogether different experience from his first two years in prison. During the first sentence, much of which he served in the Aliens Jail in Cairo, he was able to read and write and have regular visitors. In fact, security was so lax in one of the facilities where he was held that he was able to escape in 1944, approximately a year before the abolition of martial law in Egypt resulted in his full pardon.

The second imprisonment was in the Cairo Central Prison and demanded all of his survival skills. Locked in a small cell, without lighting, deprived of reading and outside contact, he had only his own thoughts to fall back on. His food consisted of a simple meal of *ful*, made of fava beans. The cell was without a chair or a table and included two buckets, one for drinking water and the other for use as a toilet. Not until a year had passed did the prison authorities supply the inmates with spoons at mealtimes and affix glass panes over the cell windows to keep the cold out in winter and the heat out in summer. The prison had a "scabies ward" since the prison's unhygienic conditions caused this condition to become widespread.

In cell 54 Sadat fixated on his marriage, finally realizing that his wife was not cut out for the life that he envisioned for himself.

His thoughts were so intense and painful that the veins in his head throbbed. He came to the conclusion that he must end his relationship with Ekbal. He asserts in his memoirs that he broke off this relationship, forbidding Ekbal from visiting him during the last nine months of his prison sentence. Like several other claims in his memoirs, this one cannot be true because one of his daughters was conceived during this period. His third daughter, Camelia, was born in 1949, well after he had left prison and several months after his marriage to Jihan.

In 1948 the state finally brought Sadat and his fellow conspirators to trial for the assassination of Amin Uthman. The hearings were closely watched and extravagantly covered in the press, and when Sadat was found not guilty, many, not just those who approved of political violence, welcomed the verdict. Sadat left prison a famous man, exalted for his courage in having rid Egypt of its most infamous pro-British politician.

Nationalistic and anti-British sentiments roiled the political environment that Sadat returned to when he left prison even more intensely than had been the case during the Egyptian uprising of 1919. During World War II Egypt had again served as a major military base as the British massed their forces to turn back Rommel's army at el-Alamein in the western desert in 1942. Whereas Egypt's polity had been marked by youth gangs and political violence during the 1930s, in the immediate aftermath of World War II, political assassinations and attempts on the lives of prominent leaders became the order of the day. The Muslim Brotherhood, with its secret cells and appetite for using violence against those who opposed its wishes, led the way. When Egypt's demands for full independence were not realized, political leaders deemed inadequately committed to the nationalist cause were earmarked as traitors and targets for assassination. The powerful prime minister, Mahmud al-Nuqrashi, who had sent Egypt into its disastrous 1948 war with the Zionists over Palestine, met his death through an assassin's bullet that same year. His executioners, members of the Muslim Brotherhood, were next in line;

an assassin gunned down their much revered Supreme Guide, Hassan al-Banna, who had never renounced violence. Not surprisingly, given the glorification of violence at the time, Sadat was accorded a hero's welcome when he emerged from prison.

One of those who admired the headstrong firebrand was a young, beautiful woman, born into a highly cultivated upper middle-class Egyptian household. The opportunity to meet Sadat at her family's vacation residence in Suez City thrilled Jihan Raouf. Arranged by Hassan Izzat, a fellow young officer and relative of the Raouf family, who, like Sadat, had been cashiered for his contacts with the German military forces during World War II and expelled from the army, the meeting was to transform the lives of Sadat and Jihan Raouf. Jihan fell hopelessly in love, and though she was only fifteen years of age when they first met, she wanted nothing more than to marry Sadat. The family was at first opposed, considering Sadat a risky marriage partner because he was without an occupation, having been expelled from the army, and possessed no obvious other job qualifications.

The Raouf clan was markedly different from the Madi village family into which Sadat had married. Jihan was the very opposite of Ekbal, his first wife, whom he was prepared to divorce once he left prison. The Raouf family was citified and sophisticated. Jihan's father was a highly respected surgeon, British educated, whose resources enabled him to maintain two residences, one in Cairo and a vacation home at Suez City. Her English mother, née Gladys Cotterill, made no effort to keep her children from growing up as devout Muslims, although she held to her own Christian religion throughout her life. Jihan would not have gone against her family's wishes and married Sadat had her family opposed. But, in fact, Sadat was able to win the parents over. The person whose endorsement he most needed was the mother, and there occurred a memorable and revealing moment in the courtship that enabled Sadat to gain the blessing of the parents. At an early meeting, Mrs. Raouf asked Sadat his opinion of Winston Churchill, having already informed him that in her estimation

Churchill was the most accomplished political leader in modern British history. Sadat did not hold back, calling Churchill a thief and attacking him as a man who had kept Egypt in colonial subjugation. Rather than being offended by this response and forbidding her daughter to have anything further to do with this young intemperate man, Mrs. Raouf admired him for holding to his views. She allowed the relationship to continue. When on later occasions Mrs. Raouf and Sadat discovered a shared passion for the English novelist Charles Dickens, she was won over. She blessed the marriage, telling her daughter that while her life might not always be easy, it would never be boring. On May 19, 1949, Sadat married Jihan Raouf, securing for himself a partner who was destined to play a major role in his life.

Mrs. Raouf's prediction that life might not be easy proved altogether too true at first. Sadat worked in a business with Hassan Izzat, whose firm did not yield much revenue and who provided Sadat and his new bride with a small salary, in their opinion much less than the business allowed. They took a modest ninth-floor apartment on Roda Island in Cairo. Jihan did the shopping, cooking, and house cleaning and usually had to walk up nine flights of stairs because the elevator was broken. The couple did not always have enough money for groceries, and they often went hungry when the funds ran short. Their lives changed, however, when Sadat was reinstated in the army in 1950, approximately thirteen months after their marriage. He owed his reinstatement to his friendship with Yusuf Rashad, personal physician to the king and head of the palace's personal army. Sadat's closeness to the palace always troubled his fellow junior officers, and the fact that Yusuf Rashad had arranged for him to return to the army raised questions about his loyalty to their goals. He regained his original rank of captain, though those officers with whom he had entered the Military Academy in 1937 were by then majors and lieutenant colonels. Still, his monthly salary of LE34 (approximately $140) gave him the financial security that the couple so desperately lacked and ended the days of hunger and deprivation.

Moreover, he had good prospects for promotion to higher ranks and higher income, quickly realized as he advanced within two years to the rank of lieutenant colonel.

Reinstatement in the army allowed the Sadats to change their residence. They moved into a villa on the Pyramid Road in Giza and made it their permanent home. Jihan furnished it elegantly over time with expensive objects d'art, acquired, she writes in her memoirs, at knockdown auction prices when wealthy Egyptians and foreigners, fleeing the country as Nasser appropriated the wealth of the large landlords and business persons, put their possessions up for sale. Questions would be raised later as to how Jihan acquired these items so cheaply, and suspicions were voiced that the couple lived well beyond their income.

Sadat's marriage to Jihan brought him a dynamic partner but also left him with many family problems, the solutions to which, not mentioned in his memoirs or in the writings of his leading biographers, revealed an extraordinarily callous side to his personality. This aspect of his personality needs to be set beside his later achievements if we are to take the full measure of this complex individual.

When Sadat first began to court Jihan, he was still married to Ekbal. Ekbal's anger at Anwar's interest in Jihan was predictable, for she had been his chief support while in prison, visiting him regularly. She had expected him to resume his familial obligations when he left prison. When she realized that he intended to marry Jihan, she agreed to allow him to take a second wife, only to learn that the Raouf family would not permit this. The divorce followed and so did Sadat's distancing himself from her and his daughters. The two younger girls, Rawia and Camelia, did not live with Jihan and Anwar Sadat until 1959, when they were ten and twelve years of age, and stayed in their household only two years before their marriages.

At the time of Sadat's marriage to Jihan two of his daughters were three and seven years old, and the third, Camelia, would be born two months after he married Jihan. They were a difficult financial burden before his reinstatement in the army, and he continued to regard them as such even after he rose to higher ranks. If the account of his third daughter, Camelia, is to be believed, he wanted to marry them off as quickly as possible and to move their financial responsibilities onto their husbands. The oldest daughter, Rokaya, was married when she was seventeen years of age. The next two, Rawia and Camelia, were asked for at ages fifteen and twelve in 1961, well after the military had seized power and Sadat had come to occupy important governmental positions. According to Egyptian law, no woman could be married unless she was sixteen years of age. If a girl lacked a birth certificate, which was the case for the two daughters, adults were required to attest to their ages. Sadat arranged to have the two most influential members of the Egyptian government at the time, Nasser and Abdel Hakim Amer, certify that Camelia was indeed sixteen years old. The only one to complain was Nasser's wife, who knew that the marriage was illegal and that her husband and Amer had sworn falsely. She wondered when the police would come to haul the two leaders away.

Camelia's marriage was a disaster. Not only did her husband beat her and keep her short of funds, but she also became pregnant and had several miscarriages because she was not yet physically able to bear children. Finally, at age fifteen, she became pregnant again, and this time, determined to have the child, she stayed in bed for the final five months of her pregnancy, delivering a healthy baby girl. Through all of this turmoil, Sadat knew that Camelia's husband was abusing his daughter, but he did nothing to stop the violence. From time to time, he helped out with small amounts of money. The only family member who came to her defense was her uncle, Esmat, who after learning about her suffering threatened the husband and informed Sadat. Sadat's response was to upbraid his daughter for having informed on her husband and offer a small token payment to her.

Not only was Sadat reinstated in the army, he rejoined the Free Officers movement and was invited to become a member of the founding committee of the organization. The Free Officers had moved to a higher stage of organization and planning by that time, and Nasser had clearly emerged as the dominant figure in the movement. Toward the end of 1949, the Free Officers had begun holding regular meetings and had expanded their membership into most of the branches of the armed forces. The organization had also formed a central committee, which at first consisted of eight individuals, to which, with some opposition, the members added Sadat. When one member queried Nasser as to why he had brought Sadat into the inner circle of the group, Nasser admitted that the choice was not an easy one. Sadat, he said, was lazy but also well connected. No doubt, Nasser was mindful of Sadat's early contributions to the movement and his courage in challenging state power. Nasser's reference to Sadat's connections within the government referred to his ties with Yusuf Rashid, personal physician to King Faruq and head of the royal guard, an elite military unit whose duty it was to protect the king from enemies. Yet it was also Sadat's connections with the palace that worried some of the group and cast a shadow of suspicion on him.

By the time that Sadat joined the Free Officers movement, the group was already a large one, boasting perhaps as many as 200 members. It enjoyed support in all military units except the navy. In addition, several developments had strengthened the resolve of the group to interject themselves into Egyptian politics, even to contemplate a seizure of power if the established parties, notably the most highly regarded of the parties, the Wafd, stumbled. The first of these developments had been the incident on February 4, 1942, when British tanks surrounded the royal palace in Cairo and forced King Faruq to replace his neutralist ministry with a Wafdist government headed up by Prime Minister Mustafa al-Nahhas. Not only did this event undercut the legitimacy of the king, but it also diminished the reputation of Nahhas and the Wafd Party as the champions of Egyptian nationalism.

The second event was even more decisive for the officers and for all of Egypt. In 1948 the Arab states led by their largest army, the Egyptian military force, went to war in Palestine to oppose the creation of the state of Israel. Plans to create an independent Jewish state out of the territory that later became British-controlled Palestine dated from the foundation of a European-centered Zionist movement in the late nineteenth century. During World War I, Zionist proponents secured a promise from the British government, known as the Balfour Declaration, according to which the British government undertook to establish a homeland for Jews in Palestine, without, however, undermining the rights of the existing non-Jewish inhabitants of that land. The British efforts as the colonial power ruling over Palestine after World War I to accommodate the demands of Jews and Arabs proved, however, to be unsuccessful, and in 1947, the United Nations voted to replace the British mandate over Palestine with indepen-dent Jewish and Arab states. No Arab state accepted this vote, and most sent troops to resist the creation of the Jewish state of Israel in May 1948. The Israeli Defense Force's military victories produced a crescendo of criticism within the Arab world against their military forces and their political leaders. In particular, the Egyptian army performed poorly, and its officers, including Nasser, who was wounded, blamed the civilian politicians, espe-cially the king, for having failed to provide the forces with effec-tive military equipment.

The 1948 war over Palestine, which in time became known as the first Arab-Israeli war, created an immense and long-lasting regional dilemma—what to do with and on behalf of the nearly three-quarters of a million Palestinian Arabs, who left, fled, or were expelled from their homes during the conflict and how to deal with the new powerful Israeli state. Those who departed from Israel retreated into the Gaza strip; Jordan; Syria, and Lebanon, and the West Bank of the Jordan River, over which Jordan exercised political control until the Six Day War in 1967; creating refugee camps in all of these lands. Many expected to return to their homeland and reclaim their homes and properties. To date, these refugees have not been permitted to return despite a 1948 United

Nations resolution (no. 194) that called on the government of Israel to allow any refugees wishing to return to their homes and live in peace with their neighbors to do so. The resolution also stipulated that compensation be paid to those who chose not to return. In 1949 at a conference at Lausanne, Switzerland, called to resolve the Arab-Israeli problems, Israel proposed to allow 100,000 to return on the condition of keeping all of the territory that it had acquired during the 1948–1949 war and being allowed to settle those who returned where it saw fit. The agreement required that Arab states sign a peace treaty with Israel and absorb the 550,000 to 650,000 remaining refugees. No agreement was reached, with the result that the rights of the Palestinian peoples consequently forced to dwell in squalid refugee camps outside Israel became a cause that no Arab government could afford to ignore.

Egypt's mounting domestic problems and its failed military effort in Palestine galvanized the Free Officers to further elaborate their visions of how Egypt should be transformed and to identify the forces that stood in the way of progress. As a beginning, the group circulated pamphlets, setting forth their ideas among their supporters. Their chief target of attack was the British, whose forces remained in occupation of the country. Egypt could not move forward economically, socially, or politically, they averred, until the country had rid itself of the British army of occupation, a task that the elected politicians seemed unable to accomplish. But the officers also complained about the power of the landed classes, the unequal distribution of income and educational opportunities, the overweening power of foreign capital, and the need for democratic reforms that would bring an end to the country's feudal institutions. The pamphlets also contained a strong Marxist emphasis, arguing that foreign capital had bought off the political elite and many intellectuals and criticizing companies like the Suez Canal Company, the Belgian utility firms, and American firms like Coca-Cola and Pepsi-Cola for having "plundered" the country.

Sadat shared these perspectives as his writings, published soon after the coup, demonstrate. Sadat, too, believed that foreign rulers retarded Egypt's development because they looked down on the people and viewed them purely as an exploitable resource. His litany of foreign oppressors began with Turkish satraps—first the Mamluks, who had ruled Egypt from 1250 to 1517, followed by the Ottomans (1517–1914). Having finally rid themselves of these tyrants, Egypt next fell under the spell of the British, who kept the country locked in an economic stranglehold to the textile industrialists of Lancashire and opposed every Egyptian effort to diversify the economy.

At the close of World War II, the Free Officers had strengthened their ties with the Muslim Brotherhood, but after the state clamped down on the Brotherhood in the late 1940s, they concluded that their group alone was capable of changing Egypt's political future. They intensified their plans for seizing the reins of government. At first, they set 1955 as the target year, believing that not until then would their message suffuse the army and their plans be well enough formulated. Yet spiraling political events forced the officers to advance the date until, finally, they decided to make their move in July 1952.

Critical in advancing the Free Officers' D-Day was the election of a Wafdist government in 1950, which won electoral support by promising an agenda of radical political and economic change. Unable to enact land reform or redistribute economic resources, the Wafdists turned their attention to expelling British troops from Egypt. To this end, they renounced a treaty that the Egyptian politicians had signed with the British in 1936 and urged the populace to refuse to supply the large British military base along the Suez Canal with workers and food. The British were in reality in flagrant violation of the 1936 treaty, which limited the size of the British forces to 10,000 soldiers and 400 airmen. The number of British forces in the canal base at times totaled 100,000 men, and the British and their American NATO allies regarded the base as a vital component in their containment of

Soviet expansionism and spread of the communist ideology and Soviet influence into the Middle East. Inevitably, countries like Egypt, with its geopolitical importance, were drawn into "cold war" politics following the close of World War II. Britain's Suez Canal base, which had been enlarged during World War II and had become the largest British military establishment in the world, stretching 120 miles long and 30 miles wide at its widest point, was in the minds of NATO military commanders a vital deterrent to Soviet territorial aims in this area. Not only did the base house a large number of troops and sophisticated weaponry, but its extended runways accommodated big, A-bomb-carrying aircrafts, which were capable of striking the Soviet Union should the Soviets launch an attack anywhere in the world. But British and American efforts to persuade the Egyptians to align with the West against the Soviets failed to overcome the primary Egyptian nationalist goal of removing all foreign troops from their soil and achieving full-fledged political independence.

In an effort to expel the British, the Wafd encouraged its supporters to use guerrilla warfare against the base, a campaign that proved so successful that the British had to fly in food supplies and bring day laborers from Cyprus and elsewhere. As one commanding officer stated, the soldiers spent more time guarding one another from guerrilla attacks than they did readying themselves for a potential cold war conflict.

Tensions came to a head on January 25, 1952, when units of the British army stormed the Egyptian police station at Ismailia, a major Suez Canal city, and killed many local policemen. When reports of the loss of life reached Cairo, the populace turned its rage against British and foreign influence. Before the government called in the Egyptian army to restore order, many British business establishments were burned to the ground. Ten British citizens lost their lives on January 26, a day that went down in the annals of the nationalist struggle as Black Saturday. Inexplicably, the massive British army of occupation stayed within the perimeters of their base despite the fact that British property was being destroyed and British lives were imperiled and the fact that the treaties signed between the British and the Egyptians gave the British forces the right to safeguard the foreign population living in the country.

Only after a long delay did the Wafdist government call in the Egyptian army. That decision clarified much for the young officers. In the first place, King Faruq removed the Wafd from power, yet the series of palace-appointed ministries that replaced the Wafd were no more successful in ridding the country of the British armed forces. More to the point, the fact that the British soldiers had remained in the canal base as Cairo burned and the monarch had to call in the Egyptian army to restore order made it clear to the young officers that the army had become the ultimate arbiter of the country's future. A military seizure of power seemed to many young officers essential and likely to succeed.

| LIVING WITH NASSER'S |
REVOLUTION, 1952–1967

IT WAS ONLY A MATTER of time before the Free Officers moved to seize power. However, fears that King Faruq, whom the young officers regarded as corrupt and responsible for the defeat in the war in Palestine in 1948–1949, was readying his supporters to move against these men accelerated their timetable. A major precipitating event was the elections to the army's Officers Club held at the end of 1950. Traditionally, the king had controlled these elections, ensuring that his cronies held the major positions in the Officers Club, especially the office of president. By 1950, however, the Free Officers felt confident enough of their rising power to run their own slate of candidates, putting forward as their choice to be president General Naguib, an older but much respected soldier, though not an early member of the Free Officers. They also ran Free Officers members for the executive committee. Although the king endeavored to postpone the election, when the final results were reported, Naguib won out as president and several Free Officers were chosen for the executive committee. The elections, however, alerted the crown and conservative, pro-palace politicians to the Free Officers movement within the army and compelled Nasser and his cohorts to speed up their plans to seize power. They shortened their timetable after learning that the king was collecting the names of his enemies within the army and was prepared to make arrests. Abandoning their already advanced deadline of November 1952, they now decided to carry out their coup in late July. The coup effort began on the evening of July 22; by the morning of July 23 the army was in full control of the government.

Sadat played a minimal role in the coup. His posting at Rafah in Sinai had removed him from most of the planning. Nasser did, however, send him a note on July 21, announcing that the coup was to take place between July 22 and August 5. Sadat returned to Cairo but, unable to reach Nasser and other Free Officers and uncertain when the coup would take place, decided to treat his family to movies at a nearby outdoor cinema. He returned home to discover a note from Nasser: "It happens tonight. Rendezvous at Abdul Hakim's, 11 pm."[1] Sadat tore out of the house, but lacking knowledge of the coup planners' password, he was stopped by sentries and not allowed to pass their checkpoint. At the last moment, by which time much of the action had already taken place, Sadat caught sight of Abdel Hakim Amer and was able to join his colleagues. Although he missed much of the action, it was Sadat himself who announced over the radio the military coup, breaking into the regularly scheduled programming to broadcast the news that the military had seized control of the Egyptian government.

Just why Sadat was chosen to make this historic announcement is not clear. Apparently, the first person asked was not able or not willing. Sadat became his replacement. It is clear that Nasser preferred to maintain a behind-the-scenes stance, and Naguib, who would soon emerge as the face of the revolution because of seniority and age, was not yet deeply involved.

The young officers who had seized power had momentous choices to make. As a member of the central organizing committee, Sadat was deeply involved in these early defining decisions. Among the crucial questions was how much of the actual running of government the officers should assume. If they chose not to take over the government, whom should they ask to form a new

A GROUP OF THE FREE OFFICERS JUST AFTER THEY SEIZED
POWER. *Nasser is in the center. To his left and seated is General Naguib;
standing behind Nasser is Abdel Hakim Amer, who became commander
of the armed forces. Sadat, who is probably the swarthiest, is seated at
some distance from Nasser.*

ministry? What should be done about King Faruq? An anathema
to the officers, they debated whether to send Faruq into exile or to
execute him. Up to this point, the uprising had been virtually
bloodless. Only two soldiers had been killed. Did the men who
now ruled Egypt want the monarch's blood on their hands?
Should the institution of the monarchy be retained if Faruq was
executed or sent into exile? And what about Egypt's parliament
and the parties that had participated in political affairs? Should
elections be held right away, the parliament reconstituted, and
the old parties allowed to reform themselves?

Even as these matters were being resolved, the central committee also had to sort out leadership questions. What form of
government should the country have? For how long should the
military hold on to power? At a central committee meeting, seven
of the eight members in attendance, including Sadat, believed
that the army needed to remain in power and govern dictatorially

for an extended period, perhaps as many as ten years, before the country would be ready for a liberal democracy. Sadat's view was that "what may be achieved 'democratically' in a year can be accomplished dictatorially in a day."[2] Sadat later elaborated on this perspective, asserting that the general belief among the leaders of the coup was that "there was no way to eliminate corruption and oppression but by dictatorial means and that there was no escape from setting up gallows in the main plaza for traitors, . . . for those who had betrayed the people."[3] Only Nasser dissented, contending that the military should hold power for six months before preparing for elections. He added that dictatorships invariably ended in violence and disappointment. Outvoted, he submitted his resignation and retired to his home. The remaining seven were thunderstruck and determined to bring their peerless leader and coup planner back. Nasser relented and returned to the executive committee, his position as ultimate arbiter of the revolution thus shrewdly solidified.

The first external move that the executive body made, having renamed itself the Revolutionary Command Council (RCC), was to ask former Prime Minister Ali Mahir to form a new government. They chose Ali Mahir because he had no party affiliation and was known as an independent and honest politician. Next, they decided to send King Faruq into exile. After intense debates, the RCC agreed not to execute the king, affirming a commitment to keep the takeover bloodless. The RCC dispatched Sadat and a few other officers to Alexandria, where the king resided during the summer months to ensure that he left the country and that no violence occurred against him or his entourage. Sadat accompanied Ali Mahir to the royal palace and witnessed the king's signature on the document of abdication, affixed twice because the first time Faruq wrote his name his hand shook so violently that the writing was illegible. By abdicating, Faruq ceded the throne to his infant son, Crown Prince Ahmad Fuad, who was to rule through a regency. Sadat stood on the deck of an Egyptian warship as the king boarded the royal yacht toting more than 200 suitcases of possessions, assembled in the six hours that the RCC allowed him to prepare for his departure. Sadat observed the twenty-one-gun salute that bade farewell to the king, having made sure that rumored plans to blow up the yacht could not be realized.

Many other dramatic developments followed the exiling of the king. In August 1952, the government enacted a major land reform scheme, appropriating more than half a million acres from the large landowning class, most notably the royal family, which possessed nearly one-third of these lands. The state redistributed these estates to small landowners and the landless. When the parties failed to purge themselves of unwanted and corrupt leaders, at least in the view of the RCC, they were abolished. The only political entity that survived the purge was the Muslim Brotherhood, which endured until 1954 when tensions between the RCC and the Brothers reached a peak. A confrontation between the Muslim Brothers and RCC supporters at the gates of Cairo University on January 12, 1954, provided the government with a justification to dissolve the organization, arguing that it had become a political body, ceasing to function as a religious group, and thus was subject to the 1953 ban on political parties. The government also arrested over 450 Brothers. An attempt on Nasser's life on October 26, 1954, provided the state with a further reason for clamping down on the Brotherhood and rounding up more of its members. Nasser let it be known that he was determined to finish off the Brotherhood once and for all. In place of the old parties, the RCC created its own political party, the Liberation Rally, which experienced various transformations and name changes. Toward the end of the Nasser years it was known as the Arab Socialist Union. Finally, the government abolished the monarchy and became a republic in early 1953.

Although abolishing the monarchy seemed an almost inevitable development once the decision to remove Faruq had been made, it marked a radical departure in the governance of Arab countries. At the close of World War II, kings were the official heads of state in Morocco, Libya, Tunisia, Egypt, the Anglo-Egyptian

Sudan, Jordan, Iraq, Saudi Arabia, Yemen, the United Arab Emirates, and Kuwait. Even before the military coup, Faruq had a premonition that monarchies worldwide were doomed, quipping that soon there will be only five kings left in the world—the King of England, the king of spades, the king of hearts, the king of diamonds, and the king of clubs. Even so, eliminating Egypt's monarchy alarmed most of the Arab states and made their leaders suspicious of the pan-Arab and antimonarchical policies that Egypt's new rulers were thought likely to promote.

As a member of the RCC, the executive organ of the Free Officers, Sadat participated in these decisions, but the record does not suggest that he played a decisive role. Keith Wheelock, who was a young American undergraduate student doing his senior thesis on Egypt at the time, provided some evidence that Sadat was often a bystander. After one of his lengthy interviews with Wheelock, Nasser suggested that Wheelock approach Sadat, who Nasser commented had lots of time on his hands.

Although Sadat was not prominently involved in many early decisions, he did surface from time to time, often when the public relations issues and the reputation of the movement were involved. In late 1952 and 1953, the RCC endeavored to burnish its reputation by putting the leading politicians of the pre-coup period on trial. It established a special tribunal, called the Treason Court, which was composed of civilian and military judges, but its trials failed to deliver the message that the military sought. Energetic and articulate ancien régime lawyers used the hearings to assault the military and to demand a return to civilian rule. In particular, well-known and still much-admired Wafdists brought before the court defended their record, arguing that their nationalist credentials were unsullied and that they should be applauded rather than blamed for what they had accomplished for Egypt. Even while these trials were going on, the former leader of the Wafd, Mustafa al-Nahhas, did not draw back from appearing in public. Using his still considerable popular support and oratorical skills, he attacked the military for suppressing freedom and demanded a return of parliamentary government, a message that received considerable support among the rank-and-file civilian population.

Dissatisfied with the results of the Treason Court, the RCC decided to intensify its attack on the old order. It established its own tribunal, selecting three Free Officers, including Sadat, as the sole judges. Unlike the Treason Court, this body, called the Revolutionary Tribunal, had the power to impose sentences, even the death penalty. The RCC's intention was to place Egypt's ancien régime under a harsh spotlight of criticism by marshaling evidence of egregious misdeeds. In announcing the formation of the tribunal, RCC officials asserted that the court's mission would be to reveal the oppressive role that foreign imperialism had played in Egypt and identify those Egyptians who had betrayed their countrymen by allowing the British to dominate the country. The Revolutionary Tribunal met between September 26, 1953, and June 30, 1954. It tried thirty-one cases and rendered verdicts of treason against four individuals who were put to death.

In the final analysis these trials were no more successful than the earlier ones. They, too, failed to strengthen the reputations of the coup leaders. Although the names of the main Wafdists were prominently featured as possible defendants, the court never brought to trial Nahhas or his wife, who was known to have made money from corrupt dealings on the cotton futures market, though both were placed under house arrest. The most prominent Wafdist politician put on trial was Fuad Sirag al-Din, the much reviled interior minister under the last Wafdist government. His trial, which lasted eight weeks, was extravagantly reported in the local press. Intended to be a show trial, the court welcomed the testimony of Sirag al-Din's most severe critics and political foes, including Makram Ubayd, whose so-called black book, originally published in 1944, listed all of the illegal and corrupt acts that the Wafd had committed to that point. The tribunal charged Sirag al-Din with accepting bribes, cornering the cotton futures market, and covering up an investigation into arms racketeering during the war in Palestine. Nonetheless, Sirag al-Din gave as good as he got, arguing passionately that his party had been the champion of Egyptian nationalism for decades. Nor for that matter, he asserted, was the Wafd to be blamed for the failures in the war in Palestine. They were the fault of the palace. In the end, the tribunal imposed a fifteen-year sentence on the defendant.

Sadat's chief function at this stage was limited to being a mouthpiece and propagandist of the regime. He was Nasser's and the RCC's most vocal and effective publicity agent, a position he obviously relished, for he opened the regime's official paper, *al-Gumhuriya*, in December 1953. While serving as its chief editor and one of its most prolific columnists, he used the paper to reflect his knowledge and interest in literature and history and his devotion to Quranic studies. He also unabashedly championed the government's programs and Nasser's indispensability. He was especially proud of his campaign against the Baghdad Pact. The British, in league with the Americans, endeavored to create an alliance of Arab states, which eventually resulted in the formation in 1955 of the Baghdad Pact, aligning Britain with Iraq, Iran, Turkey, and Pakistan, ostensibly to prevent Soviet expansionism into the Middle East but also to support the conservative, pro-Western Arab regimes that the Nasser government was putting under heavy pressure via the radio service "The Voice of the Arabs." Sadat also used *al-Gumhuriya* to attack John Foster Dulles, US secretary of state, for trying to force Egypt into the Baghdad Pact and for arguing against the policy of neutralism in world affairs, which Nasser along with many other Third World leaders strongly advocated. These and other Sadat attacks against the Americans would become major impediments to Sadat's later efforts when president to align Egypt's foreign policy with that of the United States.

Sadat saved his strongest salvoes against the Americans when John Foster Dulles in early 1956 persuaded the British and American governments and the World Bank to withdraw financial support for the construction of a new, massive dam at Aswan.

The high dam at Aswan was the centerpiece of Egypt's development strategy, a project that President Nasser attached great importance to, believing that by trapping vast waters behind it and
making them available for agriculture it would expand Egypt's
arable area and increase its agricultural output. In addition, as the
waters surged through the dam, they would generate cheap electrical supplies, which would promote Egyptian industrialization.
Dulles's decision, which he justified on the grounds that the financing of the dam was beyond Egypt's capabilities, but was in
reality intended to demonstrate to Nasser the folly of having
taken arms from the Soviet bloc, enraged Nasser. The Egyptian
president retaliated on July 26, 1956, announcing that Egypt
would nationalize the mainly French-financed and controlled
Suez Canal Company and use its toll revenues to build the dam.
A British-French-Israeli invasion of Egypt ensued, stopped only
by the diplomatic interventions of the United States and the
Soviet Union. Precisely where Sadat stood on the issue, whether
to resist, even to the extent of carrying out guerrilla warfare
against the invading forces (a position taken by Nasser), or to sue
immediately for peace (Hakim Amer's position) is not clear.
Sadat did, however, warn Nasser that the decision to nationalize
the canal meant war and that Egypt was not yet ready for war.
Nasser had a different, though ultimately, incorrect view. He believed that cooler heads would prevail and that the great powers
would see the legitimacy of Egypt's position. Even in spite of
grossly miscalculating British-French-Israeli plans to invade
Egypt, Nasser's success in resolving the crisis in Egypt's favor
solidified his reputation as the Arab world's most decisive leader,
a man whose courage and nationalist determination had overcome the military might of powerful adversaries.

Without question, 1956 saw Nasser's reputation as a Third
World leader at a high-water mark. Ousting the British, removing
a hated and corrupt monarch, carrying out a popular land reform
scheme, and opening schools and universities to more Egyptians
not only solidified Nasser's reputation at home but also abroad.

Nasser's state redistributed income and promoted social mobility. Sadat's role in these developments was a modest one. At *al-Gumhuriya*, he burnished Nasser's image as one of the Third World's most successful rulers and made his paper for all intents and purposes the official organ of the revolution.

Acutely aware of the power of the press, the Egyptian president also courted the approval of the other leading journalists in the country, including the editors of *Akhbar al-Yaum*, and *al-Misri*, and most important, Mohamed Hassanein Heikal, who eventually became Nasser's closest confidant and editor in chief of the country's major newspaper, *al-Ahram*. Nasser used all of these newspapers in his struggle with Naguib for political supremacy in Egypt. It was because he grasped the power of the press that Nasser encouraged his fellow conspirators to become involved in journalism, although the first newspaper, founded by Nasser's minister of guidance, proved too leftist for the president's tastes. Nasser was more satisfied with Sadat, who in the early years of the revolution used *al-Gumhuriya* to broadcast the government's policies. Leaving little to chance, however, Nasser made it a daily habit to visit the offices of *al-Gumhuriya* to review headlines, and, throughout his tenure in power, he continued to read the first edition of all of the daily papers, issuing instructions for changes in subsequent editions when there were items that did not meet with his approval.

Just how far removed from the seat of power Sadat found himself can be observed in his appointment as secretary general of the Islamic Congress, which the Egyptian government founded in January 1955. On the surface the appointment would have appeared to bring with it high status since the military men were eager to strengthen Egypt's ties with their Arab and Muslim neighbors. In reality, the assignment required Sadat to spend so much time out of the country that he was unable to participate in many important RCC discussions. One trip in particular, a mission to India in early 1955, was especially meaningful to him, at least if his memoirs are to be trusted, for it drove home how dysfunctional the Nasser regime was and how infighting among the leaders undermined good governance. He claims in the memoirs that his brief visit to India soured him on Egypt's leadership and persuaded him that if he were to come to power he would seek to build consensus and create a more transparent political environment.

During his visit to India, Sadat was entertained by Jawaharlal Nehru, the country's prime minister. Sadat was surprised when Nehru introduced him to an influential member of the Indian Communist Party, an outspoken critic of Nehru's Congress Party. Not only did Nehru speak generously of this man, but he allowed his critic and his wife to kiss him on both cheeks, a moment that filled Sadat with pleasure and demonstrated to him that men and women, while holding different political views, could respect one another and work for common national goals. Sadat's good feelings dissipated, however, the moment he arrived back in Egypt and was caught up in the maelstrom of political squabbling that beset Egypt's governing circles. "My colleagues in the Revolutionary Command Council," he wrote in his memoirs, "were quarreling about everything, however trivial." Unwilling to be a party to such rancorous disputes, he withdrew from the day-to-day discussions of the RCC, remaining "aloof, watching them [RCC members], sometimes in amazement, sometimes in disgust, but always with deep pain."[4] On two occasions, he tendered his resignation from the RCC but was persuaded to stay on. When, however, Nasser dissolved the RCC prior to running for election as president, Sadat told Nasser to leave him out of the new government.

In his autobiography, Sadat writes that he was asked soon after the coup what ministry he wanted for himself. He replied that he desired no portfolio because he knew "very little about politics."[5] Yet, as we have seen, he was deeply involved in the early political actions of the Free Officers. His involvement was on display during the leadership crisis in 1954, which pitted Nasser and Naguib against one another in a battle for political supremacy.

The ostensible issue dividing them was whether the military should continue to rule or should restore democratic and civilian government. Within the military itself, opposition to the power being exercised by the RCC came from the cavalry corps and was led by Khalid Muhyi al-Din, a Free Officer himself. This unit complained that its leading officers were insufficiently represented in the government.

In the power struggle with Nasser, President Naguib embraced the growing criticism of the RCC, offering himself as the champion of those who wanted the army to retire to the barracks. As Naguib was the face of the revolution to many Egyptians, his decision to resign the office, taken on February 23, 1954, left the country without a head of state and plunged it into a state of confusion.

The popular outpouring of sentiment in support of Naguib caught Nasser and the other members of the RCC off guard. So befuddled were the young officers that they were compelled to reinstate Naguib as president of the republic. Soon thereafter they also made him prime minister. Nasser and his cohort, however, had no intention of ceding power to Naguib, and they began immediately to plot his ultimate overthrow, an event that began on March 25, 1954, when Nasser issued a communiqué stating that the RCC intended to surrender its powers to a constituent assembly on July 25 at which moment the revolution would come to an end and political parties would be reinstated. Working behind the scenes, the RCC rallied its supporters, engineering a general strike on March 28, 1954, that forced Naguib to resign as prime minister on April 17 and placed the RCC and Nasser back in control of the government. On September 1, Nasser, who had taken over as prime minister following Naguib's resignation of that office, reshuffled his cabinet, bringing every single one of the RCC members into the cabinet except Naguib.

The 1954 realignment of the cabinet was in Naguib's view "a second coup d'etat."[6] It certainly dashed any lingering hopes that the young officers were committed to an early restoration of parliamentary rule, and it left the military firmly in control of the Egyptian polity. Nasser as prime minister surrounded himself with fellow Free Officers, appointing them to head up the important positions of deputy prime minister, minister of war, and commander in chief of the armed forces (Abdel Hakim Amer), and the ministers of municipal affairs, education, social affairs, national guidance, and the interior. Even Sadat, who mentions in his memoirs that he was to that point the only member of the RCC who had never had a cabinet appointment, became a minister of state. The military's dominance was total. Although Naguib stayed on briefly and only ceremonially as president and nominal leader of the revolution until November 14, 1954, "in order to maintain a semblance of unity,"[7] it was only a matter of time before he was officially placed under house arrest. Finally, on June 22, 1956, the RCC itself was dissolved, no longer necessary since all of its members had entered the cabinet. It was also at this time that Nasser became president of Egypt following a plebiscite.

Although Sadat's position as a minister of state without specific duties suggested that he was the least powerful of the military men in the ministry, an appearance confirmed by his decision in 1956 to leave the cabinet entirely, in fact, he had played a significant role as a mouthpiece of the regime's aspirations during the March 1954 crisis. He used *al-Gumhuriya* to undermine the legitimacy of Naguib and to sing the praises of Nasser. The essays that he published shortly after the crisis continued these harsh and often unfair attacks on Naguib. In these, Sadat portrayed Naguib as a free rider to the coup, a man scarcely involved in the preparations to overthrow the old order and one who was later pushed forward primarily because of his age and seniority but who then attempted to take advantage of his position to usurp the authority of others. Sadat disputed Naguib's claims to legitimacy and leadership, denying Naguib's assertions that he had joined the Free Officers movement in 1949, that he had become its president following the January 26 burning of Cairo, and that he was involved in planning the coup. In Sadat's telling, Naguib was not brought into the inner circle of the Free Officers until August 1952, well after the coup had taken place and never displayed ardor for the goals of the movement.

Although Sadat did not hold a ministerial office from June 1956 until December 1969 when Nasser made him the republic's vice president, he was far from a detached or innocent bystander. In 1957, when Egypt held its first elections since the coup, he was returned to the National Assembly, serving in the Assembly's first session as deputy speaker. Later he became speaker. In 1960, Nasser asked him to stand for election as speaker of the Federal (Syrian-Egyptian) National Assembly, Egypt and Syria having been politically unified in 1958 as the United Arab Republic. He did and won. More important, he had easy and frequent access to the president and offered his opinion on many of Nasser's policies. It is also clear, not just from Sadat's often self-serving memoirs but from the writings of other important Egyptians, that Nasser valued his counsel and frequently sought him out before making tough political decisions.

Sadat also observed the growing rivalry between Nasser and minister of war Abdel Hakim Amer, as did many others in power. The way that Amer used his friendship with Nasser and his position as commander in chief of the armed forces to build a power base within the military alarmed Sadat and many others. Like many Free Officers, Sadat had a low opinion of Amer's leadership qualities. He was especially dismayed when Nasser put Amer in charge of a special governmental organ, known as the Committee for the Liquidation of Feudalism. This body was established ostensibly to root out entrenched influences of the old landed classes. In reality, Amer used the committee to extend his influence into the countryside, rewarding local dignitaries who supported his power and punishing those who did not.

Most significant, Sadat's involvement in the two major military campaigns of the Egyptian government in the 1960s was deep and had a lasting effect on his policies when he became president. The first was Egypt's participation in the civil war in Yemen between 1962 and 1967 and later, the Six-Day Arab-Israeli war, also known as the June War, in 1967. Both went badly for Egypt, did damage to the Egyptian economy and the reputation and capabilities of the military, and provided Sadat and others with countless lessons for future actions.

On the surface a war involving Egyptian troops in the small, relatively poor state of Yemen would not have seemed to entail much danger for Egypt, the Arab world's most populous country, possessing its largest and best trained army. In reality it became much like America's involvement in Vietnam—a constant drain on resources and a blow to the prestige of the regime. To begin with, the war involved Egypt's and Nasser's strong commitment to fostering the cultural and ultimately political unification of the Arab states, a movement known as pan-Arabism that was gaining strength after World War II. Many Arab leaders believed that the Arab world could only become a force in world affairs if its many disparate states were drawn together in political unions. The union of Egypt and Syria, forming the United Arab Republic in 1958, appeared to be a first and promising step in this direction and made clear Egypt's and Nasser's ambitions to lead the Arab solidarity movement. But while many Arab leaders saw the rationale for working together politically and believed that their common language and history were strong foundations for Arab unity, they quickly fell out over which states should take the lead. Egypt's leadership aroused hostility especially among the conservative, monarchical regimes in the region, notably the monarchies of Jordan, Saudi Arabia, and Kuwait. These rulers regarded Egypt, which had replaced its monarchy with a republic and drawn close to the Soviet Union, as a formidable threat to their existence.

In September 1962, the king of Yemen died. He had ruled his land since 1948, but his increasingly heavy hand had aroused local opposition. Opponents took the opportunity of his death to install a republican form of government, and they looked to Egypt and to Nasser, as the champion of pan-Arab and antimonarchical movements in the region, to provide support. Thus, when the leader of the republican forces, Brigadier Sallal, asked for Egyptian assistance, Nasser responded enthusiastically. He dispatched Sadat to Yemen on a fact-finding mission. Nasser's reasons for selecting Sadat were hardly compelling, for Sadat had no special knowledge of the Arabian Peninsula, Yemen, or the Saudi regime, which was supporting the monarchy against the republicans and was the major power in the region. What persuaded Nasser to look to Sadat was that Jihan's sister was married to an influential Yemeni in the camp of the republican forces, Abdel Rahman Baydani. Nasser hoped that this connection would give his colleague privileged access to information and would yield political and military success. Conducting what could not have been more than a cursory study of the balance of power in Yemen, Sadat quickly signed a defense pact with the republican forces, then nominally in power in the capital Sana, promising Egyptian financial and military aid. Their opponents, the royalists, were, however, strongly entrenched in the north of Yemen where they were receiving substantial military and financial assistance from the Saudis, the Jordanian monarchy, and the British, each of whom saw the civil war taking shape there as an opportunity to damage Nasser's influence and undermine Egypt's pan-Arab aspirations.

The defense pact with the Yemeni republicans put Egypt in the middle of what became a protracted and bloody war, which by 1965 drained Egypt's financial resources and tied up 70,000 of its best troops at a distance from the homeland and from the always-present difficulties with Israel. At the outset and throughout, Sadat spoke glowingly in favor of the defense pact. In the Egyptian National Assembly, he jauntily claimed that the campaign would be "a picnic on the Red Sea" and would provide the Egyptian army with vital battlefield experience that could be used elsewhere when Egypt had to deal with more difficult foes.[8] In his autobiography, Sadat blames Amer for the military losses, asserting that Amer was not concerned with professional competence within the officer corps, only loyalty to him.

Just as the hugely unsuccessful war in Yemen was winding down, another hot spot appeared. In the spring of 1967 tensions came to a head between Syria and Israel, and, as a participant in a defense pact with Syria, Egypt was drawn head first into this arena. On April 7, Israeli fighter planes downed six Syrian planes in a major air conflict that occurred on the always-contentious Israeli-Syrian border. The Israeli pilots followed their success "with a victory loop around Damascus."[9] Then, on May 13, a Soviet intelligence memorandum warned the Egyptians that Israel was massing troops on the Syrian border in preparation for a military sortie. Although the note sent to Egypt cautioned the Egyptians "to avoid any rash action and allow the Soviet Union to defuse the crisis by diplomatic means," Nasser responded aggressively.[10] He moved large numbers of troops into Sinai. Previously, Egypt had two infantry divisions in the Sinai Peninsula, an integral part of Egypt not densely populated but affording Egypt with a contentious border with Israel. One of these divisions was in the Gaza strip, a heavily populated territory along the Mediterranean coast that had been part of the British mandate in Palestine and was slated to come under Palestinian control after the Arab-Israeli war of 1948–1949. It was, however, garrisoned by Egyptian forces and became a militarily hot border with Israel. The other Egyptian military unit was in the eastern Sinai. By June 1967, Egyptian forces in Sinai totaled 100,000 men, including 900 tanks and some battle-tested soldiers from Yemen who were being withdrawn from the conflict and sent into Sinai. These actions, in turn, led the Israelis to call up reservists and warn the population of the possibility of war.

Many reasons have been cited for Nasser's precipitous and provocative action in the lead up to the Six-Day War. To begin with, the country was in a desperate economic and political state, facing bankruptcy because of the drain on funds from the war in Yemen and the disappointing performance of the greatly enlarged public sector. As is so often the case, regimes try to divert attention from domestic problems through foreign escapades. Moreover, the constant political factionalism and infighting that character-ized the Egyptian polity had become even more intense in the 1960s and had taken a mental and physical toll on Nasser, prompting him to contemplate resignation in favor of Amer. Perhaps more telling was the constant drumbeat of criticism that Nasser was subjected to from Arab opponents, led in this instance by the Syrians. They charged Egypt with hiding behind the 4,500-man United Nations Emergency Force that was in place along the Egyptian side of the Egyptian-Israeli border, placed there after the 1956 British-French-Israeli invasion of Egypt in order to pre-vent further conflicts. Egypt's Arab critics berated Nasser as a coward and complained that the presence of the UN forces re-lieved Egypt of its obligation to come to the defense of Syria if the country was attacked.

A prideful man, Nasser took his commitments to Egyptian nationalism and pan-Arabism seriously. Stung by these attacks, he was "at his most defiant and violent," using Sadat's description of Nasser's behavior during the crisis.[11] On May 16, Egypt de-manded that the United Nations withdraw its forces, a demand that the UN acceded to two days later. The next decision that had to be made was whether the Egyptians would close the Strait of Tiran to Israeli shipping, something that the Israelis had made clear in the past would constitute a cause for war. Nasser sought the advice of an inner group of advisers, mainly non-cabinet members, including Sadat, individuals who had been close to the president for decades, some from even before the coup. He sought their advice on what was shaping up as a major regional, and quite possibly international, crisis. Nasser posed the following question to the group: Now that the UN forces have been withdrawn, should Egypt close the Strait of Tiran to Israeli shipping, knowing that by closing off the entrance to the Gulf of Aqaba, the Israeli port of Elath at the top of the Gulf would be unable to function and Israel was likely to regard this action as a cause for war? He turned im-mediately to Amer and asked whether the army was ready. Amer's reply, according to Sadat, was "on my head, be it boss. Everything is in tiptop shape."[12] The entire group, except for Prime Minister Sidqi Sulayman, favored closing the Strait. Sulayman pleaded for more time to pursue diplomatic initiatives, but the entire group, including Sadat, was confident that the Egyptian army could hold its own with the Israeli Defense Force. On May 18, Nasser closed the Strait of Tiran to Israeli shipping.

War began on June 5 and lasted six days. The Israeli air force destroyed the Egyptian air force in an early dawn attack; next, its ground forces, enjoying overwhelming air superiority, swept through Sinai, reaching all the way to the east bank of the Suez Canal. The Egyptian forces in Sinai retreated in complete disarray, and Israeli troops could have moved on to Cairo had they chosen to do so. The Nasser regime contemplated retreating to Upper Egypt and conducting guerrilla warfare if Israeli forces moved on Cairo and the delta. Syria and Jordan were also defeated militarily. Jordan lost the Old City of Jerusalem and the West Bank of the Jordan River, and Israeli forces seized the Golan Heights from Syria. Golan sat on the northern border of Israel and from its high perches the Syrian military often shelled Israeli settlements in the Galilee region. Egypt's losses were staggering. Ten thousand to 15,000 soldiers were killed, including 1,500 officers and many pilots. The country also lost $2 billion in equipment, including 320 tanks, 480 guns, 2 SAM missile batteries, 10,000 military vehicles, and 85 percent of its combat aircraft and all of its bombers. By war's end Israel was in occupation of 42,000 square miles of Arab territory, giving it control over three and one-half times the land mass that it had before the war. As part of Egypt's military campaign, the Egyptians scuttled ships in the Suez Canal during the war to prevent ships from using it. The canal was to remain closed until 1975, a huge financial loss to the Egyptian treasury.

The war, which Egyptians refer to as the reversal or setback (al-Naksa), had deep and lasting effects on Sadat. At the outset he was certain of success. On the morning when the radio announced that the war had begun, he took his time showering and shaving and put on good clothing before setting out for command headquarters. His car radio carried reports of the downing of Israeli aircraft and military successes in Sinai, and as he drove through the streets he saw crowds cheering the good news. One look at the grim countenance of Field Marshall Amer once he had entered command headquarters, however, told him a different story. The radio reports were a sham; Egypt was experiencing cat-astrophic losses. Sadat returned home distraught and in disbelief. He stayed indoors for days while the fighting was continuing and remained at home and in isolation for three weeks, interrupting his despair only by taking long walks, deep in thought. The defeat, which Sadat described as "a disgrace and humiliation," left him searching for the purpose of his life.[13] He had no doubt that Amer was responsible for the disorderly and panicky retreat of the Egyptian forces from Sinai. But he did not spare Nasser, whom he blamed for not immediately dismissing Amer, taking command of the army himself, and ordering the troops to stem the Israeli advance across Sinai by digging in along the Sinai passes. Later conversations with officers of the army convinced him that Egypt's soldiers had not failed; their commanding officers had failed them. Sadat would use but also misuse the lessons that he learned from the Six-Day War in 1973 when Egypt was again at war with Israel.

Sadat, Nasser, and the other Free Officers portrayed them-selves as revolutionaries. But were they really? They did not envi-sion themselves in this role in the early stages of their movement. Egypt's subjugation to Britain, its economic stagnation, and its military weakness dismayed them, but they were prepared to compromise with those in power in an effort to transform the country and build a new nation. Nor were they inspired by radical and agreed-upon ideological premises and priorities, nor did they possess a clear agenda for a new Egypt. If they became revolution-aries (and they constantly used the terms *inqilab* and *thawra* to describe the effects of their programs after they had seized power and began to believe that they had brought a revolution to Egypt),

they were revolutionaries only by default. If the term can be use-
fully applied to them, it is only because they seized power in 1952
after becoming disillusioned with other contenders and used
their power to effect transformative changes in Egypt. In their
youthful days, as young, raw officers, they had only inchoate ideas
about Egypt's future and their role in changing the Egyptian political dynamics. They were in touch with elements that sought a
transformed Egypt—the Communists, the fascistic Young Egypt
party, the Muslim Brotherhood, even the palace. Yet, increasingly
as they saw these groups wither under attacks from opponents,
they began to see themselves as the only agency for an economically and politically strong Egypt, independent of British power,
able to pursue a neutralist foreign policy and promote far-reaching
economic and social change.

Scholars have not been sympathetic to the revolutionary
claims of the military men. They have argued that the military
takeover was a preemptive, even preventive, revolution, keeping
more democratic and populist movements from asserting themselves. The military government of Egypt, in this perspective,
kept Egypt from becoming a more just, democratic, and open
society. Yet the transformations that these young men brought
about cannot be so easily discounted. First, they removed the
British army of occupation from the country through the Anglo-
Egyptian treaty of 1954. They expelled King Faruq and eventually abolished the monarchy. They carried out a far-reaching land
reform scheme and opened up the educational system so that
young men and women of talent could advance themselves. With
Soviet assistance, they built the High Dam at Aswan and used
its generation of cheap electrical power to promote industrial development. Yet their failures were as large as their successes, as
the latter years of Nasser's tenure in office will make clear. (See
Chapter 3.) Their economic policies, the goal of which was to raise
the standard of living for all and place Egypt among the highly
industrialized countries in the Third World, went awry. Their
dismantling of the private sector in favor of public enterprises

saddled the country with a highly inefficient and indebted public sector. Most prominently, they failed to generate popular enthusiasm for themselves. They abolished the old political parties on the legitimate grounds that they were corrupt, incapable of reforming themselves, and leading the country to a better future. But their effort to replace the old parliamentary form of government with a single party failed spectacularly. The Liberation Rally gave way to the National Union and then to the Arab Socialist Union, but few were deceived. Power rested with Nasser and his chosen subordinates.

And what about Sadat? Sadat in his early writings, while Nasser was still alive, described himself as a revolutionary, helping Nasser build a new nation on radically new foundations. Certainly, he despised much in the ancien régime, which he had endeavored to undermine through political assassinations before the seizure of power. Like the other young officers who came to power, he had no clear vision of a transformed Egypt other than the vague set of principles that animated the Free Officers in the period leading up to the coup. He and they wanted a strong army, having experienced the humiliation of military defeat in 1948. British troops must go, and Egypt should no longer be subject to the undue power and influence of foreign capital and the willingness of local capitalists to collaborate with foreign businesspersons. Yet, when many of these developments took place, Sadat found himself on the sidelines. His imprisonment had cut his early ties with fellow young officers, and his connections with the palace aroused suspicion against him. Although Nasser respected him, Sadat's influence in the governing circles was marginal until Nasser made him vice president in 1969. Even so, the office of vice president was significant only should the president be incapacitated or die. Nasser's death in 1970 was to change Egypt and Sadat irrevocably.

CHAPTER 3

| BECOMING PRESIDENT, |
1967–1973

THE 1967 WAR CULMINATED IN a series of failures that beset Egypt during the 1960s and left Nasser, and after him Sadat, with monumental political and economic problems. Although the 1950s had been an era of many accomplishments, exalting the reputation of the military men, making the country a model for newly independent states emerging from colonial rule, and elevating Nasser to the zenith of charismatic nationalists, by the 1960s one failure followed after the other. Nasser tried to deal with them, but his failing health and the severity of the problems hamstrung him and left his successor with much to do. Although Sadat had not played a prominent role in these developments, at least until Nasser chose him to be the country's vice president just one year before his death, a discussion of them is necessary in order to understand the problems that Sadat faced when he became president.

Unquestionably, the most devastating event had been the June War in 1967. Not only did it result in the loss of immense amounts of Arab territory, including Sinai, but it destroyed the morale of the people and left the country militarily defenseless. The Israeli military's chief of staff, Lt. General David Elazar, drove this point home in remarks he made at a ceremony commemorating Israeli paratroopers. "The enemy must know that *Zahal* [the Israeli Defense Force] has a long arm, and when this arm reaches the depth of his territory it turns into a fist."[1] The irrepressible Ariel Sharon, a ranking Israeli Defense Force general, was more graphic. He boasted that the Israeli army was without a counterpart in the Arab world and that, if the government wished, it could march its troops all the way to Libya and occupy all of the Arab capitals.

Sadat would have to cope with many problems when he became president. But Nasser still had three years of life left in him, and his largely unsuccessful efforts to right the ship of state added new dimensions to Egypt's difficulties. Nasser tendered his resignation as president after the 1967 military debacle, only to have the populace, spurred on by his acolytes, including members of the ruling elite, refuse to move forward without him. He, therefore, had little choice but to attempt to rebuild his shattered country, starting with the army. The first order of business was removing the military men who had performed so poorly in the June War. This meant cashiering the commander of the armed forces, Field Marshall Abdel Hakim Amer, which was no easy task because, in addition to being Nasser's lifelong friend, Amer had created his own bloc of supporters within the officer corps. But Amer had utterly botched the war, and Nasser was determined to prevail. Eventually Amer surrendered to the authorities, was imprisoned, and ultimately took his own life.

The next task was reequipping and retraining a defeated army. Here, the Egyptians had no alternative but to rely on the Soviet Union, which, following the 1956 war between Israel and Egypt, had become Egypt's chief arms supplier and a crucial resource for financial and technical assistance. It was the Soviets who constructed the new High Dam at Aswan that the Americans had refused to finance. As the Egyptian-Soviet alliance grew stronger, the Americans increasingly looked at Egypt as a Soviet client state, a position that President Lyndon Johnson made a cornerstone of his Middle-Eastern policies. The Soviets' response to Egypt's military requests was quick and decisive. Alarmed at the utter destruction of an army dependent on Soviet weaponry, they dispatched one of their top officers to oversee the military rebuilding. Marshall Matvei Zakharov left no doubt in the minds of the Egyptian elite that their forces had failed not because of the poor quality or inadequate quantity of Soviet weapons, but because of poor training and leadership. A tough and insensitive man, who did much to create resentment at the Soviet presence in Egypt, Zakharov's blanket response to repeated Egyptian demands for more and better arms was "Why do you need more arms? You only deliver them to the Israelis!"[2]

Yet the Soviets made good on their promise to reequip and retrain the Egyptian forces. No Egyptian officer could have asked for more. Within a few months the Soviet Union had provided Egypt with 80 percent of the aircraft, tanks, and artillery lost in the war, and it did so at little cost to Egypt. Within three years, some, though not all, of the top brass in the Egyptian military believed that their forces were ready to resume warfare with Israel. In so rapidly resupplying the Egyptian military, the Soviets underlined the importance that they attached to retaining Egypt within the Soviet orbit; their military commitment to Egypt exceeded the aid that they were supplying to North Vietnam and other friendly and allied countries.

After having secured Marshall Zakharov's assurance that the Egyptian army was rebuilt and rearmed, on September 28, 1969, Nasser launched a massive artillery barrage at Israeli troops dug in along the east bank of the Suez Canal, lobbing more than 10,000 bombs from 150 batteries in a period of ten hours. The bombardment made a great deal of noise but resulted in the killing of only ten Israeli soldiers and the wounding of eighteen. Still, the assault accomplished several of Nasser's goals. As intended, it demonstrated to the Israelis that, though defeated in the Six-Day War, Egypt was determined to win back the territories lost in that conflict. The shelling across the canal was also based on the premise that Egypt could absorb more casualties than the Israelis and that the attack on troops stationed in western Sinai would persuade the Israelis that having military emplacements at such a long distance from the Israeli border exposed their troops to unacceptable dangers. Alas, the strategy backfired. The Israelis retaliated, first by bombing the Suez oil refineries and the canal cities of Suez and Ismailia, and then by carrying out aerial raids deep inside Egypt, striking strategic targets and at times causing harm to innocent civilians. The bombing of the canal cities compelled Nasser to evacuate the peoples living in these densely populated parts of Egypt. Egypt's strategic surface-to-air missile system, at the time Soviet SAM 2 missiles, proved ineffective against low-flying American-made Israeli aircraft and rendered not only the peoples living along the canal but the population centers in the delta, Upper Egypt, and Cairo vulnerable to Israeli air raids.

The many losses that Egypt sustained in the War of Attrition, as this conflict came to be known, drove Egypt even more firmly into the arms of the Soviets. Nasser made a secret trip to Moscow in January 1970 to plead for additional, higher grade weapons. The outcome of his conversations with Leonid Brezhnev, general secretary of the Central Committee of the Soviet Communist Party, was to have fateful and far-reaching consequences not only for the Arabs and the Israelis but also for the Americans and the Soviets. They drew the two superpowers more deeply into Middle Eastern affairs. In Moscow, Nasser insisted that Egypt must have a more effective missile defense system and more and better fighter planes if it was to defend its people. When Brezhnev hesitated, reminding the Egyptian president that supplying these weapons would only escalate the Arab-Israeli conflict and aggravate already tense superpower relations, Nasser responded angrily. "As far as I can see," Nasser asserted, "you are not prepared to help us in the same way that America helps Israel. This means that there is only one course open to me. I shall go back to Egypt, and I shall tell the people the truth. I shall tell them that the time has come for me to step down and to hand over to a pro-American president." When Brezhnev objected that Nasser could not do this, that he was Egypt's chosen leader and must remain in power, Nasser replied: "I am a leader who is bombed every day in his own country, whose army is exposed, and whose people are naked. I have the courage to tell our people the unfortunate truth—that whether they like it or not, the Americans are the masters of the world."[3]

Nasser's threat brought a response, though not quickly enough to satisfy many Egyptians. In time, the Soviets provided Egypt with a superior surface-to-air missile defense system (SAM 3), capable of tracking and downing low-flying jet fighter planes. They also sent additional jet fighter planes, including four high-altitude supersonic reconnaissance planes (MIG-23s), though their delivery was much delayed. To man the SAM sites and fly the jet planes, the Soviet sent missile crews and fighter pilots. When, in April 1970, Israeli pilots encountered Soviet planes with Egyptian markings, flown by Soviet pilots, speaking Russian to one another, they quickly withdrew from combat and made no further deep raids into Egyptian air space. Whether Nasser ever intended to carry through on his ultimatum to seek American aid is difficult to judge. In any case, a favorable American response would have been unlikely given the fact that Egypt and the United States had severed diplomatic relations during the Six-Day War and Nasser was regarded in American circles as a man who could not be trusted. But Nasser's threat to Brezhnev was a telling one. Eventually his successor, Sadat, would carry it out.

Nasser's hint that Egypt might alter its foreign policy was not the only policy change that followed defeat in the Six-Day War. In 1968, responding to a steadily increasing number of student and workers protests, brought about because many thought that the regime had made insufficient efforts to alleviate economic distress or respond to demands for political reforms, the Nasser regime promised to alter its domestic policies. An immediate development was the March 30, 1968, declaration, which, while it offered something to nearly every segment of Egyptian society, had a decidedly liberal and democratic emphasis. First, declaring its intention to safeguard the political rights of all citizens, the regime promised that it would carry out a battery of free elections in order to ensure that those who governed the country enjoyed the support of the people. Second, in stressing the need for a more efficient and liberalized economy, the government affirmed that public-sector companies were to be held to exacting and transparent financial standards while the private sector was to be reenergized. The state would ready legislation that made foreign investment in Egypt more attractive. Unfortunately, the Nasser government had to postpone implementing most of this program because of the War of Attrition along the Suez Canal and Nasser's own deteriorating health. It was Sadat who would use the March 30 guidelines in formulating his economic and political policies.

By 1970, Nasser was a sick man. Although he maintained a heavy schedule, much too heavy in the opinion of his doctors, he sometimes had to be carried to and from his places of work, so severe was the pain in his legs. He suffered from a blood disorder, known as hemochromatosis, which causes iron deposits to accumulate in the body tissues, often leads to diabetes, as it did in his case, attacks the body's organs, and can result in cardiac arrest. That he might have prolonged his life had he cut back on his work routines is undoubted. Sadat saw him after he returned from an extensive rehabilitation treatment in the Soviet Union that featured a stay in the Soviets' astronauts' oxygen room. He looked twenty years younger, striding along the airport tarmac with "a healthy ruddy color in his face and chest thrust forward like a man of thirty."[4] But Nasser refused to reduce his commitments; nor was he willing to delegate powers to subordinates. The inevitable could not be held off; by September 1970, Egypt's president had reached a stage of utter exhaustion. Yet, despite debilitating fatigue, Nasser agreed to host a meeting of Arab heads of state, at the conclusion of which, on the afternoon of September 28, 1970, he accompanied the Emir of Kuwait to the Cairo airport. After returning home, he lay down but never regained consciousness, expiring from the cardiac arrest that many for a long time had feared would claim his life.

Nasser with his successor, Anwar al-Sadat.

One of the first officials to arrive at Nasser's home after news of his death had circulated among government officials was Sadat, at the time Nasser's vice president. Shocked and in a state of disbelief, he removed the sheet that covered Nasser's face and put his own cheek next to Nasser's. Believing him still to be alive, he implored the five attending physicians to revive him. They, too, were heartbroken, exclaiming that they had done everything in their power to save the president. They then burst into tears.

Why Nasser chose Sadat as his vice president—a decision he made in late December 1969, only nine months before he passed away, at a time when he surely knew that his days were numbered and a mere three and a half months after having had a serious heart attack—has puzzled many. Sadat's critics, who are legion, assert that Nasser never intended Sadat's appointment to be anything but temporary. Nasser's custom was to move subordinates in and out of the government, especially in the office of vice president, and so it is possible that Nasser intended Sadat's tenure as vice president to be short. According to one account, Nasser said that it was Sadat's turn when he was queried about the appointment. Nasser's daughter, Hoda, in whom he often confided, said that her father never took Sadat seriously and would not have wanted him to be president. Many thought that Nasser intended to appoint Abdel Latif al-Baghdadi as vice president after Sadat's tenure had run its course but never got around to it. On the other hand, given the fact that Nasser knew that his health was poor, it is hard to believe that he was so casual about the vice presidency. In addition, Sadat was one of only a few of the original Free Officers who still held office in 1969 and still espoused the goals of the movement. He had drawn close to Nasser in his last years, consoling him after the defeat in the June War and offering him encouragement as he coped with declining health.

Why the ruling elite agreed to select Sadat as Nasser's replacement is a matter less controversial. There were of course many aspirants to power. On the left, the man favored by the Soviets was Ali Sabri, a former prime minister, the minister of air defense, and long-time dominant figure in the Arab Socialist Union, Egypt's powerful ruling party. In the center of the political spectrum were the men in whose hands the main levers of power rested. This bloc consisted of the minister of the interior, the minister of state for presidential affairs, a minister of state, the speaker of the National Assembly, the secretary general of the Arab Socialist Union, and the minister of information. In short, this group of men controlled the police, internal security forces, radio and television stations, and the presidential guard. Moreover, they enjoyed the support of the head of the armed forces, Mahmud Fawzi, the minister of defense. On the right, favoring a rapprochement with the Americans and a liberalization of the economy, was Zakaria al-Muhyi al-Din, himself an original Free Officer and still influential in government circles. But none of these individuals had an unsullied record, and none enjoyed the standing among the people that Sadat had achieved over the years through his close association with the president and his writings in support of the regime. In addition, the ruling elite wanted a smooth transition of power. They wished to move forward constitutionally, fearing above all that the Israelis might exploit weaknesses in the Egyptian leadership to make new territorial gains. They agreed that Sadat should become acting president of the republic, as stipulated by the constitution. After that, the Arab Socialist Union (Egypt's only political party created by the RCC before it went out of existence) and the National Assembly would nominate Sadat as president, and the electorate would vote on his candidacy in a referendum.

One of the major players in promoting Sadat as Nasser's successor was Mohammed Heikal, Nasser's close confidant and a person of enormous influence as editor in chief of Egypt's most widely circulating newspaper, *al-Ahram*. He urged Sadat's candidacy on the officials of the Supreme Executive Committee of the Arab Socialist Union, cabinet members, and other key officials, arguing that the safest way to move forward was through a Sadat presidency. Heikal's major argument—one that carried the day with the other aspirants to power—was that Sadat was less ambitious than Nasser, less committed to one-man rule, and more willing to share power with others. Sadat's reputation for not challenging those in authority (his nickname being "colonel yes, yes") added to his appeal among other claimants to power.[5] To cement this understanding, the ruling elite extracted a promise from Sadat that he would honor collective leadership, not engage in one-man rule, refer all issues to the National Assembly, and allow ministers a free hand in running their own departments. Sadat also consented to have Ali Sabri, a former prime minister, long-time member of the Arab Socialist Union, and a contender for the presidency, serve as his vice president. Only Ali Sabri, not Sadat, was to be entitled to sit in on cabinet meetings.

The striking physical differences and apparent differences in temperament that distinguished Sadat from Nasser no doubt made Sadat appear a less threatening and formidable individual to those who chose him as president. Nasser was a large, muscular individual who exuded strength and commanded immediate respect whenever he appeared in public. By contrast, Sadat was wiry, less than 6 feet in height, whose appearances in public before he became head of state were rarely noticed. In addition, Sadat's swarthy complexion and his curly hair, which he inherited from his Sudanese mother, made him a person of lesser importance to those individuals in the ruling elite for whom race was a marker of status. Yet, as time would soon tell, Sadat enjoyed power, knew how to exercise it, and had as forceful a drive to stamp his personality on Egyptian society as his predecessor displayed. While Nasser was regularly referred to as *al-rais*, the boss, and Sadat never was, they both were charismatic. Nasser's appeal to people came more naturally and automatically, while Sadat used dress and a regal bearing to impress others.

The peaceful and constitutional transfer of power from Nasser to his vice president, Sadat, was by the standards of the postcolonial world in this era quite remarkable. Military coups were the order of the day throughout Asia and Africa. In the Arab world, they brought ambitious military men to power, men with whom Sadat would have to work and with whom he often found himself in conflict. Military coups occurred in Sudan in 1958 and again in 1964, finally bringing Gaafar Nimeiry to power. In Libya, Muammar Qaddafi ousted King Idris in 1969 to become that country's long-lasting strong man, while Iraq witnessed a series of coups beginning in 1958, which resulted in Saddam Hussein's assumption of power in the late 1970s. The military seized power in Algeria in 1958, while Syria experienced a series of military takeovers beginning in the 1950s that eventually brought Hafez al-Assad to power in 1970. Although Sadat was himself a military man, a participant in the original 1952 seizure of power, the orderliness of his assumption of the presidency gave him a legitimacy that many of his contemporaries in the Arab world lacked and often allowed him to scorn these men as upstarts. In addition, once he had consolidated his hold on power, his legitimacy emboldened him to remove many of Nasser's cohorts from the high political offices that they had grown accustomed to holding.

In his memoirs, Sadat asserts that he was reluctant to assume the office of president, believing that the reclaiming of the territories lost in the 1967 war should take precedence over all other issues. He proposed that he remain vice president until the showdown with Israel had taken place. He was persuaded otherwise by a note from a number of army officers pointing out that Egypt needed a firm, presidential hand at the tiller in these difficult times. In addition, he feared the influence of the men who aspired to power, believing that they had drawn too close to the Soviet Union and were out of step with Nasser's legacy.

Sadat himself sounded all of the right notes when he went before the National Assembly on October 7, 1970, as it prepared to nominate him as president. He pledged to continue Nasser's policies: "I have come to you," he announced, "along the path of Gamal Abdel Nasser, and I believe that your nomination of me to assume the responsibilities is a nomination of me to continue in the path of Nasser."[6]

Although Sadat told the National Assembly that he intended to follow in Nasser's footsteps and rarely missed an opportunity to associate his policies with those of his predecessor, some of his first acts made it clear that he was determined to move in new directions. In late December 1970, only two months after Nasser's death, Sadat ordered that the National Assembly review the sequestration and confiscation policies that the Nasser government had carried out against the wealthy and powerful classes. He followed this statement on May 31, 1971, by making the National Assembly's first item of significant legislation a law regulating sequestrations.

Sequestrations and confiscations were controversial matters. During the Nasser years, especially following the British-French-Israeli invasion of the country, the state had used the sequestration instrument to hobble the wealthy classes, mainly, though not exclusively at first, foreign residents, who had been the backbone of Egypt's private sector. They were now blamed for supporting the invasion. As state control over the economy burgeoned in the late 1950s and early 1960s, the government became suspicious of its own bourgeoisie. Attacks against Egypt's business persons became particularly savage following the breakup of the Egyptian-Syrian political union in 1961. Nasser held the wealthy classes in Syria and Egypt responsible for the rupture in relations and took his revenge on Egypt's well-off families, expropriating their wealth and turning them into wards of the state. In the late 1960s, when General Abdel Hakim Amer was riding high, the government again went after the wealthy. The Committee to Liquidate Feudalism, headed by Field Marshall Amer, was established ostensibly to ferret out those wealthy landowners, who had managed to subvert the land reform laws of the 1950s and secretly retained land that the state should have acquired. In reality, Amer used this committee to seize the property of adversaries and to distribute land and other assets to those who had linked their fortunes to his. The committee was bitterly resented by the people and did much to undermine the high regard that most people had for Nasser and his government.

That Sadat would turn his attention first to sequestrations, expropriations, and confiscations, even before approaching the Americans, was telling. It underlined a fundamental difference in the experiences and personalities of Nasser and Sadat. Nasser had chafed at the power and arrogance of Egypt's ruling elite, foreign and domestic alike. He took pleasure in meting out pain and humiliations to those who had slighted him and taken advantage of the Egyptian rank and file. He had a deep attachment to Egypt's common people and was sure that they would take pleasure in seeing their tormentors abased. In contrast, Sadat gained little satisfaction from the suffering of others (though, of course, like any man in power he was willing to inflict pain on his enemies), and indeed, he admired, certainly later in life if not in his younger days, individuals who crowned success in their careers by exercising power and accumulating riches. Nasser eschewed comforts and lived an abstemious life. He kept his personal life and family out of the limelight. Sadat was quite the opposite, luxuriating in expensive clothes and enjoying the company of famous and powerful individuals. In his memoirs, Sadat depicts Nasser as a man lacking joie de vivre and believed those who went through life carrying the burdens of the world were to be pitied. Sadat's daughter, Camelia, captured the differences between the two men in her autobiography. Describing her wedding day, a bewildering event to her because of her age but one she was determined to enjoy, she noted that Nasser's presence cast a pall over the occasion. Only after he departed was the group finally able to enjoy itself.

Another of Sadat's bold, early departures was reaching out to the Americans as Nasser had threatened to do in his January 1970 secret mission to Moscow. In this case, Sadat was altogether serious. His first overture occurred at the time of Nasser's funeral, during which he told a member of the American delegation, Elliot Richardson, how much he wanted to repair relations with the United States. Unfortunately, Richardson, not believing that Sadat would last as president and attaching little importance to his words, did not recommend a follow-up. Later, Sadat contacted Donald Bergus, head of the American interests section in the Spanish Embassy in Cairo, to whom he reiterated his interest in repairing American–Egyptian relations severed in the wake of the Six-Day War in 1967. He went even further, indicating that he was now prepared to reach an agreement with the Israelis and reopen the Suez Canal if the Israelis were prepared to return the lands taken from Egypt during the 1967 war. Unlike Richardson, Bergus was impressed. He cabled the State Department in Washington, asserting that "we can do business with this guy."[7] That Sadat was not engaging in frivolous conversation became clear in a speech he delivered to the National Assembly on February 4, 1971. In it, he said that he was prepared to clear the Suez Canal and open it to traffic if the Israelis removed their troops from the east bank of the canal and permitted Egyptian soldiers to occupy these areas. Golda Meir, the Israeli prime minister, was unimpressed, believing that the Egyptians were not offering enough to tempt the Israelis to give up highly defensible territories.

Sadat's departures from Nasser's policies did not go unnoticed. Alarmed that their new president had aspirations to power that they had not foreseen, his critics began to gather evidence that he was exceeding his authority. To this end, they employed a technique that Nasser had perfected: illegal intelligence gathering. Sadat was unaware that Egyptian security officers had bugged his residence and had turned over the records of all of his telephone and other conversations to his opponents, including Ali Sabri, Egypt's vice president and Sadat's most ardent critic. These tapes, if made public, would have harmed Sadat. They contained his secret overtures to the Americans as well as plans to remove adversaries from government positions. Sabri did not wait long before marshaling the opposition. In replying to Sadat's February 4, 1971, speech in the National Assembly on reopening the Suez Canal, Sabri argued that Egypt should not make concessions on the Canal until the whole of Sinai had been restored to Egyptian hands.

A proposal to bring about a union between Egypt, Syria, and Libya, put forward with Sadat's endorsement and debated between April 14 and April 17, 1971, would have seemed on the surface hardly the grounds for a showdown. Under Nasser, Egypt had led pan-Arab initiatives, and the union of these three countries, notwithstanding the presence of the young and irrepressible Muammar Qaddafi as president of Libya, was entirely in keeping with previous Egyptian foreign policy. Yet Sabri and many other officials seized the moment to resist the authority of a man who appeared determined to rule as forcefully and autocratically as his predecessor. Overt opposition to the political union predictably occurred first in the Supreme Executive Committee of the Arab Socialist Union, which Sadat antagonists controlled. Five of its eight members, whom Sadat considered to be so pro-Soviet that he nicknamed the committee "the Politburo," rejected the proposal outright.[8] Sadat's effort to do an end run around this body by taking the matter to the larger, presumably more accommodating Central Committee of the Arab Socialist Union also failed. Ali Sabri had been the dominant figure in the Arab Socialist Union for many years; its delegates were delighted to shoot down Sadat when he asked them to overrule the executive committee.

The challenge to Sadat came earlier than many had anticipated, in part because he had so clearly revealed his intention to dominate the polity. Predictably, it came from the men who controlled Egypt's levers of power and viewed themselves as Nasser's rightful successors. The dispute was truly joined on May 2, 1971, when Sadat dismissed Ali Sabri from the vice presidency. By removing his chief critic and the rallying figure for his opponents, Sadat forced the hand of his adversaries. Moving forcefully and quickly secured for him many advantages. The moment for action came when pro-Sadat officers within the Egyptian intelligence department delivered to his residence 3,600 pages of transcripts of conversations involving him, Heikal, and American officials in Egypt. These revealed that Egyptian intelligence had been bugging his home and was collecting evidence, or so he believed, to label him a traitor, put him on trial, and remove him from office. Sadat sought the advice of those closest to him. He turned first to his wife, who urged him to act quickly. Sayyid Marei, a close adviser and neighbor, sped back from Alexandria to offer support and met with Mohammed Heikal and others at Sadat's residence in order to devise a response to the challenge. Sadat's confidants agreed with Jihan that the president must move immediately and decisively. As an opening salvo, he removed the minister of the interior, an outspoken critic, whose portfolio gave him authority over the police and security services. Controlling Egypt's radio and television stations came next. Later, he lined up support among the managers and workers in the most important public-sector companies.

His adversaries erred in responding to Sadat's moves. On May 13, leading cabinet ministers, controlling virtually all of

Egypt's levers of coercive power, resigned en masse, believing that their resignations would expose Sadat's vulnerabilities, force him to share power, perhaps even bring about his overthrow. They miscalculated utterly. Sadat simply accepted their resignations and replaced them with his own men. Not an individual within the army, the police, the presidential guard, or the intelligence services raised a finger in protest. Nor did they oppose the bewildering array of new legislation that followed the removal of these officials.

The series of proclamations and actions that followed in swift order solidified Sadat's power and made the month of May 1971 a turning point in his ascension to power. Not only did his bold action avert political defeat, it also enabled him to populate the government with supporters, stamp his vision and personality on the Egyptian polity, and place distance between himself and the once all-pervasive legacy of his predecessor. In time, Sadat coined the term "the corrective revolution" to mark the changes that he initiated in May 1971, intimating that many of Nasser's policies had fallen short of the mark and needed to be altered. In reality, the developments that followed the ousting of his political opponents were the springboard for even more dramatic developments that came later—the October War of 1973, the journey to Jerusalem in 1977, and the 1978 Camp David accords—all of which catapulted Sadat beyond his Egyptian base onto the world stage.

The political changes that Sadat brought about in May were, indeed, breathtaking. His first steps involved reorganizing the cabinet, appointing a number of key provincial governors, and expelling members of the National Assembly who had spoken against him. He followed these actions by purging the police, intelligence, and information services of officials whom he suspected of opposing him; ordering new elections to the National Assembly; and renaming the People's Assembly and the Arab Socialist Union. In all, the Egyptian citizenry went to the polls no fewer than eight times during the last six months of 1971. They cast votes for a new slate of representatives in the professional syndicates, the Arab Socialist Union, and the People's Assembly. The electorate also participated in a referendum on a new permanent constitution. Following these changes, Sadat was truly in charge, and Nasser no longer cast a large shadow over Egyptian politics. Nor did Sadat spare his opponents. They were put on trial. A number were given death sentences, all of which were commuted to life imprisonment. Others were given long-term sentences, regularly commuted to shorter terms.

Sadat prevailed over highly placed opponents because he understood the dynamics of power in Egypt's highly centralized, top-down political system where second-tier officials were only too eager to supplant their superiors. His principal ally in the army was General Muhammad Sadiq, chief of staff under the minister of defense, General Muhammad Fawzi, who was anti-Sadat. Sadat won over Sadiq because the two of them had long shared a distaste of the Soviets. Sadat also made it clear to the officer corps that he did not hold them responsible for the failures of the Six-Day War. Instead, he blamed Nasser for the fateful decision to absorb the first Israeli military blow, which most of the high command had opposed, and Amer for the disorderly flight from Sinai. His decision to pardon 1,000 cashiered officers, censured and jailed for the war defeat, ensured that most of the officer corps would side with him. Sadat did much the same with the security forces, the police, and the intelligence services, assuring the loyalty of those just beneath the top officials.

When placing the defense minister, General Muhammad Fawzi, under house arrest, Sadat dealt with another source of opposition to his authority and to the office of the presidency, what he and others called the "foci of power" that had emerged during the 1960s. At least five relatively autonomous power centers had grown up in the latter Nasser years, the most pervasive of which was unquestionably that under Field Marshall Abdel Hakim Amer, commander of the armed forces and minister of defense until his suicide in 1967. Amer had endeavored to establish within the army a power base separate from Nasser's and then had used his high political position to win supporters outside the military. Other power enclaves included Liberation Province, the Arab Socialist Union, the media, and the ministry of agriculture and land reform. Amer's demise and General Muhammad Fawzi's dismissal in 1971 purged the leading anti-Sadat faction within the army. Sabri's removal from power, Sadat's eventual sidelining of Heikal, editor in chief al *al-Ahram*, and Sadat's friendship with the Sayyid Marei, head of the ministry of agriculture and land reform, removed these institutional obstacles to presidential authority.

Soon after removing his foes from office, Sadat publicly burned the files and tapes that the intelligence branch of the government had accumulated during the Nasser years and followed this act by promising a more open and liberal polity. To this end, he reinstated judges who had been suspended by Nasser, released numerous political prisoners, including many Muslim Brothers, and closed detention camps that held political prisoners. Sadat's new constitution, promulgated in 1971, guaranteed Egyptians all of the internationally recognized political liberties and human rights, including the right to free speech, free assembly, and religious freedom. It also forbade unauthorized searches and seizures. The 1971 constitution, while enhancing the power of the People's Assembly, especially in relationship to the Arab Socialist Union, still accorded great power to the president, who not only served as chief of state but also was the head of the government and commander of the armed forces. In cases involving national security, the president was authorized to issue decrees on his own, though these had to be ratified by referendum within sixty days. In addition, when parliament was not in session or when emergencies arose, the president could promulgate decrees having the force of law. As in the past, the president retained the power to appoint the prime minister and cabinet members, the chief of staff of the armed forces, public-sector managers, newspaper editors, judges, and party leaders. So that the people were in no doubt where the ultimate fount of authority was and where this new more open society originated. Sadat presented the constitution as a gift from the president and not as a set of principles that inhered in the people and represented their right to govern themselves. A state of emergency, which had existed most of the time in the Nasser years, was maintained and was to remain in existence during Sadat's presidency except for short intervals.

Sadat justified his "corrective revolution" on the grounds that Nasser had actually intended to move in these directions but had been prevented from doing so because of deteriorating health and the need to prepare for war with Israel. He pointed specifically to the promises made in the March 30 program of 1968 for a more open society and a more free-market-oriented economy. In actuality, however, Sadat's "corrective revolution" presaged a sharp move away from Nasser's policies, ultimately setting the stage for overtures to the Americans and a more open economy, though few could be sure at this stage how far Sadat intended to go in altering Nasser's policies. What was clear in Sadat's statements is that Nasser had led Egypt in the wrong direction. The obvious conclusion to be drawn at this juncture was that Nasser had badly miscalculated the enthusiasm for pan-Arabism when he established political unions with neighboring states and engaged in what proved to be an unwinnable war in Yemen. He had lost vital lands to Israel in the Six-Day War, expended too heavily and unwisely on the military, and had pursued ineffective socialist public-sector policies that had burdened Egypt with debt and left the country with many unprofitable public-sector companies.

Yet, even while spurning many of his predecessor's policies, Sadat did not turn away from Nasser's promise to gain back the territories lost to Israel in the Six-Day War. Nasser had announced to the world shortly after the imposition of the ceasefire in 1967 that "what was taken by force will be returned by force." In 1971, soon after consolidating his authority, Sadat reiterated this goal, proclaiming 1971 as the year of decision toward war or peace. He stated repeatedly during that year that Egypt's "main goal is the battle," and asserting "as to a permanent cease-fire . . . we shall

never concur to it. . . . As long as one single foreign soldier is stationed on my soil, I shall limit the cease-fire."[9] When at the end of
the year war had not been joined, Sadat claimed that the
Indian-Pakistani conflict in December of that year had made it
impossible to pursue a military plan because of the involvement
of the superpowers there.

Since Egypt had to prepare for war and since Sadat needed to
firm up his relations with the Soviet Union, he agreed to a treaty
of friendship with the Soviets on May 27, 1971, an arrangement
that delighted the Soviets and one that Nasser had resisted because he feared making Egypt a Soviet satellite. The Americans
were naturally alarmed and disappointed, a sentiment that was
not modified when Sadat accused the Americans of being a mere
"mailman," carrying messages between Egypt and Israel and
always taking the side of the Israelis.

Nonetheless, Sadat's relations with the Soviets were even
more conflicted than Nasser's in the late 1960s. The main bone of
contention was, as always, the supply of arms, which the Egyptians considered utterly inadequate, creating a situation, at least
in the minds of many Egyptians, of a "no war, no peace" stalemate
with the Israelis. In Sadat's view, and that of most of the Egyptian
foreign policy establishment, the situation favored the Israelis,
the Soviets, and the Americans at the expense of the Egyptians.
Compelled to maintain itself on a war footing, despite the heavy
drain that military expenditures and military training had on the
economy, Egypt's prospects for succeeding in war with Israel
were dismal. Moreover, the military stalemate imposed a pervasive paralysis on all Egyptians, putting the lives of young people
continuously on hold because compulsory military service forced
young men to delay career and marriage prospects. It is hardly
surprising that students and workers became restive and even
began to demand a once-and-for-all showdown with the Israelis.
Even were Egypt to lose, at least in the minds of this cohort of
students and workers, they themselves would finally be able to
move on with their lives.

Sadat's frustration with the Soviets as arms suppliers comes out clearly in an interview that he gave to Egyptian newspaper editors, which was published in *Newsweek* magazine on August 7, 1972. In it he said that "there has hardly been a day without some quarrel with the Russians. . . . My tongue went dry arguing with them."[10] One of Egypt's main needs was the MIG-23 supersonic jet fighter plane to counter American-built Phantom jets flown by the Israelis. The Soviet leadership rejected the request on the grounds that the plane would take Egyptian pilots five years to learn to fly—a claim that Sadat dismissed as "nonsense." Sadat was confident that Egypt's pilots could fly them in six months. Nor did Sadat's treaty of friendship produce an arms breakthrough or his two secret trips to Moscow during the first half of 1972. On June 1, 1972, Sadat sent a seven-point questionnaire to Brezhnev spelling out Egypt's needs and emphasizing that the Soviet response would, in fact, determine future Soviet–Egyptian relations. When this ultimatum did not produce results, Sadat took action that few expected. He expelled Soviet military advisers.

It should not have been surprising to the Soviet leadership, though it was, that on July 7, 1972, Sadat gave the Soviets ten days to remove all 21,000 of their military advisers from Egypt. Soviet military installations were to be handed over to the Egyptians, all Soviet military equipment was either to be sold to Egypt or returned to the Soviet Union, and all future negotiations between the two countries were to take place in Cairo. Although the Soviets complied with extraordinary speed and efficiency, carrying out the evacuation in seven days, Brezhnev demanded an explanation from Sadat of what seemed to him an irreparable rupture in Egyptian–Soviet relations. Few replies were more important in Sadat's presidential career since he still did not enjoy the backing of the Americans and still required considerable Soviet technical, financial, and military support. The president spent seven hours drafting the note, which did, indeed, lay out the reasons for expelling the Soviet military experts while still leaving the door open for continued Soviet military assistance.

In the missive to Brezhnev, Sadat averred that the main reason that the Egyptians had asked the Soviet military personnel to leave was that, in the forthcoming battle that Egypt was determined to have with Israel, Egypt must go to war on its own. Were the Soviets military advisers still in the country when war broke out and Egypt prevailed, the Soviets would gain the credit. If Egypt lost, he and his army, not the Soviets, would be blamed as they were during the Six-Day War. More important in Sadat's mind was that the battle not become "an occasion for a confrontation between the Soviet Union and the United States, knowing well that this would mean a disaster for the whole world." In the final analysis, Israel and its chief and only ally, the United States, would do nothing to change the status quo "unless Israel feels that our military strength is in a position to challenge the superiority at present enjoyed by Israel." Nor did Sadat remove the Soviets in his calculus of reasons for doing without Soviet military personnel. Sadat wrote that while the Americans had equipped Israel with "an entirely new air force, . . . the attitude reflected in your latest letter shows that for five years a partial arms embargo has been imposed on us."[11]

Sadat composed his lengthy note in an effort to explain the change in Soviet–Egyptian relations and prevent a complete rupture. Unwilling to see a strategically located country drift out of its political orbit, the Soviets responded as Sadat had hoped. They sped up their shipments of vital military equipment, including SAM 3 and SAM 6 missiles, as well as the latest antiaircraft and antitank weapons, tanks with infrared tracking devices, and bridging equipment, all of which were used with success in the October 1973 war. Sadat suspected that the reason for the willingness of the Soviets to supply weapons that they had withheld for so long was that they wished to see Egypt go to war and sustain a military defeat, thus truly forcing the country back into Soviet arms.

While Sadat was, therefore, not displeased with the Soviet response to his decision to expel Soviet military advisers, he was dissatisfied with the lack of an American response. He expected more, contemplating a renewal of relations with the United States and even hoping that the Americans would put pressure on Israel to be forthcoming in back channel talks with the Egyptians. Sadat had continued the ceasefire arrangements that the US secretary of state, William Rogers, had persuaded Egypt and Israel to accept in 1970. While it is true that Sadat was doing no more than upholding an arrangement that Nasser had originally agreed to, Nasser had made it clear at the time that the ceasefire was only a temporary measure that would allow Egypt a breathing period to improve its defensive posture against Israel. In his memoirs, Henry Kissinger criticized Sadat for not extracting significant concessions from the Americans before removing the Soviet advisers. But this would have undermined Sadat's larger strategy of keeping the Soviet Union in play should the Americans remain unresponsive to Egypt. The Americans balked at responding because they did not anticipate Egypt going to war and believed that the Egyptian condition of "no war, no peace" favored Israel and would ultimately drive Egypt to look to the United States as the only way forward. Sadat drew a different conclusion from America's disappointing response. He intensified his plans for war with Israel.

CHAPTER 4

| MAKING WAR, 1973–1974 |

EARLY ON THE MORNING OF October 6, 1973, Henry Kissinger, the recently appointed US secretary of state, was awakened with credible information that Egypt and Syria were preparing to launch a war against Israel at 6:00 p.m. their time (11:00 a.m. EST). In New York City, to attend sessions of the United Nations, Kissinger responded with alacrity, informing President Richard Nixon, who was in Florida, that a conflict with the potential to involve the superpowers was likely to unfold within hours. He also talked with top Israeli officials to ensure that the Israelis were not themselves intending a preemptive strike against their Arab neighbors. He counseled them that they should, if the information proved correct, absorb a first blow before sending their forces into action. Kissinger also spoke with Soviet officials, urging them to impose restraint on their Arab allies.

Kissinger's efforts to prevent war were unavailing. At 2:00 p.m. Egyptian time, not 6:00 p.m. as Kissinger had been led to believe, Egypt and Syria launched a massive, highly coordinated and extremely successful attack on Israeli units based in the Golan Heights and on the east bank of the Suez Canal. Within hours, the Egyptians ferried a large number of soldiers and equipment across the canal, and within twenty-four hours, Egyptian forces seized most of the Israeli fortifications along the canal. Syrian forces drove the Israeli army off the Golan Heights, which had been occupied since the Six-Day War in 1967. In control of Golan, Syrian forces once again threatened Israeli villages in the Galilee area, and Egyptian divisions, once dug in along the east bank of the canal, could contemplate moving to the Sinai passes, Gidda and Mitla, perhaps even sweeping through all of Sinai to the border between Israel and Egypt.

Although the Israelis suffered major military losses in these opening days and feared that they could not stem the advance of the Egyptian and Syrian armies, their forces weathered the first assaults. After blunting an Egyptian advance to the passes, the Israeli Defense Force drove the Egyptian and Syrian armies back, ultimately threatening the Syrian interior and imperiling the Egyptian Third Army. Through sheer determination, coupled with military blunders on the part of their adversaries, the Israelis succeeded in triumphing militarily after having absorbed wholly unanticipated and staggering early battlefield losses.

The October War of 1973 was to become a watershed event in Middle Eastern and global politics. Although it lasted less than a month, from October 6 until early November, it drew in the Soviet Union and the United States, who transported to their client states—Egypt, Syria, and Israel—immense quantities of highly sophisticated and lethal weapons. As the war progressed and the weapons were used profligately, the superpowers provided even larger quantities of arms and even more sophisticated and lethal weapons. The prospect that the superpowers could themselves clash was apparent throughout and did, in fact, lead to an American decision to place its forces on nuclear alert.

Arguably, the October War was a war that the superpowers had been preparing to fight ever since the end of World War II. Mercifully, for them, though not for the warring countries, it was fought by client states. Most of the major armed conflicts that have pitted the superpowers against each other since the Korean War have involved guerrilla warfare against decidedly superior adversaries (the Vietcong against the French and the Americans; the Afghans against the Soviets and the Americans; and the

Iraqis against American forces). The October War had no guerril-
las. It involved large armies, set battle pieces, tank assaults,
clashes of supersonic fighter and bomber planes, surface-to-air
missiles, and even worries about the use of nuclear weapons, in
the first instance by the Israelis, and then as the superpowers
were drawn into the fray by the Americans and the Soviets.
Unlike earlier Soviet-American crises, notably the Berlin airlift in
1948 and the Cuban missile crisis in 1962, the October War
found the Soviets and Americans on par in their possession of
nuclear arsenals. Both wielded enormous arsenals of mutual
destruction.

The war also had far-reaching diplomatic and political consequences, yielding winners and losers. Known to some as "Kissinger's War," the conflict enhanced the diplomatic reputation of
Henry Kissinger and achieved what Kissinger had hoped would
be its ultimate outcome. Kissinger intended for the war to prove
to Middle Eastern leaders that the only way forward was through
the United States, not the Soviet Union. Although the Israelis
won the war militarily, their unexpected early setbacks undercut
the reputation of Israeli Prime Minister Golda Meir and her
Labor Party. Finally, the Soviets' efforts to prove that they were a
reliable ally failed. Their policy of détente with the United States,
which had become a prominent feature of Soviet and American
foreign policy during the Nixon and Brezhnev era, did not survive the crisis.

In many respects, however, the primary decision maker
during the war and in many respects the true winner, politically if
not militarily, was Egypt's president, Anwar al-Sadat. It was he
who assembled the team of military strategists who drew up the
stunningly successful battle plans for crossing the Suez Canal. It
was he who decided on October 14 after getting Egypt's troops
across the canal that his forces should leave the surface-to-air
missile defense protections that they enjoyed along the east bank
of the canal and advance to the Sinai passes. When this decision
exposed the Egyptian soldiers to the full might of the Israeli air

force and resulted in catastrophic losses for the Egyptian forces, turning the military tide in favor of the Israelis, it was Sadat who pleaded with the Soviets and the Americans to impose a ceasefire on the Israelis and to save his imperiled Third Army from certain defeat. His pleas drew the Americans and the Soviets more deeply into the conflict, undercutting détente understandings and ultimately leading to an American nuclear alert. Yet, despite the losses that his forces sustained in the latter weeks of the war, Soviet and American intervention, so problematical at first and so laden with potential for a global conflict, ultimately saved Sadat and Egypt's military forces. Sadat emerged from the war in a stronger position politically than he had enjoyed prior to the conflict.

At the end of 1973, neither Middle Eastern nor global politics were the same. By convincing his own people that he had succeeded where his predecessors had failed, he came out from under the towering shadow of his predecessor, Gamal Abdel Nasser. His view, largely accepted by the populace, was that the Egyptian army, which he consistently called "his army," had finally prevailed on the battlefield. More important, he persuaded the American political establishment that he was a figure of political stature, one with whom American officials could work. The prestige that war brought him at home and internationally led him to embark on even more radical policies, eventually signing a peace treaty with Israel. Yet his successes were near failures, only achieved through extraordinary superpower interventions, including an astonishing, and in the opinion of many a provocative and unnecessary, American nuclear alert.

The outcome of the war was hardly the result of rational political calculations and cool political reasoning. Contingency, irrational behavior, and miscalculations were as much a part of this narrative as the inexorable logic of historical forces.

To highlight only the most obvious point in this regard and to call attention to the central focus of this study, had the Americans and the Soviets not come to the rescue of the Egyptian Third

Army trapped in Sinai, it is likely that Sadat's enemies, not yet fully sidelined and biding their time for the right moment to strike against him, would have been emboldened to remove him from power. Had Sadat failed to survive the October War, the Camp David framework for peace in 1978 and the Egyptian-Israeli peace accord of 1979 would have been unlikely. Yet, largely because of the interventions of the superpowers, Sadat's hold on power was secured. In fact, he emerged at home as "the hero of the crossing" (*batal al-ubur*) despite the desperate conditions that faced his Third Army in late October and despite the fact that to most impartial observers Egypt had lost the war.

As we have noted (Chapter 3), the 1967 war, known in the Arab world as the reversal (*al-naksa*), was Egypt's and Sadat's starting point. It was the essential lead-up to the October War not just for its primary combatants (Egypt, Syria, and Israel), but for the two superpowers who had fundamental and opposing interests in the region. Not only had Nasser, Egypt's president at the time, made clear Egypt's intention to repossess Sinai by force, if necessary, when he affirmed that "what was taken by force will be returned by force," but he charged his minister of war, Mahmud Fawzi, to draw up battle plans for getting Egyptian forces across the canal and advancing to the Israeli Negev border.[1] Sadat as president accepted Nasser's view that the country's first priority must be repossessing Sinai; yet he also concluded that Nasser's military planning and diplomatic actions were based on fundamental misunderstandings of international politics and military realities. In his opinion, the Egyptian army could not drive the Israelis out of all of Sinai given America's determination to maintain Israel's regional military superiority, especially the superiority of its air forces, and the Soviet Union's unwillingness to challenge this reality. Moreover, Sadat also concluded that America's commitment to Israel meant that Egypt and its Arab allies would only be able to regain territories lost in the 1967 war by coming to terms with the United States. It was, in fact, only after Sadat's efforts to engage the Americans and the Israelis on the diplomatic front that the Egyptian president concluded that Egypt had no choice but to go to war. Here, too, however, his goals were more modest and realistic than Nasser's and Fawzi's, though as we shall see, he, too, asked more of the Egyptian army than it could deliver. Nonetheless, he charged his generals with producing a military plan that would allow Egyptian armed forces to cross the canal and then hunker down along a narrow strip of land bordering it, forcing the great powers to redouble their efforts to find a peaceful solution to the conflict. He was not opposed to advancing to the Sinai passes, but unlike Nasser and Fawzi, he did not believe that the Egyptian forces could go further. He put his position well in his memoirs when he asserted: "I used to tell Nasser that if we could recapture even 4 inches of Sinai territory (by which I meant a foothold pure and simple), and establish ourselves there so firmly that no power on earth could dislodge us, then the whole situation would change—east, west, all over."[2]

The Israelis regarded the Egyptian assertions of an imminent war, whether made by Nasser or Sadat, as bluffs, intended to calm an increasingly irate domestic population and appease the country's Arab allies. They were convinced that the Arabs, led by Egypt, would not for a long time be in a position to challenge the Israeli military juggernaut, now dug in behind more defensible frontiers than it had possessed in 1967. Abba Eban, Israel's foreign minister in the period leading up to the war, was contemptuous of Sadat, mocking him as "a model of anticharisma" and claiming that his media appearances where he promised war "provoked mirth."[3] Eban described Sadat to Henry Kissinger only months before the war as "not bright," but capable of "thinking [a few] moves ahead," a statement that Kissinger disputed. In Kissinger's view, Sadat "shows no capacity for thinking moves ahead."[4] Less dismissive calculations were based on detailed Israeli military intelligence. Israeli analysts were certain that Egypt could not launch a war until it had fighter/bomber planes able to strike at airbases inside Israel and an air force able to neutralize Israeli air supremacy. These experts did not believe this situation could possibly exist before the end of 1975, if even then.

Soviet and American analysts and decision makers shared these assumptions. The Soviets dreaded a resumption of warfare. They foresaw certain Arab defeat, for which blame would be heaped on them as an unreliable ally, and the loss of significant military equipment to the Americans, thus compromising their own security. Similarly, the Americans feared that war would also produce an Israeli victory, even more territorial gains, and a deepening of Arab hostility toward the United States. American leaders thought it likely that oil-exporting Arab states would embargo supplies of oil to the United States and its allies if war broke out.

In 1971, which Sadat proclaimed as the year of decision, he and his top military men began to refine the battle plans that Nasser and his advisers had first developed. The major problem facing Egypt, on full display during the 1967 war, was Israel's overwhelming air superiority. The Soviets had diminished this capability during the War of Attrition (1967–1970) when, under pressure from President Nasser, they had created a surface-to-air missile defense system along the length of the west bank of the Suez Canal. The Egyptian air defense network, even denser than that which surrounded Hanoi and Haiphong in North Vietnam, stopped deep Israeli air raids into the interior of Egypt, which the Israelis had launched as retaliation against Egyptian shelling of fortifications on the east bank of the canal.

Still, the air disadvantage remained. If Egypt hoped to advance into Sinai, its military leaders needed to develop plans that would protect troops from the Israeli air force. It was in planning the crossing of the canal, which Moshe Dayan, one of Israel's most successful warriors and Golda Meir's minister of defense, called the greatest antitank barrier in the world, that deep divisions arose within the Egyptian leadership. These disputes would haunt Sadat and his generals throughout the war.

The first indication that military preparations were faltering took place at Sadat's residence on October 28, 1972. Having called his chief military leaders together to ascertain what steps they had taken to prepare the troops for warfare, the Egyptian president was stunned to learn that the minister of defense, Major General Muhammad Sadiq, had not notified the Supreme Council of the Armed Forces of the president's determination to go to war. No doubt, this delay stemmed from the belief, widespread even in Egyptian military circles, that Sadat's bellicose assertions were pure propaganda. Yet, in ensuing discussions that the president had with the commanders of the Second and Third Armies, he discovered that these men did not believe that the country was ready for war, citing the lack of air power and arguing that until the Egyptian military was capable of neutralizing the Israelis in the air, the battle could not be won. In this regard, his commanders' views were identical with those held by the Israelis, the Americans, and the Soviets. Sadat refused to accept this position, stating that the Egyptian planners must devise plans that would enable army units to cross the canal, thus demonstrating to all that the Israeli military did not have dominance in the region.

Immediately following this fateful meeting, Sadat removed many of the army's officers, including the minister of defense, the head of the naval forces, and several other leading generals. He replaced them with men of a different makeup, more in sympathy with his views, more committed to facing the Israelis militarily, and more talented militarily and professionally. Yet, here, too, tensions and personal differences appeared.

Three men came to the fore as the individuals who would formulate and then carry out Sadat's goal of getting forces across the canal and creating a new diplomatic reality. The first of these men was Sadat's new minister of defense, General Ahmad Ismail Ali, who had fought in all of the Arab-Israeli wars and whom Nasser had retired after the 1967 war for presumed incompetence. Sadat did not share Nasser's low opinion of Ismail Ali. At a one-on-one meeting on October 25, 1972, the retired general expressed strong support for Sadat's intention to go to war now rather than later, and believed that he and other more energetic generals could formulate plans to get troops across the canal and protect them from Israeli air strikes once they were dug in along the east bank.

The second individual was a swashbuckling paratrooper, a daring and highly decorated soldier, with whom Sadat would later clash, but who provided the plans and inspiration for the canal crossing. General Saad al-Shazli, designated Egyptian chief of staff, on May 16, 1971, was given the task of drafting plans to get more than 100,000 soldiers, tanks, antitank weapons, and big artillery pieces across the canal where their goal would be to destroy the chain of fortifications, the first line of Israeli defenses, known as the Bar-Lev line after General Haim Bar-Lev, who was serving as the Israeli chief of staff when the fortifications were put in place. Once across the canal, they were to secure, at the very least, an Egyptian foothold in Sinai. From there, the government could engage in negotiations with the Israelis, the Americans, the Soviets, and the United Nations or embark on further advances.

SADAT, GENERAL SAAD EDDIN AL-SHAZLI, AND GENERAL AHMAD ISMAIL ALI. *Shazli was the operations officer and a daring and courageous soldier. General Ali was minister of defense. They did not get along with each other, and their differences posed many problems for Sadat.*

The third soldier was General Muhammad Abdal-Ghani al-Gamasi, appointed chief of operations. His major responsibility was to secure the necessary weapons and equipment and make these resources available to the forces when and where needed. He was to prove in many ways the most capable of the Egyptian officers. He was the only one of this triumvirate standing at the end of the war, after Sadat had replaced Shazli, with whom he quarreled, and after Ismail Ali was taken sick in the latter stages of the war and the ensuing negotiations. It was hardly a surprise that General Gamasi was put in charge of the military negotiations with the Israelis after the ceasefire had finally taken hold at the end of October. Indeed, so well respected was he that he played a primary role in the negotiations between the Egyptian and Israeli military organizations following Sadat's journey to Jerusalem, right up to the gathering at Camp David where because of a falling out with Sadat he was compelled to step aside.

Unfortunately, these three men did not constitute a smoothly functioning team. Their differences plagued the military campaign from the outset. General Ismail, already suffering from the cancer which would take his life in 1974, owed his reinstatement to Sadat. He was altogether too subservient to the president. In Shazli's opinion, General Ismail was "a weak man, alternating between submissiveness and bullying. . . . He shunned the responsibility of decisions, preferring to receive orders rather than give them."[5] In addition, he and Shazli had been long-time antagonists. Their difficulties dated to the Egyptian military mission to the Congo in 1960 when, as young officers, they argued over orders and eventually came to blows. Nor did Shazli share the hostility toward the Soviets that was widespread among the officer corps. While Shazli upbraided the Soviet advisers for disrespecting Egyptian officers, describing them as "brusque, harsh, frequently arrogant, and usually unwilling to believe anyone has anything to teach them," he had opposed their expulsion. "To lose them before our men were trained would gravely embarrass us."[6]

He pleaded with Sadat not to force him to serve under a man whom he did not respect, but Sadat ordered him to do so.

The differences among these men were palpable even at the outset as they began to finalize plans for the crossing. Shazli had been part of the disastrous 1967 retreat from Sinai. He had escaped from certain capture and possible death by diving into the Suez Canal and swimming to safety on the west bank. Deeply aware of the killing power of the Israeli air force, he was profoundly opposed to exposing soldiers to air strikes. The plan that he preferred and was mainly responsible for drafting, labeled the High Minarets, was limited to getting large numbers of Egyptian troops, supplies, and equipment across the canal and then digging in while still being protected by Egypt's powerful surface-to-air missile defense system, which had a range of about 10 miles. He was suspicious at every stage of the planning, as well as during the actual combat itself, of the more ambitious plans, one of which, labeled Granite 2, called for advances to the Sinai passes, about 40 miles east of the canal. In his memoirs, he wrote that "it was impossible for us to launch a large-scale offensive or to destroy the enemy concentrations in Sinai or to force enemy withdrawal from Sinai or the Gaza strip. All that our capabilities would permit was a *limited* attack. We could aim to cross the canal, destroy the Bar-Lev line, and then take up a defensive posture. Any further, more aggressive moves would then need different equipment, different training, and a lot more preparation."[7]

It was these two quite different visions that were in play during the lead-up to the war and during the early stages of the conflict. They set Egypt's political and military leaders at odds with one another. Shazli was certain that his logic had prevailed as the day for the battle approached, but he was also aware that the Syrians, in agreeing to join the attack on Israel, had insisted that the Egyptians do more than simply get across the canal and then hunker down in anticipation of diplomatic interventions. Syrian President Hafez al-Assad's worry, based on the disasters visited upon Syria during the 1967 war, was that if the Egyptians were not constantly advancing in Sinai and putting pressure on the Israeli military, the Israelis would turn the full force of their army on the Syrians and seize even more Syrian territory, perhaps even send forces into the capital city, Damascus, which was a mere 40 miles from the border of the Golan Heights. To Shazli's dismay, the Egyptians promised Assad that they would push on to the passes once their forces were across the canal. Although the political leaders, including Sadat, sought to mollify Shazli by assuring him that they did not intend to move beyond their air defenses and had made this promise to secure the involvement of the Syrians in the attack, he was hardly pleased. In his account of the war, written from exile seven years after the conflict and intended to answer charges that his own decisions had led to significant Egyptian military reversals later in the conflict, he accused Sadat and other top generals of cynical and duplicitous behavior toward its most important ally, a fellow Arab state.

Shazli's outrage about the way the Egyptians had promised something that they were not fully intending to do revealed another problem that plagued the Arab war effort. As had been the case in the two previous Arab-Israeli wars (1948 and 1967), the Syrian and Egyptian political and military leaders failed to coordinate their plans. This difficulty occurred again in 1973 at the very outset of the war when Syria through its Soviet patron requested an immediate ceasefire. Moreover, throughout the war, Egyptian and Syrian leaders made ceasefire proposals without consulting one another and at moments when they were not in agreement.

The Egyptian and Syrian decision to go to war stunned the Israelis, the Americans, and the Soviets, though it should not have. Many telltale indications pointed toward war. Israeli overconfidence and the inability of Israeli and American intelligence to read the signs left leaders in both countries scurrying at the last minute to respond. The Soviets had been warning the Americans for some time that renewed fighting was likely if no diplomatic

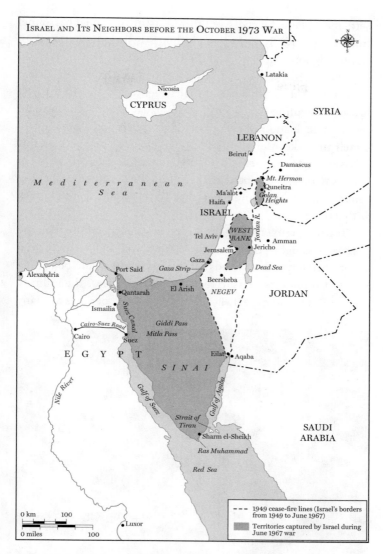

ISRAEL AND ITS NEIGHBORS BEFORE THE OCTOBER 1973 WAR

Latakia

Nicosia

CYPRUS

SYRIA

LEBANON

Beirut

Damascus

*M e d i t e r r a n e a n
S e a*

Mt. Hermon

Quneitra

Ma'alot

*Golan
Heights*

Haifa

ISRAEL

*WEST
BANK*

Jordan R.

Tel Aviv

Amman

Jerusalem

Jericho

Gaza

Gaza Strip

Dead Sea

Alexandria

Port Said

Beersheba

Qantarah

El Arish

NEGEV

JORDAN

Ismailia

Suez Canal

Cairo-Suez Road

Giddi Pass

Cairo

Mitla Pass

Suez

E G Y P T

Eilat

Aqaba

S I N A I

Nile River

Gulf of Suez

Gulf of Aqaba

SAUDI
ARABIA

*Strait of
Tiran*

Sharm el-Sheikh

Ras Muhammad

Red Sea

0 km   100

0 miles   100

- - - - 1949 cease-fire lines (Israel's borders
from 1949 to June 1967)

Territories captured by Israel during
June 1967 war

Luxor

MAP 2. ISRAEL AND ITS NEIGHBORS BEFORE THE OCTOBER
1973 WAR

settlement was achieved. Even the departure of Soviet personnel from Egypt and Syria forty-eight hours before the outbreak of war was ignored in Israel and the United States. Having learned that the attack would occur only hours before it happened, Prime Minister Golda Meir decided that Israel would absorb the first blows, overruling her chief of staff, David Elazar, who wanted an immediate and full call up of all reservists and a preemptive Israeli air strike. Meir wanted the world to be in no doubt on this occasion that the Arabs had initiated the conflict. Israel had taken criticism for its preemptive strike in June 1967. Moreover, her top military analysts assured her that Israel would counterattack with lethal force.

The Egyptian crossing went even more successfully than the planners thought possible. At one time, well before the actual events, Sadat had thundered that the Egyptians would be willing to lose 1 million soldiers to reclaim lost territories. The military men in Egypt did expect significant casualties, perhaps as many

One of many pontoons that the Egyptians put in place to allow them to cross the Suez Canal.

as 20,000, and were astonished when in the first three hours of the crossing they had landed 30,000 soldiers, their equipment, and many tanks on the east bank of the canal and had lost only 280 soldiers, 5 aircraft, and 20 tanks. "The battle of the crossing had been won," Shazli later boasted.[8]

In fact, the Bar-Lev line was a mirage intended to frighten the Egyptians more through its very existence than through its military capabilities. That it was intimidating to the Egyptians is undoubted. Shazli wrote that while the canal was "only 195–220 yards wide, but to all who saw it the Suez Canal seemed an impassable barrier."[9] Not only would it be difficult to cross, but gigantic sand dunes arose on the east bank, erected by bulldozers to the height of 60 feet and thick at the base, behind which were a series of thirty-five forts, each of which was self-contained and equipped with supplies to hold out for up to a week until Israeli soldiers could rush across Sinai to the rescue. Only the Israelis were aware of how weak these defenses actually were. As a result of inattention and a belief that the Egyptians would be intimidated simply by the sight of the defenses and by the daunting prospect of eventually facing the full might of the Israeli army in Sinai, the Israeli military had allowed the fortifications to fall into disrepair. The most telling example of their lack of attention was their failure to respond to Egypt's raising of sand ramparts above those that the Israelis had erected on their side of the canal. Able to look from their high perches at Israeli activities behind their dunes and protected from Israeli observations, though not from American aerial reconnaissance, the Egyptian soldiers practiced crossing activities day in and day out and brought up heavy crossing bridges and massed soldiers and equipment along the west bank of the canal. By mobilizing and then demobilizing their forces on a number of occasions in 1973, the Egyptian buildup in early October was seen in Israel as yet another false alarm, intended to force Israel to engage in an expensive and unnecessary mobilization of its forces.

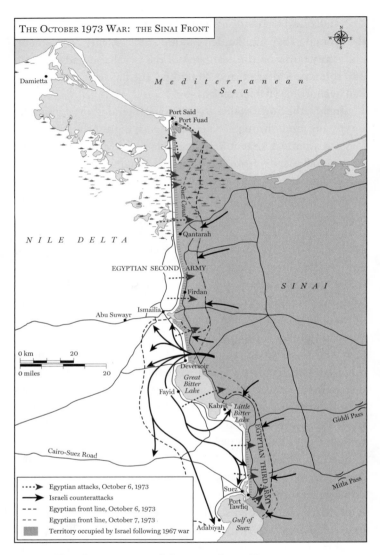

The October 1973 War: the Sinai Front

MAP 3. The October 1973 War: the Sinai Front

The Israeli Agranat Commission, which investigated the war after its conclusion, placed primary responsibility for the early unanticipated losses in the war on the shoulders of the military leaders, notably the chief of staff, David Elazar and the head of Israeli military intelligence. It cleared the political leaders, Golda Meir, the prime minister, and Moshe Dayan, the minister of defense, but the citizenry did not. Although Meir did not accept Dayan's offer to resign during the war, he did step aside after the war, in response to a groundswell of public criticism. Meir's days as prime minister and leader of the party were also numbered.

In Egypt, the crossing had an energizing effect. It enhanced the reputation of Sadat and restored the standing of the military. Thought by many Egyptians to be a weak figure, unlikely to remain in power long, made fun of as a yes-man to Nasser, who many thought never intended him to be his successor, and considered the lucky survivor of a botched coup attempt carried out by more capable leaders in May 1971, Sadat saw his image transformed. Overnight, he went from the butt of jokes to Egypt's new strong man, a leader able to accomplish what Nasser and the military had been unable to achieve in 1948 and 1967: defeating the Israeli army. Pictures of captured Israeli soldiers, which were regularly displayed in Egyptian newspapers, delighted the people, lifting the mood of despair that had descended on the country after the 1967 war. Sadat's most triumphant moment came on October 16 when he addressed the People's Assembly and received a warrior's welcome. Having basked in the adulation of the crowds as he traveled through the main streets of Cairo and exulting as the citizenry shouted out his new nickname, "hero of the crossing," he catalogued Egypt's military accomplishments before the Assembly's rapt representatives. Claiming that the results of the first six hours of the battle were "magnificent" and that a wounded nation had finally had its honor restored, he went on to talk about peace—a peace based on justice that would reclaim the lands lost in the 1967 war and "respect and restore the legitimate rights of the Palestinian people." He concluded by asserting that Egypt would accept a ceasefire if the Israelis would withdraw to the 1967 borders.[10]

Although Sadat celebrated October 16 as a day of triumph, Egypt had already begun to suffer significant battlefield defeats. On the very day that Sadat addressed the People's Assembly, the Israelis were pushing military columns across the Suez Canal. Egyptian intelligence discounted the first reports of this Israeli thrust "into Africa" as some Israeli generals dubbed their crossing to the west bank, claiming that a mere seven tanks had made it across the canal and were now being destroyed. In reality, an Israeli military presence on the west bank posed serious military challenges for Egypt. First, the Israeli forces, as they were strengthened, sought to take up positions where they could cut off the supply routes to the Second and Third Egyptian Armies in Sinai. Second, the Israeli forces on the west bank set about destroying the Egyptian antiaircraft units, so vital for protecting the Egyptian soldiers on the east bank. Third, if the Israelis could get large numbers across the canal, their forces could threaten population centers in Cairo, the delta, and Upper Egypt.

The Israeli crossing occurred at the worst possible moment for the Egyptian forces and at the most propitious time for the Israelis. Spurning Shazli's constant reminder to keep the Egyptian troops under their air defense umbrella, the top brass, urged on by Sadat, decided to go on the offensive on October 14. The highly controversial decision to advance to the passes was a turning point in the war. Throwing everything into the advance, including forces that had been held back on the west bank of the canal to protect the country from a possible Israeli counterattack across the canal, the Egyptians saw the momentum of the war shift to the Israeli side. The advance revealed an incautious, perhaps one might also say, reckless side to the president's decision making, one that was to reappear later at crucial moments.

The major Egyptian discussions about the decision to come out from under the surface-to-air missile defense system, dealt with in the memoirs of Sadat, Gamasi, and Shazli, are murky and confusing, but two factors were clearly at play. In the first place, plans to advance to the Sinai passes had always existed and had been agreed to by all of the top brass, including Shazli. They awaited only the right moment for implementation. Having crossed the canal, some military men pressed for an immediate surge toward the passes. More conservative views prevailed, however, on the grounds that the armies should first secure their strongholds on the east bank before embarking on further attacks. Second and more vitally, President Assad of Syria, under intense pressure from Israeli counterattacks that had already reclaimed the Golan Heights and threatened interior Syrian cities, even Damascus, pleaded with the Egyptians to relieve pressure on his country. Sadat came to the rescue, thinning out his forces on the west bank to carry the assault to the passes. Had the Egyptians carried out this strike in the early days of the war when the Israeli forces were not yet fully mobilized and were reeling from bloody defeats, the thrust might have succeeded. Eight days later, with the enlarged Israeli forces dug in at the most defensible Sinai locations, the advance was doomed. The Egyptian losses in tanks and men were staggering, and the Egyptian troops had no choice but to retreat at the end of a bloody and bitter day of fighting.

Numerous commentators have called the battle of October 14 one of the greatest tank battles in the history of warfare, even comparing it with the massive engagement of tanks between the Soviet forces and those of Nazi Germany at the battle of Kursk in July 1943, a turning point in World War II. The Sinai battle involved more than 2,000 tanks joined in battle along the entire length of the Suez Canal. By nightfall, the Egyptians had lost 264 tanks and sustained 1,000 casualties to Israel's loss of only 20 tanks. On the very next day, as the Israelis prepared to move units across the Suez Canal, another major battle ensued that also went in favor of the Israelis and enabled them to push large numbers of soldiers and equipment across the canal. On this occasion, however, the fighting was hardly one-sided. Ariel Sharon, who was in command of most of the Israeli units in this engagement, described the fighting as the bloodiest in the history of the Israeli Defense Force. His description of the battlefield at its conclusion is one of the most chilling on record:

> As the sky brightened, I looked around and saw hundreds and hundreds of burned and twisted vehicles. Fifty Israeli tanks lay shattered on the field. Around them were the hulks of 150 Egyptian tanks plus hundreds of APCs, jeeps, and trucks. Wreckage littered the desert. Here and there Israeli and Egyptian tanks had destroyed each other at a distance of a few meters, barrel to barrel. It was as if a hand-to-hand battle of arms had taken place. And inside these tanks and next to them lay their dead crews. . . . No picture could capture the horror of the scene, none could encompass what had happened there.[11]

A second momentous event that went against Sadat and the Egyptians and continued to turn the military tide in favor of Israel was the Israeli thrust across the canal onto the west bank. Ariel Sharon had been an early and constant advocate of this initiative, having noted the gap between the Egyptian Second and Third Armies before the crossing and anticipating that these two armies would not link up once in Sinai. Sharon was a headstrong commander, resented by many fellow officers, but admired for his boldness and military acumen. He had wanted to make the crossing even in the early days of the war, but the central command rejected his advice. When he continued to insist, he was even threatened with dismissal and court martial. In truth, the decision not to cross when Sharon first wanted to but to await an anticipated Egyptian advance to the passes proved decisive militarily. Once the Israeli soldiers had crossed to the west bank and had solidified their position with additional troops and equipment, they found themselves largely unopposed because the Egyptians had thrown so many forces into the rush to the Sinai passes. Not only were they in a position to imperil the Egyptian Second and Third Armies by cutting off supply lines, but they could also threaten civilian populations in the canal cities, the Nile delta, and Upper Egypt.

Sadat never ceased to dismiss the Israeli crossing as unimportant. He called it a television and propaganda event, comparing it to the German Battle of the Bulge of World War II, which he described as a Goebbels publicity stunt, militarily suicidal, but intended to reassure the population at home. Similarly, Sadat insisted that the Israelis never threatened the Egyptian forces or the Egyptian people and that his troops could have wiped out the Israeli bridgehead on the west bank if he had issued the orders to do so. Instead, he claimed to prefer a peaceful route, pursuing a ceasefire, a new relationship with the Americans, and negotiations with the Israelis.[12]

Public statements aside, Sadat and his generals were acutely aware of their desperate plight once they had detailed information of the Israeli crossing. Their responses, inadequate when it came to dislodging the Israeli bridgehead, again revealed the deep divisions and differences among the leaders of the war effort. Sadat ordered Shazli, Egypt's chief of staff, to deal with the Israeli forces on the west bank, but then refused Shazli's request to transfer units of the Third Army from Sinai to the west bank. Shazli was beside himself with anger, having watched his armed forces be torn to pieces when they were compelled, against his better judgment, to advance to the passes. Now, he saw the Third Army imperiled, possibly destroyed, if the Israeli bridgehead on the west bank was extended southward where it would be able to cut off the vital supply routes, located in the southern region of Sinai. At a contentious meeting, involving Sadat and Generals Gamasi, Shazli, and Ismail Ali, Sadat claimed that the consensus was that the Egyptian forces had "nothing to worry about" from the Israeli crossing. The president issued an order not to withdraw, "not a soldier, not a rifle, nothing."[13] He also insisted that Shazli "never . . . speak of withdrawal."[14] Should he do so, Sadat threatened to court-martial him. Gamasi and Ismail Ali sided with Sadat, fearing that withdrawing units from Sinai would sow panic among the troops, reminding these men of their desperate and leaderless retreat in the 1967 war. In their view, it was likely to cost Egypt the Sinai territorial gains that the crossing had accomplished and that Sadat and others saw as vital in forthcoming negotiations.

Shortly after this dispute, Sadat removed Shazli as chief of staff, replacing him with Gamasi, though he did not announce this publicly for fear that the announcement would reveal the divisions that existed inside the high command of the Egyptian army. Much later, when some of this information began to leak out, Sadat defended his decisions, claiming that Shazli had in fact suffered a nervous breakdown, a charge that many others, even Sadat enthusiasts, disputed.

One of the major reasons that Sadat went to war was his belief that the region required a shock that only a powerful conflict was capable of producing. He sought superpower involvement and believed that only through drawing the Soviet Union and especially the Americans into the dispute could Israel be forced to give back the lands that it had occupied in the Six-Day War. In this regard he was not mistaken, although he could hardly have foreseen the acute crisis in superpower relations that his actions provoked or the dire straits that his armies found themselves in, mainly owing to the extraordinarily successful resupply effort that the United States carried out on behalf of the Israeli forces. By the end of the second week of the conflict, the Egyptian military situation had become so precarious that Sadat was compelled to make desperate appeals to the Americans and the Soviets to save his forces from destruction.

Inevitably the October War involved the superpowers, at first as suppliers of armaments to their client states and then, as the conflict went against Egypt and Syria, as arbiters of the war's final resolution. From the moment that American officials realized that Egypt and Syria would attack Israel, they entered into close consultation with the Israelis. The Soviets were also committed to their Arab allies despite having had their military personnel expelled from Egypt and wishing to strengthen détente with the Nixon administration. They undertook to supply vital weapons to Egypt and Syria as soon as the conflict was joined. Under acute pressure from the Israelis, the Americans responded in kind, agreeing to make good on any losses that Israel sustained on the battlefield. Ultimately, the American resupply program outdid that carried out by the Soviets and turned the tide of the war in favor of the Israelis.

Soviet military supplies began to arrive in Syria and Egypt on October 9. Huge military transports carrying antitank weapons, the hand-carried stagger guns that had proved so deadly against Israeli tanks, and large amounts of ammunition landed with precise regularity at the main Syrian and Egyptian air bases. Ships loaded with equipment that could not be transported by plane passed through the Dardanelles on the way to Syrian and Egyptian ports. An American intelligence agency picked up neutron emissions from a Soviet merchant ship transiting the Bosporus and bound for Alexandria, raising the specter of nuclear warheads being offloaded in Egypt.

The American secretary of state, Kissinger, was determined to overcome any reluctance that existed in official circles and to outdo the Soviets in supplying America's ally. He badgered and pleaded with James Schlesinger, secretary of defense, to go all out in backing the Israelis militarily. They were to do so even if, as proved to be the case, the overt American resupply program jeopardized important economic interests in the Middle East and brought on an oil embargo against the United States and its European supporters.

Kissinger's insistence on resupplying Israel with all the requests that it made, which approached $1 billion before the war was at an end and totaled $2.2 billion in the immediate aftermath of the war, was part and parcel of his diplomatic/military strategy for advancing American interests in competition with the Soviet Union in the Middle East. Kissinger's desired outcome for the war was an Israeli military victory, which, while not humiliating the Arab states, drove home the message that the United States was the one and only arbiter of Middle Eastern affairs, the only power that could help them reclaim lost territories. In this regard, then, supplying Israel with more and better military equipment than the Soviets could provide to Egypt was essential.

The American resupply effort was fully in progress by October 14. Not only was it massive; it was also completely visible. Fearing retaliation from the Arab states, American officials had at first attempted to conceal US involvement. They asked the Israelis to use their own El Al jet airliners to move the equipment but discovered that El Al had only seven big jets and would be unable to carry the required tonnage. Next, in an effort to deflect criticism, Schlesinger and Kissinger approached American commercial carriers with a request that they allow the Israeli government to charter their airplanes, a proposal that failed utterly. American carriers feared Arab retaliation and a loss of business, even being deprived of landing rights in the Arab world. Left with no alternative, the Americans undertook the campaign openly. The tonnage was staggering, prompting Alexander Haig, who was Nixon's chief of staff, to observe that "the resupply effort was larger in terms of tonnage delivered than in the Berlin airlift."[15]

The Americans succeeded in outdoing the Soviets, shipping enormous quantities of ammunition and equipment, and did so in many different ways. Huge C-5 military transports, capable of carrying loads as bulky as four M-60 tanks, five or six Skyhawk aircrafts, and antitank weapons landed at Lod airport outside Tel Aviv often at fifteen-minute intervals. So visible was the resupply that residents came out to see the planes, the size of which had never been observed in the country, and to cheer the effort. One of the major resupply items was F-4 Phantom jets, long-range supersonic interceptor fighter/bombers, having a top speed of Mach 2.2 and capable of carrying 18,000 pounds of weapons, including air-to-air and air-to-ground missiles. Unable to obtain overflight permission from their NATO allies, except from the Portuguese who allowed the use of only one base in the Azores, these planes leap-frogged from one aircraft carrier to another in the Mediterranean before landing in Israel.

On October 19, Sadat decided that he must seek a ceasefire. He informed his chief ally, President Hafez al-Assad of Syria, "that I was not afraid of a confrontation with Israel but that I would not confront the United States. I would not allow the Egyptian forces or Egypt's strategic targets to be destroyed once again."[16]

The American resupply effort was so large that Secretary Schlesinger worried about American war readiness. He cautioned that the transfer of thirty-four F-4E aircraft to Israel brought the United States Air Force assets to six squadrons below authorized strength. By transferring 172 M60 tanks, drawn from stocks in Europe, the American capability was reduced by seven armored battalions, and if the United States shipped 1,000 more tanks to Israel, as requested late in the war, the Americans would not attain full strength in tanks for thirty-three months. Schlesinger pointed out similar shortages in TOW antitank launchers, Maverick missiles, armor-piercing tank gun ammunition, CH53 helicopters, and A4 aircraft. He concluded his report by noting that "many of the transfers are significant in terms of those special items which we depend on to give us the military edge over Soviet forces."[17]

The American resupply effort proved both militarily and psychologically decisive to the Israelis. Confident that the Americans would replace any losses on the battlefield, and do so promptly, the Israelis launched offensives against Egypt and Syria. Their military successes were unqualified, exactly what the Americans and the Soviets had expected at the outbreak of the war. They were so successful in repulsing the Egyptian thrust to the passes, landing large numbers on the west bank of the canal, and advancing within twenty miles of Damascus, that the Soviet Union and the American government worried about how the war would end. Would Israeli troops overrun Cairo and Damascus, underscoring the message of previous wars that Israel was the dominant military force in the area? Would Sadat and Assad remain in power? Would the Soviet Union be seen as an unreliable ally, as Kissinger had hoped? Moreover, was the outcome that seemed to be taking shape—a total victory for Israel and the destruction of the Egyptian Third Army—desirable from anyone's point of view, except Israel's?

Although Kissinger sought an Israeli victory, the steady back-channel communications between Egypt and the United States and the frequent friendly personal messages exchanged between Sadat and Nixon had suggested to the American secretary of state that the United States might well have found a potential ally and negotiating partner in the Egyptian president. Under these altered circumstances, the Americans, unlike the Israelis, became apprehensive about a rout of the Egyptian army, the humiliation of Sadat, and a possible leadership change in Egypt. Aware that the Israeli government thirsted for revenge against a man who had brought them so low at the outset of the war, Kissinger began to wonder how the Americans could rein in the Israelis' appetite for vengeance and save the Egyptian Third Army and Sadat's standing in Egypt.

Sadat had resisted the early appeals for a ceasefire. The blunting of the thrust to the passes and the appearance of Israeli troops on the west bank of the canal radically changed his perspectives. Even while boasting that the Israeli salient on the west bank could be removed at a stroke, he implored the Americans and the Soviets for a ceasefire. His appeals to the Soviets left no doubt, at least in the minds of Politburo members, that the Egyptian president feared for his country and for his own position. According to Soviet intelligence, the Egyptian leadership was in a state of panic as early as October 16, already drawing up plans for withdrawing to Asyut should the Israeli forces advance on Cairo. From Upper Egypt, they planned to carry out guerrilla warfare. The new military situation alarmed Leonid Brezhnev, general secretary of the Central Committee of the Communist Party, who felt compelled to stand by his Arab allies. His first action was a cautionary letter

to President Nixon in which he stated that "unless Israel with-
draws from the Arab lands it seized there will not be peace in the
Middle East. This is the essence." Further and more insistent
Soviet notes finally caught the attention of the White House, the
State Department, and the Defense Department, persuading
these officials that the Soviets did indeed attach the utmost importance to maintaining Sadat in power.

The Soviet Union had made a call for a ceasefire within hours
of the crossing, an appeal summarily rejected by the Israelis, desperate to reverse their early setbacks in Sinai and on the Golan
Heights, and by the Egyptians, buoyed by their early successes.
The Soviets continued to press for an end to the fighting, and
when they finally received Sadat's plea to end the fighting on
October 20 they shouldered the primary responsibility for rescuing Egypt from total defeat. On October 20, General Secretary
Leonid Brezhnev sent an urgent message to President Nixon
asking the American president to send his secretary of state to
Moscow for consultations. Nixon agreed, conferring full powers
on Kissinger, who flew to Moscow, accompanied by the Soviet
ambassador to the United States, Anatoly Dobrynin, on that
very same day. Fully aware of the military situation in the Middle
East and not yet determined to save Sadat but wishing to give the
Israelis as much time as he could in order to strengthen their
bridgehead along the west bank of the Suez Canal and to complete their encirclement of the Egyptian Third Army, Kissinger
unsuccessfully sought to postpone discussions for a day.

In the discussions in Moscow, the American position on
ceasefire arrangements prevailed. Kissinger rejected the Soviet
proposal that linked the ceasefire to Israel's return of all the territories seized in the 1967 war. Instead, he persuaded the Soviets to
accept a straightforward ceasefire. The two powers agreed to
sponsor a joint ceasefire resolution before the Security Council of
the United Nations, demanding only that troops remain in place.
Seeking to give the Israelis extra time to solidify their military
positions, Kissinger stipulated that the ceasefire motion, once

adopted by the Security Council, would take effect twelve hours later.

After leaving Moscow, Kissinger flew to Tel Aviv to apprise the Israelis of the agreement. In fact, when Kissinger met with the Israeli leadership in Herzliyya, just outside Tel Aviv, he heard only bitter reproaches and complaints that the Americans and the Soviets were dictating terms to the Israelis. In particular, several Israeli military officers pleaded with the US secretary of state to give Israel two or three more days to destroy much of the Egyptian army, thus dealing a blow to the Egyptian military establishment from which it would likely not recover for many years. Kissinger made no objection at this meeting to this Israeli proposal, and, after hearing a full military briefing dealing with the Syrian and Egyptian fronts, he expressed only admiration for the way in which the Israelis had conducted the war and were in the process of achieving victory. In other words, at this point, Kissinger had not concluded that preventing Israel from encircling and cutting off all supplies to the Third Army was a priority in American policy. Even earlier, he had indicated to the Israelis that he and other American officials would understand if the Israelis required "some additional time" after the ceasefire came into effect to solidify their military positions.[18] The Israelis were to take full advantage of this comment and other remarks that Kissinger made while in Israel.

The Security Council debate, which commenced on the evening of October 21, was, if anything, a travesty. Time was of the essence if the Egyptian and Syrian armies were to be rescued. Yet, some of the debaters, often with the best of intentions, were not brief. The result was that the resolution did not come into effect until 12:52 p.m. that evening, and as agreed, the shooting was not required to cease for another twelve hours.

Unfortunately, many violations occurred well after the ceasefire came into effect. The violations, in truth, occurred on both sides, but no one was in any doubt, neither the Soviets nor the Americans, which side benefited. The Israelis sought unquestioned military advantages, seizing the city of Adabiya, south of Port Suez, advancing on Port Suez, which resisted with astonishing effectiveness, and further cutting off the Third Army. The Egyptian violations were acts of desperation, futile efforts to break through the Israeli blockade and to escape to safety from what appeared to many of the troops as certain death.

In Egypt, Sadat reacted even more insistently to the failure to enforce the ceasefire, firing off notes to the Americans and the Soviets, alternately pleading with them and upbraiding them for their failure to implement the ceasefire. On October 23, just a day after the ceasefire had come into effect, Brezhnev characterized the Israeli actions as "a flagrant deceit" and in another message suggested that the Americans had colluded with the Israelis, remarking "Why this treachery was allowed by Israel is more obvious to you."[19] By the morning of October 24, after Israeli troops had taken Adabiya, Brezhnev could barely contain his anger. "These defiant actions have been taken by the presumptuous leaders of Israel only several hours after the last confirmation by the Security Council of its decision about an immediate ceasefire and after your firm statement that the United States takes full responsibility for implementation by Israel of a complete termination of hostilities."[20] Sadat's demands also became more urgent and insistent to the point that he pleaded with the Americans and the Soviets jointly to send troops into the area to enforce the ceasefire.

Sadat's request for Soviet-American troop involvement posed a serious risk to Kissinger's vision of the American role in the area but also indicated how dire the military and political situation was for the Egyptians. To this point, the American strategy had succeeded beyond Kissinger's most optimistic expectations. It had driven home the message that the Soviets were ineffective actors and the United States the only power capable of bringing real change to the region. But the introduction of Soviet troops into the area was something that he could not tolerate. The Americans were quick to notify Sadat that they would not join with the

Soviets in sending soldiers to enforce the ceasefire. If the Egyptians or any other power introduced such a resolution in the Security Council, the United States would veto it.

At this point, the drama spiraled out of control. The Soviet Politburo, under heavy pressure from their Egyptian and Syrian clients, met to consider what steps to take. Enraged at what they thought to be open and blatant Israeli violations of the ceasefire, the members of the Politburo drafted a strong letter to President Nixon, which was to be sent under Secretary General Brezhnev's signature. Ambassador Dobrynin read the document to Kissinger, who later described it as "brutal and threatening," referring in particular to one passage in the message, which subsequently was learned to have been written by Brezhnev himself and inserted without consultation with other members of the Politburo. The message represented the increasing frustration and anger that the Soviet leader felt: "I will say it straight that if you find it impossible to act jointly with us in this matter, we should be faced with the necessity urgently to consider the question of taking appropriate steps unilaterally. We cannot allow arbitrariness on the part of Israel."[21]

This message arrived at a time of heightened tension within the United States. The Nixon presidency was enmeshed in the Watergate crisis, which was at the very moment that the Brezhnev note arrived at a high pitch of anxiety. Two weeks earlier, on October 10 when the war was only a few days old, Vice President Spiro Agnew had resigned because of misconduct earlier in his career. Although Nixon had already nominated Gerald Ford as his replacement, Ford's nomination was not to be confirmed until November 27. Thus, throughout most of the crisis the United States was without a vice president. On the day that the Brezhnev missive arrived, President Nixon had fired Archibald Cox, the special prosecutor in the Watergate affair, because of Cox's insistence that the president release the White House tapes. Cox's dismissal prompted the resignations of the attorney general and deputy attorney general and was quickly dubbed the Saturday night massacre. Increasingly preoccupied with Watergate, Nixon found it difficult to concentrate on affairs of state. He was mentally exhausted, often inebriated. On the night that a response to the Brezhnev message needed to be drafted, he had drunk heavily and needed to go to bed. When Kissinger inquired of General Al Haig, Nixon's chief of staff, whether the president should attend the meeting, as required by US protocol if serious political decisions likely to involve a nuclear alert were to be made, Haig responded that Nixon was in no condition to attend.

Prior to assembling a small group of top officials, Kissinger informed Haig of the hotline message from Brezhnev, no doubt emphasizing the sentence that Brezhnev had inserted. Kissinger added the following observation so that Haig would be in no doubt that Kissinger wanted a strong American response. "I think that we have to go to the mat on this one."[22] In anticipation of the meeting, Haig apprised the president of the Soviet challenge and Kissinger's views. The president indicated that he would not attend the meeting and stated: "You know what I want. Al, handle the meeting." Haig went on to write: "We knew what he wanted: a worldwide military alert of United States military forces tied to a strong reply to Brezhnev."[23]

The meeting got underway at 10:30 p.m. on October 24 and lasted until 3:30 the next morning. Whether the group that met had the legal authority to take the action that it did and whether this body represented the Washington Special Action Group, an interdepartmental committee composed of senior officials from the State and Defense Departments and the CIA and given the responsibility of gathering information for the president on the use of US military forces in a time of crisis, which had been meeting regularly throughout the crisis, or the National Security Council, remains unresolved to this day. The only semiofficial record of the discussion made available in the State Department's recently published volume of documents on the October War is the diary of Admiral Moorer, chairman of the Joint Chiefs of Staff. It is hardly a complete account.[24] Only seven men attended the meeting.

In addition to Kissinger, Schlesinger, and Moorer, were Al Haig, chief of the president's staff, Major General Brent Scowcroft, deputy assistant to the president for national security affairs, William Colby, director of Central Intelligence, and Jonathan Howe, a senior staff member of the National Security Council. The Moorer record reveals that Kissinger dominated the discussions, though several external accounts of the meeting suggest that the level of dissent to his recommendations was considerable.

Kissinger's main argument for a robust American response was that the Soviet threat to send troops was a serious one. He noted that big Soviet transport planes, which had been making frequent flights to Egypt and Syria in the resupply effort, were not in use. He feared that they were being readied to move to the Middle East perhaps as many as 50,000 airborne soldiers who had been placed on alert in the early stages of the war. Just before midnight, the group decided to put all American forces on a general nuclear alert, invoking the third stage in the American alert formulas, known as DEFCON 3 (Defensive Condition 3).

The American defensive arrangements or defensive conditions (DEFCON) involved five stages, moving from DEFCON 5, which had the appellation "fade out" and indicated little likelihood of global conflict to DEFCON 1, also nicknamed cocked pistol, which meant that the United States anticipated an imminent nuclear war. Although, then, DEFCON 3 was only an intermediate stage, the United States has in fact only been in the DEFCON 3 stage on three occasions, two of which are well known to even the most casual observer of American foreign policy. They are the Cuban missile crisis of 1962 and September 11, 2001. Except for a few foreign policy experts, most Americans to this day remain unaware that on the evening of October 24, 1973, the country's armed forces were put on a high state of alert. Their ignorance was not for lack of information since, much to the surprise and chagrin of the secretary of state, the decision to put the country's forces on a nuclear alert was blazoned across the headlines of the major newspapers of the world in the morning editions of October 25, including the *The New York Times* and *The Washington Post*. Entirely preoccupied with the events of the Watergate crisis, American citizens paid little attention to the crisis unfolding in the Middle East.

That the American military took the alert seriously is unquestioned. It moved the aircraft carrier *John F. Kennedy* from west of Gibraltar into the Mediterranean, where it joined the *Roosevelt* and *Independence*. The call put American forces in Europe on alert as well as the 82nd Airborne division, based in the United States. The military recalled seventy-five B52s from Guam. The potential for an unfortunate incident in the Mediterranean Sea was elevated since that region swarmed with American and Soviet naval vessels, including many submarines.

To Kissinger, the introduction of Soviet troops into the Middle Eastern conflict represented the worst possible outcome for the Americans: snatching a certain American diplomatic victory from the jaws of a Soviet defeat. Instead of a diminished Soviet presence in the area, Kissinger faced the prospect of a massive Soviet troop intervention, enhancing the Soviet reputation as saviors of the Egyptians and Syrians. Yet, had the secretary of state consulted more widely, especially with Soviet intelligence experts in the CIA, State Department, and Defense Department, as Ray Cline, an analyst in the State Department at the time, later pointed out, he would have learned that a consensus existed that the Soviet Union had no interest in dispatching troops to the Middle East. Had they been consulted, they would have told him that the Soviet note to President Nixon expressed the deep frustration toward Israeli ceasefire violations and should have been seen as a plea to the Americans to rein in their ally and a last-ditch effort to save the Third Army and the position of President Sadat.[25]

Although Kissinger did not expect the newspapers to learn of DEFCON 3, he knew that the Soviets would pick up its signals once the American forces began to move. He was hopeful that its existence would deter the Soviets from sending troops to the region.

The Americans had good reason to worry. The alert decision shocked the Soviets, who had already decided not to send troops and had intended their note to stir the Americans to control their ally. Yet the strong, unanticipated American reaction caused the Soviet leaders to reconsider their policies in the region and toward the Americans. At an eight-hour Politburo meeting, Nikolai Podgorny, chairman of the Presidium of the Supreme Soviet, summed up the Politburo's shock at the aggressive American action when he remarked: "Who could have imagined that the Americans would be so easily frightened?"[26] Hawks in the Politburo insisted on a strong Soviet countermeasure, demanding that Soviet forces be put on alert. Brezhnev was deeply angry, and Dobrynin, who knew how emotional Brezhnev could be when challenged, feared that the Soviet leader "might do something irresponsible."[27] The Soviets already had 1,500 troops in Syria, and Marshall Andrei Grechko, the Soviet minister of defense, wanted them to occupy the Golan Heights, a suggestion rejected by Andrei Gromyko, Soviet minister of foreign affairs, and Alexei Kosygin, chairman of the council of ministers of the USSR. Finally, after having remained silent for most of the time, Secretary General Brezhnev asked the group what was likely to happen if the Soviets made no response. Because no one thought that the Americans would do anything, this became the Soviet policy.

Although Kissinger claims in his memoirs that the nuclear alert was required in order to prevent the Soviets from sending troops into the area, such a strong message would seem in hindsight an overreaction. Even some of Kissinger's statements made at the time suggest that he had second thoughts. In a telephone conversation with Ambassador Dobrynin, who questioned the secretary of state about the need for DEFCON 3, suggesting that the crisis was an "artificial' one, Kissinger chose not to dispute this explanation. He stated that the policy was invoked for "domestic purposes," thus shifting the blame to Nixon and his Watergate difficulties.

In invoking DEFCON 3, the Americans undercut détente and failed to honor many obligations that they had made with the Soviets at a Soviet-American summit meeting held in Moscow in May 1972, designed to smooth relations between the United States and the Soviet Union. At those meetings, the two powers had agreed to prevent "the development of situations capable of causing a dangerous exacerbation of their relations. Therefore, they will do their utmost to avoid military confrontations and to prevent the outbreak of nuclear war. They will always exercise restraint in their mutual relations."[28] An additional agreement on the prevention of nuclear war, signed in June 1973, stipulated that "if relations between countries not parties to this agreement appear to involve the risk of nuclear war . . . [the two powers] shall immediately enter into urgent consultation with each other and make every effort to avert this risk." More surprisingly, Kissinger, author of *Nuclear Weapons and Foreign Policy* (first published by the Council on Foreign Relations in 1957), a book that urged world leaders to think through all of the consequences of their diplomatic and military decisions, failed to consider many of the ramifications of this decision. In particular, no one had thought through what actions the Americans would take if the Soviets did indeed send troops to the area. Not only did the Soviet leaders regard the alert as "incomprehensible" but "they considered it an irresponsible act in a nuclear age." Nor did Kissinger fully understand DEFCON 3, believing that it could be kept secret from the world. In reality, the alert was "ineffective, potentially dangerous, and ill-conceived." Lacking credibility and made in haste, with "little attention to its details, its risks, or its likely consequences," the decision increased the potential for confrontation rather than diminishing it.[29]

What lay behind the complex, often tortuous, American-Soviet diplomacy, and lost sight of in the American nuclear alert, was the major Soviet goal at that moment: preventing the destruction of the Egyptian Third Army. In fact, once the American nuclear alert was withdrawn, within twenty-four hours, the

Americans and the Soviets settled in to work for this common
end: rescuing the Third Army and saving Sadat. Critical to this
effort was the provision of food and medical supplies, a development that the Israelis opposed. They did so for many reasons.
Prime Minister Meir was under daily attacks for her conduct of
the war and for the considerable loss of life, which the Israelis
were at pains to point out to the Americans exceeded the American loss of life in the Vietnam War by an order of three to one, if
calculated as a proportion of the population. Moreover, they
wanted to use their stranglehold on the Third Army as a bargain-
ing chip in the exchange of prisoners, in high demand in Israel at
the time, and finally but far from least, as proof that the Labor
Party had indeed won the war and deserved to be kept in power.
A general election, scheduled for the end of December, was looking increasingly difficult for Labor. Opposition groups to the
Labor Party, led by Menachem Begin and Ariel Sharon, the hero
of the Israeli counterattack, were gaining popularity and mounting attacks on Meir and her minister of defense, Moshe Dayan.

A crucial exchange of telephone messages between Kissinger
and the Israeli ambassador to the United States, Simcha Dinitz,
on October 26 crystallized the chasm between the Israeli and
American positions. Kissinger's proposal that the Israelis simply
open up an escape route for the Egyptian Third Army brought a
scornful response from Dinitz: "We will not open up the pocket
and release an army that came to destroy us. It has never happened in the history of war." Kissinger's rebuke was equally
strong: "It has never happened that a small country is producing
a world war in this manner," to which he added: the Egyptian
Third Army would never surrender, "no matter what you do,"
since surrender would mean that the Egyptians had lost the war.
It would destroy the Egyptian government.[30]

A hotline message from Brezhnev to Nixon on October 26
made it clear that while the Soviets did not intend to send troops
they refused to see the Syrian and Egyptian armies destroyed.
Complaining that the Soviets had done nothing to provoke the

American nuclear alert, Brezhnev returned to a familiar theme. The Americans must restrain their regional ally. With Soviet military intervention no longer an issue, Kissinger was free to respond, turning the full power of the American government on the Israelis. He informed Ambassador Dinitz that Israel's "course is suicidal. . . . You will not be permitted to destroy this army. You are destroying the possibility of negotiations which you want. . . . It is inconceivable that the Soviets will permit the destruction of the Egyptian army and that the Egyptians will withdraw their army. It will bring down Sadat. It is not something that we will agree to."[31]

The Israelis had little choice. Yet they relented grudgingly, at first agreeing only to allow a single convoy to replenish the Third Army on October 27 and making no promises about further convoys. The crisis confronting the Third Army was far from resolved. More to the point, the Egyptians had not agreed to release Israeli prisoners, nor had they lifted their naval blockade at the Bab al-Mandab Strait at the base of the Red Sea where it opens into the Indian Ocean between Yemen on the Arabian Peninsula and Eritrea on the African continent. By blocking it with warships, the Egyptians prevented ships from reaching the port of Eilat on the Gulf of Aqaba. As a result, the Israelis had refused to permit additional convoys to reach the beleaguered Egyptian soldiers before Golda Meir met with the Americans in Washington in early November.

Further American-Israeli, high-level meetings on the cease-fire and provisioning of the Third Army took place at the State Department and the White House on November 1, 1973, during Prime Minister Meir's visit to the United States. Here, too, the Americans argued for permitting Egyptian convoys to provision the Third Army with nonmilitary supplies, and the Israelis insisted that allowing convoys through should be tied to a release of prisoners and the end of the naval blockade of Eilat. An agreement to permit provisioning of the Third Army and an exchange of prisoners was finally achieved only after Kissinger met with

Sadat in Egypt on November 7 and then extracted agreement from the Israeli cabinet. Although, in fact, the Egyptian Third Army remained encircled by Israeli forces until the first Sinai disengagement agreement of January 19, 1974, it was no longer in danger of being strangled for want of food, water, and medicines. (For a further discussion of the Egyptian-Israeli disengagement agreements of 1974 and 1975, see Chapter 6.) Sadat could begin to put forward his vision of the war as an Egyptian triumph, which did, in fact, change the political landscape of the Middle East and prepared the way for his 1977 trip to Jerusalem and the 1979 peace agreement with the Israelis.

When Kissinger visited Egypt and met with Sadat on November 7, he took with him a highly regarded American diplomat, Hermann Eilts, who was to become the American ambassador to Egypt on February 28, 1974, after diplomatic relations had been restored between the two countries. Kissinger and Eilts formed decidedly different impressions of the Egyptian president. Kissinger writes in his memoirs that he quickly took the measure of Sadat and found him to be "a great man," adding that "the difference between great and ordinary leaders is less formal intellect than insight and courage."[32] While not unaware of Sadat's character flaws—his expensive clothing, his preening, and his infatuation with important world figures—he noted his roots in the Egyptian countryside, commitment to his country, and drive for peace. In Kissinger's view, Sadat was a subtle and sophisticated leader, able to grasp nuances in the American political system, to understand the personalities of the presidents with whom he had to deal (Nixon at the time; later on, Ford, Carter, and Reagan), and thus to wring concessions for Egypt from each leader.

Eilts saw a different man. "Let me tell you, when I first got to know him in November of 1973, the war had already taken place. He was at the time one of the most insecure persons that I have ever run across, and I say this as one who has a deep and abiding admiration for Sadat and what he did in the end. He was uncertain of himself. He had been unsure whether the military operation would work. He had been pushed into it in a sense, because he had perhaps talked a bit too much in the previous year about 'this is the year of decision.'"[33] In Eilts's view, only later, after prolonged negotiations with Kissinger and the Americans, and especially after addressing both houses of the United States Congress in 1975 where he was enthusiastically embraced, did Sadat achieve the status of a world leader.

The events catalogued here would suggest that Eilts's view is more accurate than Kissinger's. In fact, Sadat had lived a life full of high risk up to the October War, being imprisoned by the British, put on trial in 1948 but found innocent in the assassination of the Egyptian collaborationist politician, Amin Uthman, nearly absent from the July 1952 coup that brought the Egyptian military to power, mainly sidelined by Nasser, then appointed as vice president only months before Nasser's death, and a survivor of plans to overthrow him in May 1971. The October War was a high-wire act that ultimately succeeded, politically if not militarily, against deep odds, in part because the Americans, prodded and then threatened by the Soviets, came to Egypt's rescue. If it did nothing else, the decision to call for a nuclear alert awakened the American political leadership to the importance that the Soviet Union attached to preventing the destruction of the Egyptian Third Army. Going forward after the withdrawal of the nuclear alert, Kissinger and Nixon put relentless pressure on the Israelis to allow Egypt to resupply its forces, an action bitterly resented by Golda Meir, but one that rescued Sadat. Saving the Third Army also saved Sadat's government and made it possible for him to burnish his reputation as an astute political and military leader. It facilitated a new relationship with the United States and provided a springboard for dramatic departures in Egypt's relationship with Israel that would soon follow.

CHAPTER 5

| OPENING EGYPT TO THE |
OUTSIDE, 1974–1977

THE SUCCESSES IN THE OCTOBER War, however limited, enhanced Sadat's reputation at home and gave him an opportunity to repair other defects in the country's economy and polity. In fact, according to many comments that Sadat made after the war, Egypt's nearly bankrupt economy had left him no alternative but to proceed to war. His memoirs recount remarks Sadat made to the country's National Security Council on September 30, 1973, just a week before the crossing, during which he warned that "our economy has fallen below zero. We have commitments (to the banks and so on) which we should but cannot meet by the end of the year. In three months' time, by, say, 1974, we shan't have enough bread in the pantry."[1] He made similar statements to student leaders in Alexandria in late August 1974. The army, he claimed, was costing Egypt LE 100 million a month in 1973, or $40 million at the official exchange rate, at a time when the intake of taxes for the whole year was only LE 200 million or $80 million. "There was nothing left but to enter the battle, whatever happened. We were in a situation such that if nothing changed before 1974 we would have been hard put to it to provide a loaf of bread."[2]

Although Sadat was given to exaggeration and may have overstated the severity of Egypt's fiscal woes, there can be little doubt that the economic condition of the country in 1973 was desperate. A few figures make the point. In 1970, when Sadat became president, Egypt was able to stave off creditors only because of large loans from Arab oil-exporting allies and the Soviet Union. Much of the Soviet financing was, however, of little help in balancing the budget. Intended to promote economic growth and provide security, it was used to purchase arms, construct the High Dam at Aswan, and promote industrialization. It was the oil-rich states of Saudi Arabia, Kuwait, and Libya, offering Egypt on average $286 million per year, who saved Egypt from bankruptcy, papering over a fiscal gap marked by yawning and ever-increasing deficits. The external assistance was not cost-free, however, for Egypt's debt repayments rose catastrophically in the 1970s. In 1970, the country's total indebtedness already stood at a massive number; $5 billion. Debt payments ran at $240 million annually and were increasing. The cautious and careful economic historian, Galal Amin, mindful of Egypt's troubled economic history, compared Egypt's financial distress to that which had afflicted the country during the reign of Khedive Ismail (r. 1863–1879), a period most Egyptians were painfully aware of and regarded as fiscally disastrous. During Ismail's tenure in power, the country had actually gone into financial receivership, turning over the vital ministries of finance and public works to British and French advisers and sliding inexorably into a British armed invasion and British overrule. Amin regarded the period between 1967, the year of the June War, and 1975, when disengagement agreements with Israel (see Chapter 4) allowed Egypt to reopen the Suez Canal and pump oil from wells in Sinai, as "one of the bleakest in [Egypt's] modern history."[3]

Since war had become Egypt's highest priority, once overtures to the Americans and the Israelis had failed, Sadat concluded that desperately needed economic reform and new political programs could not be undertaken until the conflict with Israel had been joined. War's end freed Sadat to approach the Americans and international financial organizations and to embark upon radical new economic initiatives. Changing the orientation of an economy and altering a political system are imposing challenges. Dismantling Egypt's powerful public sector, repairing relations with the Americans, opening the economy to outside investment, and ultimately approaching Israel publicly, not in secret, were to test the mettle of the man and his leadership qualities and also expose him to increasing levels of criticism. Transforming a public sector–dominated and largely closed economy to one that was open to outside investment—was to prove as difficult as going to war with Israel.

The first indication that new policies were under consideration occurred on April 18, 1974, in Sadat's speech to a joint session of the Central Committee of the Arab Socialist Union and the People's Assembly, only months after the October War had ended. After making his customary obeisance to Nasser's policies, singling out the National Charter of 1962 and the public sector as significant achievements, Sadat asserted that the only way forward was to revitalize the private sector and champion electoral reform. In dealing with economic matters, he employed the term *infitah*, or open door, echoing a word that was on the lips of many. This speech, which subsequently was labeled the October Paper after the October War, argued that a new and potentially beneficial economic phase was opening in the Middle East, one in which Egypt needed to be a major player. The spectacular rise in the international price of oil, a direct result of the October War and the embargo placed on oil exports to Europe and the United States, had endowed Arab oil-exporting countries with massive dollar reserves that were in search of profitable investment opportunities. Egypt should ready its institutions and its legal system to attract these funds.

Sadat also devoted remarks to Egypt's political institutions. Here, in his view, Nasser had failed Egypt badly. Because there had already been much discussion in public forums about free elections and the benefits of a multiparty democracy, Sadat explained why he still rejected this call. Egypt was not yet ready for full-bore political democracy, he averred. Although the Arab

Socialist Union had failed to generate popular support, Sadat believed that something in between, something that would move away from the single-party state, still highly popular in Africa and many other parts of the Third World, needed to be devised.

As a direct follow-up to the October Paper, Sadat slowly but systematically began to replace those Nasser appointees who had survived the 1971 purge with individuals loyal to him. By April 1975, the transition to a new set of ministers had taken place. Sadat's new top-level bureaucrats were mainly men and women outside the military, chosen primarily for their technical proficiency. His new prime minister, Mamduh Salem, had spent his career in the security services and had sided with Sadat during the May 1971 crisis. Sadat also removed Hussein al-Shafei as his vice president, thus ridding himself of the last of the original group of Free Officers holding high office in the government. His replacement, Husni Mubarak, had distinguished himself as commander of the air force during the October War and as a military man, though not a Free Officer, and ensured continuing support for Sadat within the armed forces. Finally, Sadat tapped Zaki Shafei, dean of the Cairo University economics faculty, to be the minister for economy and economic cooperation. He was assigned to lead the campaign to open the economy to foreign investment and reinvigorate the private sector.

The new cabinet of April 1975, rightly considered a watershed moment in the history of modern Egypt, saw Sadat replace the Nasserites, Socialists, and pan-Arabists, who had dominated affairs up to then, with individuals sympathetic to the liberal political and fiscal agenda that Sadat wished to implement.

Sadat also carried his campaign to root out Nasser's favorites in the press. One of the first to go was the former president's close confidant, Mohamed Heikal, who, as noted, was influential in effecting the transition from Nasser to Sadat and supported the president during the May 1971 crisis. As editor in chief of the country's most prestigious newspaper, *al-Ahram*, Heikal used the paper, especially his Friday editorial columns, to champion Nasser's domestic and foreign policies, turning *al-Ahram* into the official organ of the state. Nonetheless, Heikal's low opinion of Sadat, whom he regarded as inferior to Nasser and whom he had sometimes upstaged in the presence of foreign reporters, infuriated the president and eventually cost him his job. After reading a series of *al-Ahram* editorials critical of the government in the 1970s, Sadat appointed Ali Amin, well known for his conservative political and economic views and his pro-American stances, as the paper's new editor in chief. His twin brother, also an influential journalist, whose battles with Nasser had resulted in imprisonment, became editor in chief of the daily newspaper, *al-Akhbar*. Even closer to Sadat were Musa Sabri, made editor in chief of *al-Akhbar al-Yaum*, once Egypt's most widely circulating newspaper, and Anis Mansur, a prolific professor of literature at Cairo University, chosen to be editor in chief of the *October* magazine. Sadat also made him his major speech writer.

Sadat's second landmark speech, delivered on September 28, 1975, the fifth anniversary of Nasser's death, to a joint session of the Central Committee of the Arab Socialist Union and the People's Assembly, set out in detail the new directions in which he intended to take Egypt. It took him four hours of rambling remarks, spoken entirely in colloquial Egyptian, to make it clear to the delegates that the country was no longer functioning in the shadow of Nasser. He began his speech by reminding Egyptians that they should not make the mistake of idolizing Nasser and the Nasser years or lose sight of the fact that Nasser was a human being whose stature "would not be diminished if we said that he had both virtues and shortcomings."[4] As proof of Nasser's shortcomings, Sadat catalogued the regime's main defects, emphasizing arbitrary arrests, detention camps, competing foci of power, and the failure of the Arab Socialist Union to reflect the wishes of the people. Sadat also stressed the gains that Egypt would derive from his new policies, emphasizing the extraordinary long-term fiscal returns that were already flowing from the 1974 and 1975 disengagement agreements with the Israelis. The opening of the Suez Canal in 1975 and concessions signed with multinational oil companies for explorations in Sinai and the eastern and western deserts had boosted access to hard currencies.

Although Sadat had previewed many of these initiatives during the May 1971 corrective revolution, it was not until after the October War that he was in a position to implement them. And it was only then that Sadat's attack on Nasser's policies became strident. Those who argue that Sadat carried out a systematic de-Nasserization effort, however, overstate their case. Sadat did, indeed, criticize many aspects of Nasser's rule, but he was always effusive in praise of his predecessor's achievements. He never shrank from commending the revolution for ousting a corrupt monarch, passing land reform legislation, nationalizing the Suez Canal Company, constructing the High Dam, opening the educational system to the entire population, and restoring Egypt's dignity in international affairs. These undoubted achievements were Nasser's. In truth, Sadat saw himself as advancing Nasser's agenda rather than opposing it and described his tenure as president as moving Egypt to a new, yet evolutionary stage in the country's development, an era that urgently required the country to open itself to the global economy and to promote political and intellectual freedoms.

Sadat initiated the political aspects of the agenda at the Arab Socialist Union's National Congress in July 1975. In the session, in which the party nominated him for a second term, its members also championed his political vision. Rather than embrace multiparties, which the congress, in accord with Sadat, believed Egypt not yet ready for, the delegates opted for the creation of political platforms (embryonic political parties, so to speak) with all, however, functioning under the umbrella of Egypt's dominant party, the Arab Socialist Union. The first of these platforms (*minbars* in Arabic) to come into existence called itself the Social Democratic platform, but within six months no fewer than forty-three additional groups clamored for recognition. Believing that the matter had spiraled out of control, Sadat created the Committee on the Future of Political Work in Egypt to review these applications and recommend a more controlled creation of platforms. This body, headed up by one of Sadat's closest advisers, Sayyid Marei, proposed that at least for the time being Egypt should have only three platforms, representing left, center, and right perspectives. It also stipulated that each of the platforms should endorse the principles of the July 23, 1952 revolution and the May 15, 1971 corrective revolution.

The National Progressive Union Party, known in Egypt by its shortened name, *tagammu*, emerged to represent the left platform. Headed by Khalid Muhyi al-Din, a former Free Officer well known for his Socialist/Communist leanings, it scooped up the leftist and Nasserite groups and was destined to clash with Sadat as he moved to repair his relationship with the United States and to promote private-sector initiatives, especially those that threatened the public sector. Moreover, as heirs of Nasser's pan-Arabism, *tagammu* was critical of any effort to diminish Egypt's obligation to promote the rights of the Palestinian Arabs to self-determination.

The center party was at first called the Egyptian Socialist Organization and only took the name of the National Democratic Party on July 9, 1978. From its origin until the overthrow of Husni Mubarak in the uprising of 2011, it dominated Egyptian politics. At first Sadat chose to remain aloof from the party, seeking to portray himself as the father of the nation and as a fair-minded, ultimate arbiter of Egypt's hurly-burly politics. Still, the selection of Mamduh Salem, the Egyptian prime minister at the time, to head the Egyptian Socialist Organization left little doubt that the party enjoyed the president's backing.

On the right was the Liberal Socialist Organization, led by Mustafa Kamel Murad, himself a former Free Officer. This group supported most of Sadat's political and economic initiatives. It favored *infitah*, a strengthened private sector, and sought closer links to the International Monetary Fund and the World Bank.

Yet its members worried about Sadat's authoritarianism and his flirtation with the Muslim Brotherhood.

The Arab Socialist Union had angered Sadat by opposing him during the May 1971 crisis. He did not get around to abolishing it, however, until June 29, 1977, and not before the legislature placed restrictions on the creation of additional political parties. At that moment, the People's Assembly enacted a law that forbade the creation of political parties based on religion, geographical region, or class. In essence, the law made Socialist and Communist parties illegal on the grounds that they were class based and would represent only the interests of the lower classes. In addition, the law made a Muslim Brotherhood party illegal because it would be based on religion.

The one party that endeavored to establish itself outside the framework of the political platforms was the Wafd, which tried to win popular support in the late 1970s by reminding the populace of the 1919 revolution and the nationalist career of Egypt's most celebrated opponent of British overrule, Saad Zaghlul. Nasser's Revolutionary Command Council had abolished the Wafd and other political parties almost immediately after seizing power, arguing that these parties had not only failed the country before the revolution but had shown no willingness to purge themselves of corrupt and unpopular leaders. When some of the individuals who had been prominent in the Wafd in the 1950s approached Sadat with a request that they be permitted to revive their party, arguing that they would serve as a counterweight to the rising appeal of the Muslim Brotherhood and others who were opposed to Sadat's overtures to the Israelis (see Chapter 6), Sadat saw only an upside in allowing the Wafd to reappear. He was certain that the people, aware of the failings of the prerevolution political system, would not regard the New Wafd, as it was renamed, as a serious challenger to the National Democratic Party.

As had been the case in the first years of the revolution, the president grossly underestimated the Wafd's appeal (see Chapter 3). The leader of the New Wafd, Fuad Sirag al-Din, now in

his seventies, was hardly a spent force. He had galvanized opposition to the Revolutionary Command Council in 1953, and he was
able to do so again. Labeling the 1952 military seizure of power,
which the military leaders called a revolution or *thawra* in Arabic,
as nothing more than a coup (*inqilab* in Arabic), Sirag al-Din reminded the people of the revolution of 1919, the leadership of
Zaghlul and Nahhas, and argued, with stunning success, that
while Sadat's efforts to liberalize the polity were much appreci-
ated, the government had failed to go far enough. Further recall-
ing that Egypt had enjoyed free elections, a free press often critical
of the government, and freedom of assembly before the military
takeover, he succeeded in drawing to his party much of the dis-
content that had accumulated against the autocracy and secrecy
of the military regime. Caught by surprise by the outpouring of
interest and sympathy for a party that the president and his supporters scorned, the government refused to recognize the New
Wafd as a political party. It was also at this moment, and as a riposte to the popularity of the New Wafd, that Sadat established
the National Democratic Party and assumed leadership of it.

Although Sadat had devoted much of the October Paper to
political reform, the focus of the document was economics. Sadat
believed that economic reforms and an opening to global capitalism were essential and far more beneficial to Egypt at this moment
than political reforms. In his view, Egypt had finally arrived at
that stage in its progress when it could experience rapid economic
growth and rising standards of living, an ambition that had
largely eluded rulers from the turn of the nineteenth century
straight down through the Nasser regime. The significant transformations that had occurred in global economic trends, starting
first and foremost with the abrupt rise in the world price of oil,
were producing cataclysmic shifts in global economic power and
providing new opportunities to grow economically. Sadat's formula, spelled out in skeletal form in the October Paper and then
elaborated in more detail later in speeches, press releases and articles, and legislative enactments, was that Egypt, a populous,

strategically located territory in the very heart of the Arab world, could become one of the fulcrums of this new world economic order. To be precise, the country would make its many resources available to global capital, accumulating at an astonishing rate in oil-exporting, underpopulated Middle Eastern territories, and blend these two ingredients with Western technology. The economic growth rates that the Nasser governments had projected for Egypt, some in the neighborhood of 8 percent per annum and that had unfortunately not been realized, in large measure, in the opinion of Sadat's new economic team because of flawed economic formulas, would now be attained. Egypt was about to usher in a new era of progress.

Critical to economic success was reining in the ambitions of those bureaucrats who administered Egypt's highly powerful public sector, thereby creating space for private capital. But such an endeavor required not only passing legislation that safeguarded foreign and domestic investment from the nationalizations and expropriations that had marked the Nasser years but also persuading Egypt's ruling circles that many of Nasser's public-sector policies, especially the state's attack on the private sector in the mid-1950s and early 1960s, had been harmful to the country.

To understand the obstacles that Sadat faced in opening an economy to global capital, it is essential to look back at the Nasser era and the emergence at that time of a powerful public sector. When the military came to power in 1952, Egypt's public sector was a small one, confined to transportation and communications, the irrigation system, and a single bank. By the time that Sadat took over in 1970, the public sector had grown by leaps and bounds as had the government bureaucracy. The number of governmental administrative units grew from less than 20 in 1952 to 1,600 in 1970, including 29 ministries, 50 public authorities, and 381 public-sector enterprises. In 1952, the state employed 350,000 individuals. By 1970, the number had expanded nearly four-fold to 1,200,000, and the state employed about 60 percent of all university graduates.

The explosive rise of the public sector had begun almost un-intentionally, the result of the British-French-Israeli invasion of Egypt in 1956. The Nasser regime responded to this aggression by sequestrating almost the entirety of British and French assets, including business firms, along with many assets belonging to the Jewish community living in Egypt. The total value of these properties was around L260 million (roughly $100 million), the major portion being business firms that formed the core of Egypt's private sector. These businesses were then turned over to a governmental body known as the Economic Organization for ultimate disposal. As the 1956 war itself lasted only a matter of weeks, it would have been feasible to restore business firms to their original owners, or, if this was not considered to be in the longterm interests of the country, to dole them out to inter-ested Egyptian businesspersons. But the postwar years were marked by an emphasis on economic planning, state interven-tion in economic affairs, a suspicion of free-market economics as an inefficient method for promoting economic progress, and a belief that the Soviet Union through its five-year plans and rapid industrialization had found the formula for rapidly overcoming economic backwardness. The Egyptian state decided, accord-ingly, not to disband the Economic Organization but to make it the oversight body for an expanding public sector. Further na-tionalizations and expropriations followed in rapid succession, often spurred on by political events. The breakup of the Syrian-Egyptian federation in 1961 provided the state with more pre-texts for expropriating the assets of Egypt's haute bourgeoisie, including its business firms. Troubles in the Belgian Congo in 1960 led to the nationalization of Belgian businesses in Egypt. By the time the expropriating and nationalizing zeal had run its course, Egypt possessed a dominant public sector and an atro-phied private sector. Few large-scale businesses had escaped the reach of the state, and Egypt found itself virtually off limits to the world's big multinational corporations. To be sure, the coun-try had lots of small-scale enterprises—small manufacturers and traders—and private urban and rural property holders still existed, but their activities were carefully regulated by the state through agricultural cooperatives or through progressive taxation rates.

There was only one problem with Nasser's state-led industrialization and economic planning. It did not work. The industrialization drive, which had been focused on import substitution and heavy industries, unfortunately produced severe trade imbalances, the result of importing large quantities of intermediate and capital goods that the country's exports, mainly cotton, did not cover. By the second half of the 1960s, per-capita income growth had slowed dramatically. Investment and saving rates had also declined while the state budget skyrocketed as the public sector expanded. Increasingly, public-sector enterprises became employers of last resort, often only able to attract the least desirable employees. The result was that as the numbers of Egyptians finding employment in the government bureaucracy, including public-sector enterprises, soared, the output per bureaucrat declined sharply.

Sadat's first choice to lead the open-door policy push was Abdel Aziz Higazi, former dean of the faculty of commerce at Ain Shams University in Cairo and, from 1968, Nasser's minister of finance. Sadat retained Higazi as minister of finance when he became president, made him deputy prime minister for economy and finance just after the October War, and then prime minister on September 25, 1974. Well known for his belief in liberal economics, he promoted Sadat's economic and fiscal agenda. In a speech to the People's Assembly, he warned that Egypt's trade imbalances, massive external debt payments, and heavy military expenditures had created an unsustainable economy. The war in Yemen had been little short of a disaster, he insisted, forcing the state to allocate no less than 33 percent of the national income to the armed forces. In his view, and that of his president, Egypt's economy, as constituted in 1974, was doomed to fail unless far-reaching structural reforms were carried out.

Law Number 43 of 1974, passed through the People's Assembly in June of that year, was intended to be the cornerstone of a radical change in the Egyptian economy. It set aside many of the laws enacted during the Nasser years that restricted foreign and domestic capital. Specifically, it exempted all private-sector firms, even those functioning jointly with public-sector enterprises, from the labor laws that mandated labor representation in the management of firms, profit sharing with workers, and tenure for workers. Further, the law contained explicit guarantees against nationalization and expropriation and lifted the requirement that Egyptians hold a majority of company shares and seats on the boards of directors. The law also permitted foreigners to exercise total ownership of companies, except banks, and to own up to 49 percent of the shares of public-sector enterprises.

A month after the passage of this law, the People's Assembly enacted Law Number 111, which put an end to the General Economic Organization, the public sector's oversight body, thus preparing the way for offering shares in public-sector enterprises to private investors. The law did stipulate, however, that these enterprises must first of all offer their shares to their employees.

The face of Sadat's economic program was not, as one might have anticipated, a wealthy foreign businessperson or a multinational corporation. It was not, for example, David Rockefeller, head of the Chase Manhattan Bank. Despite being featured in many photo-ops with the Egyptian president, talking up Sadat's economic initiatives and establishing a joint enterprise with one of Egypt's state-run banks, Rockefeller was never deeply involved in Egyptian economic affairs. Nor was it any number of wealthy Persian Gulf sheikhs who might have been attracted to Egypt. Egypt's window of opportunity for attracting Arab investment would close abruptly once Sadat journeyed to Jerusalem. It was, in reality, an Egyptian businessman, Osman Ahmed Osman, head of the Arab Contractors Company, an individual who had first made his mark in the business world fulfilling construction contracts in the Arabian Peninsula, Iraq, and Libya. Born in

Ismailia in 1917 and taught by Hassan al-Banna, the founder of the Muslim Brotherhood, Osman became a Muslim Brother in his youth, but left the organization because of the pressure of work. After building up his firm outside Egypt and establishing many subsidiary companies, he returned to Egypt and put his business acumen at the disposal of the Egyptian state. Although Nasser nationalized the Arab Contractors Company in 1961, he wisely allowed Osman to run the company without state interference, a notable exception to the customary state involvement in public-sector enterprises. Among the many projects that the Arab Contractors carried out during the Nasser years, and the one that gained the greatest press notoriety, was its work in the building of the High Dam at Aswan. Although the firm did no more than crush rock and pour cement, its publicists promoted the idea that the company had virtually singlehandedly built the dam. Still, Osman kept his distance from the state, refusing all overtures to run for parliament or become a minister. After Nasser's death, the reason for his distance from the state became apparent. Osman became one of Egypt's most outspoken critics of Nasser's policies.

It was thus hardly a surprise that Osman became Sadat's most ardent *infitah* booster and a close family friend. The two men enjoyed walks together, Sadat looked to Osman for economic and financial advice, and cemented his relationship with Osman's family when his daughter married Osman's son. Osman's steady complaints against Nasser's economic policies undoubtedly pleased the Egyptian president. Osman's memoirs, *Safahat min Tajrabati*, published in the year that Sadat was assassinated, 1981, offered a devastating critique of the Nasser era. He was notably savage in commenting on the consequences of the June 1967 war, which, in his opinion, had left the country with the task of "clearing ... debris, especially the bleeding of all of Egypt's resources.... Instead of aiming our efforts at building our country, we are now aiming our efforts at liberating our land. . . . Egypt abandoned hope and embraced despair [under Nasser] until Sadat came and

lifted her face from mud."[5] Osman regarded Nasser's nationalizations "as a great mistake that victimized all Egypt," establishing
the state "as another God on earth."[6]

But, as the face of *infitah*, Osman was more than a publicist.
The Arab Contractors Company, which the Sadat government
quickly privatized, became the showpiece of a reinvigorated private sector and had many achievements on its record. Its war
record was exemplary. In the lead-up to the October War, the
firm erected the silos that protected the SAM missiles. It also
built the ferries that carried troops and heavy military equipment
across the canal during the campaign. After the war, the company
led Egypt's reconstruction programs. It built the October Sixth
Bridge, which spanned the Nile River in Cairo and eased traffic
congestion, as well as the tunnel under the Suez Canal that linked
the heartland of Egypt to Sinai. Arab Contractors took on the
massive task of reconstructing the canal cities (Suez, Ismailia,
and Port Said), which were devastated during the War of Attrition and forced to be evacuated. Nor did Osman refuse Sadat's
invitation to assume government office as he had resisted Nasser's efforts to recruit him. Under Sadat, he became minister of
reconstruction, supervisor of the food production program,
chairman of the National Democratic Committee for Popular
Development, and head of the engineers syndicate.

Osman's and Sadat's showiest project, one that was supposed
to demonstrate how private initiatives outperformed public enterprises, was a desert reclamation program at Salhia, which was
carried out in 1980. Salhia was 4,000 acres of largely desert land
20 miles west of Ismailia, which the Arab Contractors Company
undertook to reclaim as part of a larger campaign to make arable
150,000 acres of desert land per year, up to 3 million acres by
the year 2000 and to do so more cheaply than Nasser's state had
done in the 1950s, when it used increased water supplies from the
High Dam at Aswan to reclaim desert land around Alexandria in
Liberation Province. Alas, neither Salhia nor Liberation Province
was a financial success. If anything, they proved that the Egyptian

deserts could be made to bloom only if a lot of money was expended.

Sadat had believed that *infitah* would unlock Egypt's economic and business creativity, which had been too long suppressed by an autocratic state, and produce strong economic growth. The overall economic statistics were impressive, but a closer look at them reveals that the progress had little to do with the open door and more with the end of belligerency with Israel. The gross domestic product (GDP) grew at an outstanding rate of 9 percent per year between 1968 and 1975, and the investment rate doubled from 13.7 percent of GDP in 1973 to 28.7 percent in 1985. These achievements stemmed directly from the aftermath of the war. They were the result of the reopening of the Suez Canal in 1975, remittances sent back home by Egyptian workers who poured into the Gulf states as their economies boomed, a large increase in tourism, an increase in oil production stemming from oil explorations in Sinai and the eastern and western deserts, and that ever-important standby of the Egyptian economy, foreign assistance and loans. Happily, these improvements did not result in the maldistribution of income or an increase in those living in poverty as many feared. The numbers of those living in poverty and the mortality rate declined while life expectancy increased from fifty to fifty-eight years.

In contrast, *infitah*'s contribution to Egypt's striking economic progress under Sadat was slight. Law Number 43 of 1974, designed to attract foreign capital, failed badly. Of the LE 5 billion, which was committed under this law, more than half (61 percent) came from Egyptian businesspersons, not foreigners; only 23 percent originated from the program's main target, businesspersons from the oil-rich Arab states. Moreover, of the total promised investment, only 32 percent materialized. The *infitah* problems were legion. In the first place, the law was cumbersome, requiring substantial revisions in 1979. Opposition to allowing the private sector a free hand had so many critics that investors worried about how secure their investments truly were. Although the regime dominated organized labor, prohibiting strikes, the main labor federation, the Egyptian Trade Union Federation, mobilized opposition, and government bureaucrats created a climate of go-slow throughout the country in processing applications for new projects. Most important of all, the hope that the drafters of the *infitah* program had of spurring industrialization through a combination of Arab investment, Egyptian resources, and Western technology never materialized. Not surprisingly, most private-sector investment poured into tourism, housing, and luxury construction. As a result, Egypt's trade deficit, which an export-oriented economy was designed to eliminate, ran at the alarmingly high rate of 20 percent of GDP. External indebtedness continued apace. In 1977, the country's external debt stood at $5.7 billion, a robust 42 percent of GDP, a figure that alarmed Egyptian economists and showed no signs of abating. It was destined to rise to $41 billion by 1993. One critic's claim that overall *infitah* was an "utter failure" is not far from the mark.[7]

A direct result of Sadat's *infitah* policies and the restoration of diplomatic relations with the United States in 1974 was that the major international financial institutions became involved in Egyptian finances and economic plans. As the economy failed to respond as rapidly or effectively to the opening to foreign capital as had been hoped for, the state was compelled to look to the International Monetary Fund and the World Bank for advice and financial assistance. In particular, the International Monetary Fund became increasingly involved in recommending fiscal and administrative reforms that would make Egypt a more attractive investment arena and would promote economic growth. The Fund's most energetic agent in Cairo, Paul M. Dickie, argued that only radical fiscal reforms, notably the devaluation of the currency and the slashing of food and other subsidies, would enable Egypt to truly prosper.

That governmental subsidies were a major element in governmental budgetary deficits was unquestioned, and that they had to be reduced was well understood in government and international financial circles. But how these cuts were to be carried out, whether gradually, the government's preference, or dramatically and all at once, which was the view of the International Monetary Fund, led to intense debates and ultimately to the severest popular challenge to the Egyptian government since the 1919 revolution.

Egypt's government subsidy program dated back to 1941 when, as a wartime measure, the government, seeking to make necessities available at reduced prices, introduced price controls on a number of widely traded commodities. The main price-controlled items at the time were bread, flour, edible oil, sugar, tea, and kerosene. But a program that had functioned on a small scale during the 1950s expanded rapidly in the next two decades. By the 1970s direct subsidies existed on more than twenty commodities. Not only did the state control the prices of such essentials as bread, flour, lentils, beans, rice, edible oil, sugar, tea, and cooking gas (*butagas*)—items that were undeniably critical to the budget of ordinary Egyptians—it also expanded the list to include a number of items such as frozen fish, frozen meat, and chicken, for which the case that they were essential to survival was difficult to make. Nor did the state limit availability to its most needy and vulnerable citizens, as would have been the case had it issued food stamps. Any Egyptian citizen could obtain a ration card. Nearly all Egyptians had cards, even though some of the subsidized items, notably coarse *baladi* bread and coarse *baladi* wheat flour, were overwhelmingly consumed by the poorer classes.

By 1975, direct subsidies on food and other items accounted for no less than 43 percent of total government expenditures and 13 percent of GDP. There were, in addition, many indirect or implicit subsidies that did not show up as line items on the budget but added enormously to the government deficit. Indirect subsidies were widespread and included innumerable public-sector enterprises run at a loss, particularly public utility enterprises that distributed water, gas, and electricity at controlled prices, as well as the salaries of redundant employees in the state bureaucracy and public enterprises, estimated by one economist at 30 percent of the wage bill of these bodies. By the time that Sadat became president, direct and indirect subsidies were eating up virtually the whole of Egypt's tax revenues.

In late 1976 and early 1977, the Egyptian government engaged in negotiations with the International Monetary Fund for a large loan, which it needed in order to meet its debt-servicing obligations. Under pressure from the International Monetary Fund, the government agreed to cut back on subsidies. The cabinet discussions on how to trim subsidies were intense and difficult because everyone understood how vital most of the subsidized products were to family budgets. In his memoirs, Heikal blames the International Monetary Fund for leaving the government little alternative except to accept the draconian demands of this body. Heikal claims that both Zaki Shafei, the minister of economy, and Abdel Aziz Qaissuni, the deputy prime minister in charge of economic affairs, were opposed to the International Monetary Fund recommendations, but they had no choice but to accept "commands rather than recommendations."[8] Sadat adds that Qaissuni, in charge of economic affairs at the time, informed the cabinet that subsidies would have to be lifted if the country wanted to get help from the International Monetary Fund and the World Bank. Prime Minister Mamduh Salem, a former police officer and security expert, then warned the cabinet to expect unrest as a result of the rollback of subsidies, but Qaissuni said that he was getting pressure from conservative Arab states as well as the International Monetary Fund, the World Bank, and the American Embassy. The latter argument, more than the dicta from the World Bank and the International Monetary Fund, persuaded Sadat that Egypt had no alternative.

Qaissuni's announcement to the People's Assembly on the evening of January 17, 1977, carried in all of the newspapers the next morning, sent shock waves throughout the land. The reaction was instantaneous and violent. On the morning of January 18, Sadat was being interviewed at the government rest house in

Aswan, one of his favorite locations, preparing for the visit of President Tito of Yugoslavia, when he saw smoke rising from Aswan City. What is that, he exclaimed to the reporter. Her response took him utterly by surprise. She informed him that riots had broken out that morning in Cairo and Alexandria and were erupting in all of Egypt's cities. Briefly, Sadat found himself personally threatened, for an unruly group of Aswan protesters was marching to present their demands to him. His security team, determined to prevent a confrontation, flew him back to Cairo where they readied a plane to whisk him and his family away to Iran should the protest movement threaten his regime. As soon as he arrived in Cairo, he conferred with the commander of the armed forces, the much decorated General Gamasi, who, as we noted, had served Sadat and the country so well during the October War. Gamasi reminded Sadat that the army had not been called in to restore order since the 1952 revolution and that its leaders were opposed to using the army against the people. Gamasi agreed to suppress the protesters but only if the state reinstated the subsidies. Sadat agreed, and the military units moved in, and over a three-day period (January 18 to 20) locked Egypt down with a dusk-to-dawn curfew, thus ending the uprising. The loss of life was considerable. According to official figures, disputed by the protesters, 73 individuals died, 800 were injured, and 1,270 were arrested.

It is shocking that Egypt's president was so completely out of touch with the populace, considering how widely the issue of subsidy cuts had been discussed in the lead-up to the legislation. Rumors abounded; many feared that the austerity package favored by the International Monetary Fund, the World Bank, and the American Embassy would result in these international financial organizations and the American Embassy assuming control of the Egyptian economy. Prime Minister Qaissuni's speech to the delegates in the People's Assembly on the evening of January 17, intended to calm people by showing that the government had stood its ground and refused to cut many subsidies, was not persuasive. Many in the Assembly raised their voices in protest. But their protest paled next to the popular and violent outpouring of dissent.

The January 1977 subsidy riots dismayed Sadat and made him aware that the prestige that he drew from the October War was fading. The populace wanted more to show for their many sacrifices than a mere end to warfare with the Israelis. The open door had failed to take root, obstructed, as it was, by a recalcitrant state bureaucracy and by a thus far unenthusiastic group of foreign backers. In Sadat's opinion, more was needed for Egypt to move forward economically and politically; Egypt required further psychological jolts and deeper challenges to Nasser's policies. Sadat's vision for Egypt's future entailed even more radical departures, this time in Egypt's most sensitive area of foreign policy, its relations with Israel. The journey to Jerusalem and the peace treaty were direct outcomes of the January food riots.

CHAPTER 6

| MAKING PEACE, 1974–1979 |

ALTHOUGH THE MILITARY ASPECTS OF the October War were over at the end of 1973, much remained to be done. The ceasefire so laboriously negotiated between Egypt and Israel held, but territorial arrangements between Egypt and Israel needed to be resolved. Even more pressing, however, was disengaging the Egyptian and Israeli armies, awkwardly stationed around the Suez Canal. The potential for renewed fighting was ever present. Sadat had achieved one of his major goals in going to war: he had brought the attention of the superpowers to the unresolved problems in the Middle East and reignited stalled diplomatic negotiations. In 1977, though, most of Sinai still remained in Israeli possession as did the Golan Heights, the West Bank of the Jordan River, and Gaza. Because these were the territories that the Egyptians and Syrians entered the war to reclaim, their leaders could hardly consider the war a success.

The first order of business for the Americans, Israelis, and the Egyptians was separating the armies. Henry Kissinger, the US secretary of state, took the lead, shuttling back and forth between Egypt and Israel, but Sadat also provided decisive support, often to the dismay of leading Egyptian officials. Egypt and Israel signed two disengagement agreements, the first on January 18, 1974, known as Sinai I, and the second more than a year later on September 4, 1975, known as Sinai II. The first agreement obligated the two armies scrupulously to observe the ceasefire, which had gone into effect on October 22, 1973, but was frequently violated. It also confined the forces to well-defined zones, separated from each other by a United Nations Emergency Force. The Israelis were to withdraw their forces from the west bank of the Suez Canal and also to pull back from the east bank of the canal. Both sides were to limit the size of their armies in Sinai.

Kissinger anticipated difficulties in limiting Egypt's Sinai army, given the fact that the Egyptians had expended so much effort and lost so many lives in crossing the canal. He believed that the Egyptians would insist on being allowed no fewer than 250 tanks within the small zone that was to be allotted to them on the east bank of the canal. To Kissinger's delight and surprise, Sadat agreed to limit the number of troops to 7,000 and the tank force to 30, a concession that profoundly troubled Egypt's generals. General Gamasi, who was Egypt's chief military negotiator during these discussions, was so deeply wounded at this concession that he withdrew to a corner of the room and wept. The Egyptian Foreign Minister, Ismail Fahmy, expressed well the discomfort that many on the Egyptian negotiating team felt about the decision, remarking that "Sadat had singlehandedly given away all that the Egyptian army had won with great effort and sacrifice without consulting anyone." He also described Sadat as being "oblivious to details," a comment made later many times as other Egyptians observed Sadat in his dealings with the Americans and the Israelis.[1] Fahmy criticized the Egyptian president for being too trusting of Kissinger and too eager to please the Americans to whom he appeared to have hitched his future.

In the second disengagement pact Egypt and Israel agreed not to use force, threats of force, or military blockades to resolve conflicts between them, another agreement that distressed Fahmy and other Egyptians since it effectively ended the state of belligerency between the two countries. The Israeli forces withdrew to the passes of Sinai, and a new buffer zone was established

Sadat and Henry Kissinger in negotiations in Cairo in 1975.

between the Israeli and Egyptian lines, maintained, as before, by United Nations Emergency Forces. The Egyptian and Israeli armies also agreed to limit the number of troops and armaments in Sinai.

Sadat's decision to reopen the Suez Canal on June 5, 1975, taken before the second disengagement agreement but exactly eight years after the commencement of the June War, also distressed many. Believing that the canal should remain closed in order to incentivize the Israelis to sign a more comprehensive disengagement agreement, Fahmy complained that the decision to open the canal and reconstruct the Suez Canal cities at a time when Israeli forces were still able militarily to threaten the canal and the Suez Canal cities sent a message that Egypt was no longer prepared to go to war. In his opinion, Sadat used the opening of the canal on the very day that the Six-Day War had begun as a blatant effort to boost his reputation at the expense of Nasser's. It highlighted Sadat's ability to reclaim what Nasser had lost, a message not well received by the still substantial Nasser admirers in Egypt.

Fahmy was right about Sadat's inattention to diplomatic details and even his lack of preparation when complex negotiations required close study. In truth, Sadat had little interest in the intricacies of diplomacy and would often compromise with Israeli negotiators on issues that he considered inconsequential. Yet, in dwelling on Sadat's diplomatic deficiencies, critics underestimated his impressive and at times intuitive grasp of the main principles that he believed were needed to guide Egypt's foreign policies. He derived his foreign policy priorities largely from the frustrating experiences that Egypt had had with the Soviet Union and the Americans in the 1960s. The Soviets appeared to him an unreliable military ally, delaying the supply of essential arms and withholding offensive weapons. All of this had convinced him that "the Americans held ninety-nine percent of the cards" in Middle Eastern affairs, a statement that Sadat made repeatedly. In addition, the war showed him that while the United States was ready to back Israel to the hilt, the Soviets would not do the same for their Arab allies. Hence, in his view, Egypt had no alternative but to come to terms with the Americans. Nasser himself, who had tied his success so closely to the Soviets, had begun to understand this reality when he threatened to change his allegiance to the Americans. But it was Sadat who carried through on Nasser's threat.

Sadat's belief that the Americans were the primary actors in the region was not confined to military affairs or the high priority that the Americans gave to guaranteeing Israel's security. It had a strong economic dimension. He believed that an accommodation with the Americans, which was likely to entail ending the Egyptian state of belligerency with the Israelis, would unlock American and international financial coffers and provide vital assistance to a still beleaguered Egyptian economy.

The disengagement agreements called upon the interested parties to work toward a peaceful resolution of the Middle Eastern conflict. These discussions, involving the Arab confrontation states (Egypt, Syria, Jordan, and Lebanon), Israel, the Soviet

Union, and the United States, took place in Geneva under the auspices of the United Nations. Unfortunately but predictably, little was achieved, and thus no progress had been made beyond the separation of the combatants and Egyptian and Israeli promises not to go to war before Jimmy Carter became president in January 1977.

An admitted novice in foreign affairs, who had cut his political teeth as governor of Georgia, Carter was, nonetheless, acutely aware of the dangers in the Middle East. Even before becoming president, he had come to the conclusion that the Arab-Israeli conflict held the greatest potential for global instability and therefore decided to make the Middle East a foreign policy priority for his administration. Moreover, as a devout and born-again Christian, steeped in the Bible and possessing a strong attachment to the Holy Land as well as a longstanding commitment to human rights, he thought American morality and humanitarianism could be forces for good in this troubled region.

The two individuals whom Carter chose to lead his foreign policy team—Cyrus Vance, his secretary of state, and Zbigniew Brzezinski, head of the National Security Council, shared his worries about the Middle East. They also brought a wealth of experience to their tasks. Brzezinski, who was a professor of political science and international relations at Columbia University and a renowned expert on the Soviet Union, recognized Carter's lack of knowledge of foreign policy. Even before the election Brzezinski undertook to bring himself up to date on the Middle East, which he thought would loom large in American foreign affairs. A fact-finding trip through the Middle East, which he undertook before the presidential election, convinced him that Kissinger's step-by-step diplomacy had run its course. Without a comprehensive diplomatic breakthrough, he feared that war was imminent, would involve the superpowers in an even more lethal confrontation than had occurred in 1973, would undermine the standing of the conservative pro-American Arab states, and would elevate the influence of the Soviet Union in the region.

Vance, too, shared this view, and in discussions with Carter in the summer of 1976, he and Carter came to an additional conclusion about the Middle East, one that would have far-reaching implications for American policy. In their view, the crux of the Arab-Israeli problem was the question of the Palestinian peoples, who, dispossessed of a homeland in the 1948 and 1967 Arab-Israelis wars, had created a vehicle for their political aspirations in 1964, the Palestine Liberation Organization, and found a charismatic leader, Yasser Arafat, to champion their demands for an independent state.

In Sadat, the American foreign policy triumvirate found a willing, even eager, partner. Although Carter had not met any Arab leader before he became president and had been to the Middle East only once (a trip to Israel), the two men hit it off from the outset. They met for the first time in early April 1977. Carter was swept off his feet, claiming that "a shining light burst on the Middle East scene for me." The contrast with the Israeli prime minister, Yitzhak Rabin, whom Carter had met a month earlier, was striking. Whereas Carter found Rabin to be reticent, introspective, and distant, barely willing to discuss the prospects for progress in the Middle East, Sadat impressed him as "charming and frank, and also a very strong leader who would not shrink from making difficult political decisions. He was extraordinarily inclined toward boldness and seemed impatient with those who were more timid or cautious. . . . The prospects for peace in his troubled region might not be dead."[2] Vance, too, was immediately taken with Sadat, valuing those very traits that alarmed so many Egyptians. He described Sadat as "a truly extraordinary man. A patriot, he was wise and visionary, bold and courageous, yet at the same time, private and sensitive. Once his trust was gained he would stand with you unfailingly. From our first meeting in Lebanon, I was drawn to him by his warmth and charm." While agreeing with Sadat's critics that the man was "intuitive rather than methodical . . . strong on principles, weak on implementation" he believed that Sadat's ability to see the big picture and to ignore lesser details made him the area's most promising and creative negotiating partner.[3]

The new American foreign policy team had little to show for their work and their new-found ally in Sadat during the first nine months of Carter's presidency. Only toward the end of October did this situation change, the result of an unusual handwritten and hand-delivered letter from Carter to Sadat, dated October 21, 1977. Carter's note, a mere 129 words, contained a powerful message. It reminded the Egyptian president of "your promise to me [made during a meeting in April] that at a crucial moment I could count on your support when obstacles arose in our common search for peace in the Middle East. We have reached such a moment, and I need your help. . . . The time has now come to move forward and your early public endorsement of our approach is extremely important—perhaps vital—in advancing all parties to Geneva." Coincidentally and unbeknownst to the Americans, the note arrived at a time when dramatic developments were occurring in Egyptian–Israeli relations, though not toward a gathering of the interested parties in Geneva, the direction that the Americans were advocating. Sadat had, in fact, concluded that the prospects of achieving anything lasting through multiparty negotiations in Geneva were doomed and had initiated secret high-level contacts with Israel. On September 16, 1977, Hassan al-Tuhami, a Sadat confidant, met Moshe Dayan, the Israeli foreign minister, in Morocco under the auspices of King Hassan. In these conversations, Tuhami made clear Sadat's interest in separate Egyptian–Israeli discussions leading possibly to a comprehensive peace accord.

The year 1977, however, hardly seemed a favorable moment for approaching the Israelis. In May of that year, the electorate had voted the Labor Party out of office in favor of an ultraconservative and expansionist-minded Likud coalition government, led by Menachem Begin, who became prime minister in June. The Labor Party, whose leaders represented a veritable who's who in Israeli politics, including such worthies as David Ben-Gurion,

Moshe Dayan, Golda Meir, and Yitzhak Rabin, had dominated Israeli politics for three decades from the creation of the state in 1948 until the 1977 elections. But the opprobrium of the early days of the October War, when Israel seemed on the verge of a catastrophic military defeat, contributed to the triumph of the Likud coalition. Likud posed many problems for the Arab states, owing much of its electoral victory to the increasingly large and strongly anti-Arab Sephardic Israeli community, many of whose members had fled to Israel from Arab countries and held a grudge against their former governments. Moreover, Begin was the Israeli politician who was thought least willing to make concessions to the Arabs. A disciple of the Zionist zealot Zeev Jabotinsky, Begin was on record in favor of occupying all of Eretz Israel, the Land of Israel, a vague and often contested term that referred to the Biblical lands of the Israelites. Eretz Israel usually included the West Bank of the Jordan River, which had come under Israeli occupation during the 1967 war.

Sadat's trip to Romania in late October, arranged even before receiving the note from Carter, however, rescued Carter's and Sadat's diplomatic initiatives. The Egyptian president used the occasion to query the Romanian president, Nicolai Ceausescu, about Begin. Sadat asked Ceausescu, one of the few Soviet bloc leaders to have maintained contacts with Arab and Israeli leaders, whether Begin truly wanted peace with the Arabs and whether he was strong enough to push an agreement through the Israeli Knesset and persuade the electorate that an agreement was in Israel's interests. Ceausescu's answers were unequivocally positive and were followed by a plea to Sadat to use all of his personal resources to bring an end to this long and bitter conflict.

On November 9, 1977, Sadat made what many have come to regard as the most consequential speech of his presidency. The occasion was the opening of the new Egyptian parliament, and Sadat's address, which was in the tradition of the US president's state of the union address to congress or the British monarch's speech to parliament at the beginning of each new legislative year, began unexceptionally and unexcitedly as a review of the agenda to be dealt with during the year by the People's Assembly. After reminding the delegates of the achievements of the 1952 revolution and the 1971 corrective revolution, well-worn themes in Sadat speeches, he alerted the delegates to their most important legislative duty for the year: reforming the taxation code. It was only toward the end of his remarks that he turned his attention to "the whole picture of the external situation." At first, Sadat dilated on the many rebuffed overtures that he had made to the Israelis, praising Jimmy Carter at the same time for bringing the attention of the world to the Palestinian question despite the pressure "shamelessly" exerted on Carter "to revert to the stand of total support to Israel, whether right or wrong, as the former President Johnson did in the past, and not to deviate one step from the Israeli position." Next, he spoke about Arab solidarity, praising the Palestinian leader, Yasser Arafat, who was in the audience, as the hope for the future. He stressed Egypt's willingness to go to Geneva to discuss Middle Eastern issues but added the sentence that was to be the most memorable part of the speech: "Israel must be greatly surprised to hear me say that I am even ready to go to the Knesset to discuss with them."[4]

Sadat's sentence about going to Israel came at the end of a very long, rambling, and frankly boring address, for which he had made no advance preparation or offered any follow-up. It received routine applause not notably different from the standard applause that greeted many of Sadat's remarks. Arafat even applauded. It would appear that few in the audience grasped the significance of what Sadat said. Ismail Fahmy believed that the statement was one of Sadat's frequent divergences from the formal text and was meant to be little more than a rhetorical flourish, not to be taken seriously. Sadat later claimed in a remark to Fahmy that the statement had been a slip of the tongue, and he asked that it be removed from the formal text, since it was intended to be little more than an embellishment of a remark made on many occasions of his willingness to go to the ends of the world to prevent more bloodshed in the Middle East.

If Sadat's sentence was merely a slip of the tongue, in fact to be expunged from the formal text of the speech, the president grossly miscalculated the attention that the foreign media would make of it. While the Israeli press focused on his tirade against the Israeli political leaders, notably his claim that their intransigent and expansionist policies prevented peace, the headlines in European and American newspapers highlighted the offer to go to the Knesset. Once Walter Cronkite and Barbara Walters began to focus on the remark, there was no retreat. Sadat had crossed his Rubicon and now had little alternative but to allow the local newspapers to report the entire speech.

Begin was, at first, slow to respond, believing like many that Sadat's speeches could not be taken seriously. His first comment was that he was ready to meet and talk with Sadat anywhere and suggested that they should convene in Geneva. In response to questions from visiting American Congressmen, however, Begin went further, assuring them that Sadat would be received in Israel with all the honor that is conferred on a head of state. On November 12, three days after Sadat's speech in the People's Assembly, Begin formally invited the Egyptian president to come to Jerusalem, concluding his remarks with the Arabic expression, *ahlan wa-sahlan*, meaning "welcome."

Not only did the statement that Sadat was ready to go to Jerusalem and address the Israeli Knesset catch many Egyptians off guard, it also brought the resignations of Egypt's two leading foreign policy officials. The first to resign was Ismail Fahmy, whom Sadat had made his foreign minister in 1973. The individual whom Sadat designated as Fahmy's replacement, Muhammad Riad, and who had been serving under Fahmy as the minister of state for foreign affairs, also refused Sadat's invitation, a refusal normally not permitted in the Egyptian bureaucracy and hence an even more obvious indication of the depth of opposition to the president.

Fahmy's complaints were telling, and they represented the views of many in Egypt's political elite and intellectual classes. His main criticism was that Sadat had failed to consult before he made his remark in the People's Assembly and before he finally agreed to go to Jerusalem. The Egyptian foreign minister let the president know that he was strongly opposed to going to Jerusalem. He informed the president that he would have supported the policy if, after discussing the matter with top officials, the president was still determined to go. Sadat refused, screaming, "I will not discuss it with anybody. I don't care for anybody's opinion."[5] To Fahmy, Sadat's Jerusalem journey was further proof of the president's impulsiveness, his inability to focus on long-term policy goals, his willingness to overturn fundamental Egyptian policies on his own, and his penchant for proceeding day by day, "in fact from moment to moment, dealing piecemeal with problems as they arose."[6] To Fahmy, the twin principles of Egyptian foreign policy were pan-Arab solidarity and neutrality—principles that Nasser had been faithful to and that Sadat was in the process of discarding.

The worries expressed in Egypt about Sadat's offer to go to Jerusalem paled in comparison with the venom that poured out of the other Arab states. Although Arafat had applauded the statement at the time, he regretted this action and later expressed anger, hurt, humiliation, and resentment. He now claimed that he had been brought to Cairo on false pretenses and forced to listen to a remark that undermined his mission. King Khalid of Saudi Arabia guiltily admitted that he prayed that the plane that carried Sadat to Jerusalem would crash.

Sadat's offer to address the Israeli Knesset constituted a radical and provocative departure from Arab policy toward the state of Israel. No Arab state had recognized the state of Israel, and no Arab official, let alone an Arab head of state, had ever met formally with Israeli officials though there had been many secret backchannel communications. Sadat's offer to travel to Jerusalem, to be met, even to shake hands, with the top Israeli officials, and to address the Knesset was beyond the imaginings of other Arab leaders and drew immediate and nearly universal condemnation in the Arab world.

Some of Sadat's critics dismissed the offer and the speech that he made in the Knesset as publicity stunts, little more than Sadat's egomania and his compulsion to be the center of attention getting the better of him. In reality, there were many reasons that this policy made sense for Egypt. The country assuredly was suffering from Palestine fatigue. Four wars with the Israelis and heavy expenditures on armaments had drained the Egyptian exchequer and imposed innumerable burdens on Egyptian families, not the least of which was the loss of loved ones. Egypt's combined war losses between 1948 and 1973 were extraordinary. A total of 39,000 Egyptian soldiers had died, 73,000 had been wounded, and another 61,000 disabled while 2.1 million people living in the canal cities twice had to be evacuated—in 1956 and again after 1967. The hardly pro-Sadat magazine *Ruz al-Yussuf* expressed the disillusionment over Palestine well, running a cartoon showing two well-dressed, obviously well-off Arabs entering a posh café commenting that they were going in to struggle on behalf of the Palestinians. Sadat had an even more telling statement, remarking after hearing strong critical comments about his journey to Jerusalem coming from Algerian officials and the Algerian press. The Algerians, he claimed, were determined to fight to the last Egyptian soldier. In truth, Egypt had borne the brunt of the fighting in the conflicts with Israel and would always be the primary target for the Israeli army in any Arab-Israeli war since the Egyptians had the Arab world's largest and most formidable army and the force that the Israeli Defense Force was determined to defeat before dealing with any other Arab army.

Nor did Fahmy's complaint that Sadat had undercut the two main principles of Egyptian foreign policy—neutralism and pan-Arabism—carry the historical weight that they had possessed in the 1950s and 1960s. Union with Syria had failed, and intervention in Yemen had been expensive and unsuccessful. The enthusiasm surrounding Third World neutrality, so vivid two decades earlier when decolonization was sweeping across Asia and Africa and had been championed by Nehru, Sukarno, Nasser, and Nkrumah, had faded badly by the 1970s. The Arab countries had not succeeded in playing one superpower off against the other as so many Third World leaders had hoped in the 1950s. Was it then any wonder that Sadat concluded that Egypt needed to repair its relationship with the Americans and that Egypt's stance toward Israel required rethinking?

Sadat flew to Israel on November 19, 1977, landing at Ben-Gurion Airport, the beginning of a thirty-six-hour visit, which was to be culminated by his address to the Knesset. On arrival he was

Sadat Presenting a Gift to the Israeli Prime Minister Golda Meir During his Breakthrough Visit to Jerusalem in 1977.

accorded the customary twenty-one-gun salute and then shook hands with Golda Meir, the former Israeli prime minister, but did not kiss her hand as some of his critics charged, passing along the greeting line, where he shook hands with other leading Israeli politicians and military men, including, of course, the famous Moshe Dayan, hero of many campaigns against the Egyptian armies. He and his entourage, which included his wife, Jihan, his new minister of state for foreign affairs, Boutros Boutros Ghali, later secretary-general of the United Nations, his prime minister, Mustafa Khalil, and many others who one year later would travel with him to Camp David, were then taken by motorcade to Jerusalem along routes lined by exuberant Israeli citizens, holding Egyptian and Israeli flags and placards welcoming the Egyptian president.

The moment that everyone awaited took place the next day, November 20, when Sadat ascended the podium of the Israeli parliament and addressed its delegates and numerous important invited guests. The proceedings were televised around the world. Husni Mubarak, Egypt's vice president, had asked Boutros Boutros Ghali to craft Sadat's speech in English. Ghali at first balked, uncertain about the president's policies toward Israel and also excusing himself on the grounds that English was only his third language, after Arabic and French. He relented after being assured by Mubarak that Sadat had no intention of "relinquishing any rights concerning either the Palestinian issue or Arab territories occupied by Israel since 1967. The speech must clearly reflect this."[7] Ghali enlisted Magdi Wahba, an esteemed professor of English literature at Cairo University, to assist him. The two men worked from 10:00 a.m. to 4:00 p.m. before presenting the draft to the president. Consider the surprise that Ghali must have felt and the disappointment he experienced when he heard Sadat's first words, delivered in Arabic, and realized that they bore no relationship to the text that he and his colleague had labored over.

Sadat began by asserting that he was a man of peace and that war, however noble, brought irreparable costs and inflicted unspeakable suffering, causing families the loss of loved ones. The

Middle East, which had experienced too many bitter conflicts, must put warfare behind it, but to do so it must overcome psychological barriers that now made it impossible for Arabs and Jews to see one another as human beings with resolvable differences. Sadat averred that his decision to go to Jerusalem was designed to overcome these barriers, which even prevented Arabs and Israelis from meeting one another. The peoples of the region must "stretch out our hands with faith and sincerity so that together we might destroy the barrier." When, however, Sadat turned to the ways that these psychological barriers could be dismantled, he presented the standard Arab negotiating positions. First and foremost, citing the Security Council Resolution 242, passed in 1967 shortly after the conclusion of the Six-Day War, he affirmed that there could be no enduring peace unless and until Israel returned all of the lands that it had seized in that war. A separate agreement between Egypt and Israel, he noted, "has no place in Egyptian policy. . . . This peace could not endure in the absence of a just solution to the Palestine problem." Yet the most memorable words in the speech were ones that no Arab head of state had ever uttered: "I tell you today and declare to the whole world that we accept to live with you in durable and just peace." Returning to the occupied lands and the Palestinians, he stressed that the Arabs would never accept Israeli occupation of Arab lands and called on Israel to reject expansionism and withdraw from the occupied territories, including Arab Jerusalem, that portion of Jerusalem that had been under the control of the government of Jordan before the 1967 war, proclaiming that the Palestinians were the crux of the Arab-Israeli dispute and must have the right to establish a state in their land.

The reactions were predictably mixed. The Egyptian delegation, relieved that Sadat had not deviated from the standard Arab positions on Israel and had reiterated the demand for the return of all of the territories taken in 1967, was even more delighted when the president stressed the rights of the Palestinians to a state and argued that "Jerusalem must be a free city, open to all the faithful." His statement against signing a separate peace accord with the Israelis was probably his most reassuring remark because many in the delegation feared that he was willing to sacrifice the cause of the Palestinians to bring peace to Egypt. His new minister of state for foreign affairs, Boutros Boutros Ghali, who had assumed the office reluctantly, described the speech as "wonderful" and complained that Begin's response, which was little more than a standard Israeli response to what had been a standard Arab statement, was a "hectoring" speech.

In replying to Sadat's speech, Begin summarized what Israeli leaders had been saying since the end of the Six-Day War, namely that Israel had no obligation to return all of the lands taken in that war, certainly not without the Arab states' recognizing Israel's right to exist, that Israel had annexed the city of Jerusalem, including East Jerusalem, and regarded it not only as a unified and indivisible city but the country's capital. He reiterated a position that all Israeli politicians at the time held: an unwillingness to

MENACHEM BEGIN, JIMMY CARTER, ANWAR SADAT, AND MOSHE DAVAN WHILE THE DELEGATIONS TOOK A BREAK FROM THEIR NEGOTIATIONS AT CAMP DAVID IN 1978 TO VISIT THE AMERICAN CIVIL WAR BATTLEFIELD AT GETTYSBURG. *Begin was Israel's Prime Minister, and Dayan was at the time the Israeli Foreign Minister.*

allow a Palestinian state to come into existence especially in light of the fact that the Palestine Liberation Organization was committed to the destruction of Israel.

Sadat's speech failed to inspire Moshe Dayan, though the man did. Not even Sadat's decision to come to Israel had persuaded Dayan that the Egyptian president's visit augured a significant change in Egyptian–Israeli relations since Sadat had said on many occasions that he was prepared to go anywhere to bring peace to the region. Moreover, Dayan, who incorrectly said that Sadat delivered his remarks in English, found little to praise in Sadat's delivery, which he claimed was marked by stumbling over phrases and groping for words. But the man himself had an entirely different impact on Israel's most famous warrior. Dayan commented on the "sincerity" that Sadat radiated and the force of personality that made it appear as if he were speaking personally to each individual in the audience.[8] More typical of the Israeli reactions to Sadat's hardline speech came from Israel's defense minister, Ezer Weizman, who later became a Sadat admirer. In the middle of Sadat's outline of what was needed to bring about peace, Weizman scribbled a note to Begin: "we have to prepare for war."[9]

Sadat had flown to Israel from the military airport at Abu Sueir but returned to the Cairo International airport to a hero's acclaim from a large and admiring Egyptian crowd, shouting his name and singing his praises. Certainly, there were those, especially among the professional and intellectual classes, who were critical of Sadat for having broken with a longstanding Egyptian and Arab injunction of meeting openly with Israeli officials. Yet, in truth, Jerusalem became a defining moment for Sadat, unfortunately for him far more abroad than at home, transforming his image from that of a third-rate dictator into a statesman of vision and courage. Overnight Sadat achieved international superstar status, a person in demand for television appearances and newspaper interviews. Although his command of English was far from flawless, his radiance and charisma, so well noted by Dayan, allowed him to command any gathering.

Nonetheless, the follow-up to the trip to Israel proved unpromising, and the momentum of the journey quickly diminished. Many commentators jumped to the conclusion that the journey to Jerusalem was destined to be merely a trumped-up television moment designed to call world attention to Sadat but unlikely to have lasting importance. Still, Israel felt under pressure to do something in return for Sadat's huge gamble. Begin accordingly announced that Israel would offer self-rule to the Palestinians living in the West Bank and Gaza. His offer, however, fell well short of national self-determination, hemming in the powers that the Palestinians would exercise. Moreover, Israeli citizens would be permitted to buy and sell land in the West Bank and Gaza, a right denied to Palestinians wishing to acquire land in Israel. Although an elected Palestinian council would be empowered to establish a local police force, the ultimate responsibility for public order and security was to remain with Israeli authorities. Finally, Israel reiterated its longstanding claim to sovereignty over the West Bank, which Begin, as was his custom, referred to as Judea and Samaria, employing its Biblical names, and the Gaza district. By recognizing that the political status of the West Bank and Gaza was contested, the Israelis agreed to leave the question open for future negotiations. Not surprisingly, the Palestinians rejected Begin's proposal.

On December 25, 1977, the occasion of Sadat's fifty-ninth birthday, Israeli and Egyptian delegations met in the city of Ismailia along the Suez Canal as a follow-up to the Jerusalem visit. Although expectations ran high, the concrete results were entirely disappointing. The meeting started poorly for the Israelis, who noted how coolly they had been received, especially in light of the exuberance of the Israeli welcoming of Sadat to their country. Pictures of Sadat adorned the city streets, but there were none of Begin and his team. Nor for that matter were the local residents who watched the motorcade waving Israeli flags. The one accomplishment—a decision to create separate Egyptian-Israeli political and military committees to discuss future military and political arrangements—fell well short of what the two sides thought that they could accomplish.

A singular positive development did emerge from the Ismailia meetings, however: the beginnings of a friendship between Ezer Weizman and Sadat that was to prove crucial in the months to come. Weizman, the minister of defense, had previously not thought highly of Sadat, "regarding him more or less the stereotype of a totalitarian Arab ruler." Prior to the Jerusalem visit he had endorsed the general Israeli view that Sadat was a man of much lesser talents than Nasser, given to bombast despite his broken English—"unsophisticated, undemocratic, a fanatical Muslim nationalist who could be toppled by the slightest shove." But the October War and the decision to address the Knesset proved "Sadat's indisputable gifts as a statesman and strategist."[10]

Weizman admired Sadat for having alerted the world to the danger of a political stalemate in the region, but he also believed that the election of his Likud Party offered unique opportunities for peace. The Likud Party, on the right and known for its hawkishness in foreign affairs, especially toward the Arab states, was, in his view, less exposed to criticism if its leaders made territorial concessions to Egypt and other Arab states. In his opinion, had the Labor Party been in power when Sadat addressed the Knesset, its members would have been so fearful of the Israeli right wing that they would not have responded favorably and quickly to the Egyptian president's remarks. Weizman thereafter went out of his way to befriend Sadat and to argue with suspicious colleagues that the Egyptian leader was a forthright individual whose promises could be trusted. He believed that Sadat, while evincing little interest in diplomatic details, had a firm grasp of the essentials of foreign policy. In his opinion, if any Arab leader could make peace with Israel, that man was Anwar al-Sadat. Weizman's commitment to Sadat was long lasting. It was evident throughout the Camp David accords and the Egyptian-Israeli Peace Treaty of 1979, and even beyond. He resigned from

Begin's government in 1980 in protest against Israeli policies that he believed violated the spirit and even in some cases the actual text of the peace treaty and undermined the position of Sadat not only within the Arab world but within Egypt.

For many months, the political and military committees met with little to show for their discussions. Seemingly the last gasp of goodwill was exhausted at the Leeds Castle negotiations, held in Kent County, England, in July 1978, which involved the foreign ministers of Egypt (Ibrahim Kamil), Israel (Moshe Dayan), and the United States (Cyrus Vance). Both Sadat and Kamil blamed the Americans and asserted that unless the United States became a full partner in the negotiations, not just a mediator, the talks would fail.

Carter took up the Egyptian challenge of greater involvement, dispatching his secretary of state, Cyrus Vance, to the Middle East with handwritten notes to Sadat and Begin inviting them to come to Camp David to engage in face-to-face negotiations

ISRAELI DEFENCE MINISTER EZER WEIZMAN SHAKES HANDS WITH SADAT. *Weizman was one of Sadat's strongest supporters among Israeli ministers.*

under American auspices and promising his own personal in-volvement. Both men accepted the invitation, bringing about an extraordinary meeting of three influential heads of state. The last time that three political leaders of such stature had met had been more than three decades earlier when in 1945, Churchill, Roosevelt, and Stalin came together at Potsdam to discuss ar-rangements for the postwar world.

Camp David had been constructed during World War II as a retreat and location for contemplation for the president and other high-ranking American officials. A heavily wooded area, 70 miles from Washington, located in Catoctin Mountain Park, it was 6 miles away from the nearest town of Thurmont, Maryland, which was hastily readied to house the large number of domestic and foreign journalists who assembled there to report on devel-opments. The responsibility for briefing reporters fell to Jody Powell, White House press secretary, who was permitted to tell the reporters only which individuals had met one another and for how long but was prohibited from giving any indication of how the talks were going.

It was only natural that Carter would choose Camp David as the site for these crucial discussions, for his family had made much use of the grounds during his presidency. Carter believed that the lush, mainly evergreen trees and the attractive cabins, each bearing the name of a tree and set aside to house the delega-tions, would afford frequent opportunities for the teams to meet, to talk about issues, and ultimately to find common ground. An optimist and a tireless worker himself, he expected agreement to be reached within three days, but he also extracted a promise from the delegations that they would stay together until they had hammered out an accord or concluded that no agreement could be achieved. To ensure that the only business conducted each day was the Middle East, contact with the outside world was severely limited. Thus, in a unique historical moment, three major heads of state undertook to be away from their countries, largely iso-lated from the events taking place in the outside world, so that

they could devote themselves to reaching accords that would prevent warfare and offer solutions to a range of problems that had
bedeviled the countries of the region for decades.

Carter's optimism was sorely tested from the outset. At the
suggestion of Rosalyn Carter, the president's wife, who knew
how vital religion was to all three leaders, Carter asked Sadat and
Begin when they arrived if they would call on the world to join
them in a prayer for success. The suggestion delighted Sadat, who
arrived two hours before Begin, but Begin revealed a trait that
would be in evidence throughout the negotiations. He insisted on
examining the text of the prayer, word for word, before agreeing
to the call for prayer. Nor for that matter did the aesthetics of
Camp David appeal in the same way to the Middle Eastern residents as it did to Carter. Weizman did not like the place, complaining that the profusion of trees, which blocked out the sun,
created an atmosphere of gloom. Sadat's preference for places of
contemplation ran to arid climates and housing surrounded by
sand and water.

The attitudes toward the prayer mirrored the way the teams
had actually prepared themselves for Camp David. The American team spent countless hours drawing up detailed briefing
books, sitting with legal and Middle East experts, drafting position papers, and anticipating the stances that the Egyptians and
Israelis would take. Early in their discussion, they concluded that
they would probably have to put forward a compromise proposal
and exert pressure on both sides to achieve an agreement. The
Israelis also left no stone unturned, discussing in great detail
how forthcoming they could afford to be toward Egyptian demands on Sinai and the Palestinian question. In contrast, the
Egyptian delegation was slow to get preparations underway,
much to the annoyance of Ibrahim Kamil, the foreign minister.
At first, Kamil was enthusiastic about Camp David, believing
that only two outcomes were possible, both of which would benefit Egypt—either a comprehensive settlement or no agreement,
in which case blame would be affixed to Israel. But Sadat's fasting

during the month of Ramadan, which occurred in the lead-up to the Camp David meetings, led in Kamil's view to "listless indolence" on the part of the president. Kamil contended that Muslim law did not require such a strict observance because of the seriousness of the impending negotiations. He also worried that the pleasure that Sadat derived from moving from one guest house to another and the time he spent in the evenings organizing his new National Democratic Party left the Egyptian delegation woefully unprepared.[11] Even more alarming to Kamil and others was Sadat's presentation to a meeting of the Egyptian National Security Council held on August 30, less than a week before the delegation was to fly to Camp David. Sadat informed the council members that he felt entitled to speak on behalf of the Palestinians and asked the council to discuss what territorial concessions Egypt might concede to the Israelis on the West Bank to secure a peace agreement.

Kamil was the most outspoken member of the Egyptian delegation. His deputy foreign minister, Boutros Boutros Ghali, also found the Egyptian preparations deficient, noting in particular that the Egyptian team entered the negotiations lacking a general strategy. He, too, feared that Sadat's driving ambition to regain Sinai would come at the expense of the Palestinians. Both Ghali and Kamil were appalled at Sadat's negotiating style, noting his failure to keep his team abreast of the private discussions he undertook with Carter and the Israelis.

Despite the Egyptian delegation's fear that Sadat's eagerness to regain control of Sinai would lead him to sacrifice Palestinian interests, its members had no cause for alarm at Sadat's opening statement at Camp David. He put forward the full Egyptian demands for peace, stressing the return of all the lands taken in the 1967 war and the right of Palestinian refugees to reclaim their homes, adding a demand that had not been a prominent part of the Egyptian case: an obligation on the part of Israel to pay indemnities for the use of oil and land in Sinai. The entire package dumbfounded the Israeli delegates, and they only agreed to continue the discussion when Carter said that the American team also rejected the Egyptian position, even as a starting point, and that Sadat had told Carter that he would be more flexible going forward.

Still, the first round of discussions went so poorly that three party meetings had to be abandoned after the third day. Despite the fact that Begin and Sadat had similar backgrounds, both having secretly and violently opposed British authority as young men, in truth, their styles and ways of life were utterly dissimilar and tended to grate on each other. Begin was an intensely formal man, appearing so even in the relaxed setting of Camp David, where he nearly always wore a coat and a tie. He was deeply, one might even say neurotically, concerned about negotiating details and examined literally every word before agreeing to it, as perhaps befitted a leader profoundly scarred by the experience of the Holocaust. His approach to negotiating was framed by his upbringing in Poland and his later studies where he had concentrated on "Jewish history with a special emphasis on the memories of the holocaust and the democratic ideas of the basic rights and the rule of law."[12] His home life, austere and simple, contrasted with Sadat's, whose preference for expensive and well-tailored clothing and luxurious living quarters was on display even at Camp David. Although Sadat mainly wore sporting outfits at Camp David, they were always highly fashionable. His insistence on keeping to the strict regimen that had been his habit in Egypt made it difficult for anyone to encounter him by accident. He took long walks every day, ate alone, and asked and was provided with a small, private place where he could pray. Nor was he a man willing to immerse himself in the details of texts as Begin did. Although Carter had placed Sadat's and Begin's cottages close together in hopes that the two men would run into one another, converse, and perhaps even develop a friendship, in fact, for the last ten days of the Camp David discussions they never spoke to one another.

It was Carter who finally devised the method for breaking through the hostility that had come to exist between the Egyptian and Israeli delegations, though he did not devise his formula until September 10, almost five days into the discussions. Carter's formula took account of the radically different negotiating styles of Begin and Sadat, assuming in particular that Sadat trusted the American president while Begin feared accepting any arrangements that might jeopardize Israeli security. Later, when criticisms mounted about the final results of Camp David, Carter would write that "it was soon to be obvious that Sadat seemed to trust me too much and Begin not enough."[13] Carter's method entailed approaching Sadat first with a set of American proposals since Sadat's assent was easier to obtain than Begin's, and only then, armed with a dictionary and thesaurus and aware that the Israeli delegation would weigh and parse every word, taking the proposals that Sadat had accepted to the Israeli team. Even so, the first American efforts failed. The Israeli delegation crossed out all references in an early American draft to Security Council Resolution 242, which stated that territories could not be acquired by force and changed references to the Palestinian peoples to Palestinian Arabs. It was not until September 12, following a full week of intense discussions, that the Americans concluded that the chief stumbling block between the Egyptian and Israelis teams was the Palestinian issue and that success could only be achieved if Palestinian issues were separated from a peace agreement between Egypt and Israel.

The final agreement, which was signed on the lawn of the White House on September 17, 1978, a full thirteen days after the delegations arrived at Camp David, was not achieved without severe last-minute setbacks and dramatic moments when the likelihood of failure seemed imminent. In all, the Americans prepared no fewer than twenty-three separate sets of proposals. At significant moments each side was ready to leave. Two days before reaching the final agreement, Carter called the American delegation together and told its members that they had to discuss how to present the failure of Camp David to the world. Prior to that dismaying moment, Carter had pleaded with and then bullied Begin to get him to agree to proposals that he had up to then steadfastly resisted. In particular, Carter challenged the Israeli claim that Security Council Resolution 242 did not apply to the lands that they had taken in the June War on the grounds that the war was defensive. Carter bristled with resentment and pointed out that all previous Israeli leaders had accepted the Security Council resolution. Carter made it clear at this stage that if the Israelis walked out on this issue they would incur world displeasure. His mainly unrewarding encounters with Begin, whose inflexibility alarmed the president, ultimately persuaded Carter to bypass the Israeli prime minister and to work instead through the Israeli jurist and former law professor and dean of Hebrew University School of Law, Aharon Barak, whom Begin had designated the delegation's legal adviser.

Of utmost importance in finally winning Begin's support was the intervention of General Abraham Tamir, one of the military experts who was part of the Israeli delegation. For Begin, a major sticking point was Sadat's insistence that all of Sinai be returned to Egypt, the Israeli settlements there dismantled, and the air bases that the Israelis had constructed in eastern Sinai returned to the Egyptians. While Begin understood that Sinai did not form part of Eretz Israel, its defensive significance could not be minimized, and the dismantling of the settlements, small in numbers, compared with those on the West Bank, would pose great military and political risks to him and his party. He was prepared to hold firm on these matters even as it became increasingly apparent his insistence would ruin the negotiations because Sadat would not yield on Sinai. Only General Tamir's request that Begin telephone Ariel Sharon, his minister of agriculture and the Israeli cabinet member most deeply committed to settlements, saved the day. Sharon's assurances to Begin that giving up all of Sinai, however distasteful and difficult, was a price worth paying to achieve a durable peace agreement with Egypt and, thus, persuaded Begin to stay on and eventually to sign the accord.

On September 15, day eleven of the meetings, another firestorm erupted within the Egyptian delegation. Sadat told his group to pack their bags and ready themselves for departure, largely, it would appear, because of his dissatisfaction with the Israeli stance on the Palestinians. Sadat's decision to leave had the agreement of most of the Egyptian delegation, according to Ibrahim Kamil, but Secretary Vance prevailed on the Egyptian president to hear Carter out one more time before he finalized his decision. The meeting between Carter and Sadat was entirely a one-on-one affair, and the only record that we have to date comes from Carter's memoirs. Sadat emerged from the meeting appearing to his delegation a changed man, happy and relaxed for the first time since arriving at Camp David. He proceeded to inform the Egyptian delegates that Carter had solved the problems and left him "completely satisfied." When pressed on just exactly what Carter had promised, Sadat said at first that the provision that the agreement had to be ratified by the Israeli Knesset and the Egyptian People's Assembly offered both sides a final review of the terms. Pressed even more, he said, "I shall sign anything proposed by President Carter without reading it." Then, "he turned on his heel, left the terrace, and entered the bungalow." For Kamil, Sadat's remarks to his delegation were little short of disgraceful, demonstrating what he and others had suspected about him, namely that his eagerness to have an agreement to take back to his countrymen and to win the favor of Carter and the Americans had caused him to capitulate "unconditionally to President Carter who, in turn, capitulated unconditionally to Menachem Begin."[14] Kamil tendered his resignation as foreign minister but agreed at Sadat's urging to postpone his announcement until after the signing of the accords. His absence from the signing ceremony put many on notice that the Egyptian foreign minister opposed the agreement.

Precisely what Carter promised Sadat is unclear. There is no doubt that he used all of his presidential authority and persuasiveness to win over the Egyptian president. He told Sadat that his departure would put an end to peacekeeping efforts and the special relationship that had been developing between Egypt and the United States and probably Carter's hopes for winning a second term and then added "something that is very precious to me, my friendship with you . . . The president later told his wife, Rosalyn, that 'he had never talked with anyone else in his life the way he talked with Sadat, except maybe my children.'"[15] Sadat's deputy foreign minister, Boutros Boutros Ghali, confirmed this view of the meeting, stating that Carter had said that if the Egyptians left he was likely to lose the next election, but if they stayed and a peace treaty was concluded he would get a second term and then would fulfill all of Egypt's requests.

One issue that may have been discussed at that crucial meeting was the question of Israeli settlements in the West Bank and Gaza. The American team was adamantly opposed to any expansion of Israeli settlements, believing that every new settlement and every expansion of an existing one made the chances of a comprehensive peace accord more difficult. To this end, the Americans believed that they had extracted from the Israeli delegation a promise to freeze all settlements, those already in existence and those contemplated for the future, until the negotiations for Palestinian autonomy had commenced. The Israelis differed, contending that they had agreed to freeze settlements for only three months, the time allocated for the signing of an Egyptian-Israeli peace treaty, a position that Secretary Vance had difficulty accepting. Vance observed in his memoirs that "it is difficult to understand how Begin could have so totally misinterpreted what the president was asking."[16] Whether Carter conveyed his understanding on the settlement freeze to Sadat during their private meeting is not known, but if he had, it would have played an important role in Sadat's decision to stay, sign the accords, and place his trust in the Americans.

A last-minute glitch with the possibility of destroying all of the hard work appeared at the very moment that Carter, Begin, and Sadat were preparing to leave Camp David for the signing ceremony at the White House. It had to do with the status of Jerusalem, long a bone of contention between the Israelis and the Egyptians. As part of his willingness to stay, Sadat had extracted from Carter a restatement of the American position on East Jerusalem, namely that this part of Jerusalem, which had been in Jordanian hands before the Six-Day War, still constituted occupied territory according to the Americans and therefore potentially returnable to the Arabs. When the text of the American note was shown to the Israeli Ambassador, Simcha Dinitz, he said that it was unacceptable, and when Begin saw it he told the Israeli delegation to pack their bags. Dayan's opposition was even more forceful. He informed the American president that, had the Israeli delegates known that the Americans would articulate this position at Camp David, they would not have come. Carter dispatched Vance to find some kind of a compromise, and his secretary of state did indeed work his diplomatic magic, finessing the Jerusalem problem by removing all references to Jerusalem from the approved Camp David text but appending to it three letters from Begin, Sadat, and Carter laying out the positions of each country.

First, Sadat sent a letter to Carter which stated the Egyptian position that Arab Jerusalem was an integral part of the West Bank and therefore subject to Arab sovereignty. Carter then dispatched Sadat's letter to Begin, affirming the American position on Jerusalem but in much vaguer language than Carter had originally employed, stating simply that the American position was that which had been put forward by the American Ambassador to the United Nations on July 14, 1967. Begin next replied to these two notes in a letter addressed to Carter and then sent on to Sadat, noting that on July 28, 1967, the Knesset passed a decree vesting the Israeli government with legislative and administrative powers over any part of Eretz Israel and establishing the city of Jerusalem as "the unified, indivisible capital of the state of Israel." In these arcane and mysterious ways the Camp David negotiations were brought to a conclusion, and the delegates sped to the White House, where in a public ceremony on the lawn the three men signed the agreed-upon text.

Although the world thought that the Camp David accords brought peace to Egypt and Israel and would serve as a road map for a more comprehensive peace agreement between the Arabs and Israelis, in actuality they provided only a framework for peace. Before the actual treaty could be signed, first the Knesset and the People's Assembly had to give their assent to the accords, and then the Egyptian and Israeli delegations had to hammer out the specific terms of the peace treaty. These latter negotiations dragged on for nearly six months, well beyond the three months that the delegates at Camp David had allotted for working out the details. The treaty was finally initialed on the lawn of the White House on March 26, 1979, but only after President Carter had traveled to the region, shuttling back and forth between the two countries and applying pressure on both sides.

The Camp David Accords framework, which formed the basis of the final peace agreement, was divided into two sections. The first dealt with Egypt and Israel and stated that Israel would return all of Sinai to Egypt within three years from the signing of the peace treaty and would remove the Israeli settlements in Sinai. It also stipulated that the Israelis would turn over their military air bases in Sinai to the Egyptians, who, however, were to use them only for civilian purposes. Egypt and Israel undertook not to use force to settle disputes and agreed to negotiate a peace treaty within three months. Israeli ships were to be given unobstructed passage through the Suez Canal, the Strait of Tiran, and the Gulf of Aqaba, while the Egyptians agreed not to station more than one military division within 50 kilometers east of the Gulf of Suez and the canal and to allow United Nations forces to position themselves in Sinai between Egyptian forces and the Egyptian-Israeli border.

The Sinai arrangements reflected Sadat's determination to reacquire all of Sinai and to make no territorial concessions in that area to Israeli settlements and Israeli military installations. Begin was to come under criticism at home for agreeing to dismantle the Sinai settlements, failing to maintain a military presence in Sinai, and weakening the Israeli defensive posture on the Egyptian front. But he was persuaded, having harkened back to the words of Ariel Sharon, that peace with Egypt was a modest price to pay even if Israeli had to leave Sinai. The Knesset agreed and gave a strong endorsement to the accords.

The Palestinian arrangements were far more complex and controversial, subject to conflicting interpretations. To begin with, Egypt, Jordan, Israel, and representatives of the Palestinian people were to engage in negotiations for the resolution of problems relating to the future of the West Bank and Gaza. These negotiations were to proceed in stages with the first stage leading to the creation of a self-governing Palestinian authority, the ultimate goal of which was "full autonomy to the inhabitants." As soon as the self-governing Palestinian authority (also called the administrative council) had come into existence, the Israelis would withdraw their military government and civilian administration from the West Bank and Gaza but in a way that was both consistent with the principle of self-government for the inhabitants and at the same time assured "the legitimate security concerns of the parties involved."[17] The Israeli military forces would redeploy into specified security zones. No later than three years from the establishment of the self-governing authority, Egypt, Israeli, Jordan, and representatives of the Palestinian people would carry out negotiations to determine the final status of the West Bank and Gaza and its relationship with its neighbors and seek to bring about a peace treaty between Israel and Jordan. The agreement on the final status for the West Bank and Gaza would be submitted as a referendum to the inhabitants of the West Bank and Gaza.

The three heads of state each played their own vital roles in achieving the peace agreement. Begin's reputation as an Israeli hawk and his well-known right-wing, expansionist views insulated him from attacks from those elements in Israeli society most disposed to retaining the lands taken in the Six-Day War. Carter was the indefatigable negotiator, refusing to accept failure and repeatedly finding saving formulas when discussions came to a dead end. He knew how to motivate the other two principals, playing to Sadat's image of himself as a peacemaker and a reasonable compromiser and threatening Begin with international opprobrium when his delegation displayed its most inflexible side. But it was Sadat who made the decisive concessions, especially on the Palestinian question, based largely on his belief that Egypt could not move forward domestically or internationally as long as its territorial integrity remained compromised. He held onto this bedrock principle despite near-universal condemnation within his own delegation and the protests that he knew the accords would provoke at home and throughout the Arab world. He had lost his foreign minister and deputy foreign minister when he decided to go to Jerusalem and then lost the foreign minister whom he took with him to Camp David when he agreed to initial the accords.

Sadat's concessions were indeed monumental, and they were to cost him dearly, ultimately, of course, his life. He allowed the final text to be stripped of all references to Jerusalem and to refer only in general terms to Security Council Resolution 242. He signed the accords even after learning that Begin's freeze on settlements would last only three months, not for the entirety of the Palestinian autonomy negotiations. For him, what counted was ending warfare with Israel, restoring all of Sinai to Egyptian sovereignty, distancing Egypt from the Soviet Union, which had proved itself an unreliable ally, and aligning with the Americans, who, he believed, were certain to provide critical financial and technical assistance for his free market, *infitah* policies. Moreover, it has to be doubted that he could have gotten more from the Israelis. Begin was subjected to intense criticisms for giving away too much to the Egyptians in Sinai. Dismantling the Sinai settlements proved every bit as difficult as he had feared. The prospect of returning to Egypt empty handed may well have appealed to most of his delegation, but not to Sadat. Failure to reach an agreement with Israel would have left much of Sinai in Israeli hands, made the resumption of warfare likely, and exposed the canal and the canal cities to Israeli military threats.

Although the Camp David accords were acclaimed in the West and led to the honoring of Sadat and Begin with the 1978 Nobel Peace Prize, they aroused a storm of protest in the Arab world. Arab leaders at a summit meeting in Baghdad between November 2 and November 5, 1978, repudiated the agreements and warned the Egyptian president that signing an Egyptian-Israeli peace treaty would bring about a severing of political and diplomatic relations with their states, the cutting off of loans, and the boycott of Egyptian companies. Following the signing of the Egyptian-Israeli peace agreement, which involved a step that Sadat had thought would not happen in his lifetime—the exchange of ambassadors—the Arab states at a follow-up summit meeting, also held in Baghdad, carried out the warnings that they had made to Sadat. They broke off diplomatic relations with Egypt, suspended aid payments, expelled Egypt from the Arab League, and moved the seat of the Arab League out of Cairo.

Throughout these long months of arduous negotiations, leading up to the peace agreement, Sadat's chief failing was his choice to proceed alone. He allowed a vast chasm to arise between him and the ruling elites in Egypt and throughout the Arab world. Although he believed that his policies were in Egypt's and the Arab world's best interests, in fact, the only viable alternative available to Egypt, he confided in almost no one. He failed to gain the backing of those officials with whom he worked most closely. It should have come as no surprise that the way forward would see him lose control over events and fear attempts on his life.

| LOSING CONTROL, 1979–1981 |

SADAT RETURNED TO EGYPT FROM the peace treaty signing ceremony in Washington, D.C., hoping for approbation but facing
stern opposition. As expected, the People's Assembly strongly
endorsed the treaty, and the referendum that the president called
for also provided the customary 90 percent approval rating. But
even in these controlled environments, evidence of dissent appeared. In the People's Assembly, thirteen delegates spoke and
voted against the treaty, characterizing it as a separate accord that
left the Palestinians to fend for themselves. Their opposition infuriated the president, who dissolved the Assembly and called for
another election, during which twelve of the thirteen dissenting
delegates lost their seats. Nor could the referendum on the treaty
be proclaimed an unalloyed triumph. The actual turnout, though
officially claimed to be high, was in the estimation of unbiased
observers embarrassingly small. Independent journalists asserted that no more than 10 percent of eligible voters cast ballots.
Even more ominous for the regime was a stinging verbal attack
launched by colleagues of the president, former Free Officers, and
holders of high office during the Nasser years. They joined their
voices to those of many others that said the accord shamed Egypt
by forsaking the Palestinians.

Sadat defended his decisions for war in 1973 and peace in 1979
on the grounds that they were economic and political necessities.

In his opinion, Egypt in the 1970s had no choice but to look to its own economic development and poverty alleviation. The country could remain on a war footing no longer. And, in reality, the economic payoffs from war and peace during Sadat's tenure in office were impressive, many of which stemmed directly from decisions to go to war and to conclude peace with Israel. American assistance, which flowed abundantly after the peace treaty, filled the gap created when the oil-rich Arab countries withdrew their financial support. It totaled $1.8 billion in 1980 and made Egypt the largest recipient of American aid next to Israel. The American embassy expanded rapidly, rising from a six-member staff when diplomatic relations were restored in 1974 to become the largest American embassy in the world by 1980, a virtual beehive of economic reports and projects. The sharp rise in the price of oil that had accompanied the October War also brought huge financial returns to the country, rising from $312 million in 1976 to $2.85 billion in 1980. Suez Canal revenues, which Egypt had been without since the 1967 war, totaled $1.7 billion in 1980, all paid for in hard currencies, as were the comparable revenues from tourism, which were on an upswing in large measure because of the peace treaty. Remittances from Egyptians working overseas, mainly in the Gulf where the rise in the international price of oil spurred rapid economic development and expensive building projects, skyrocketed from $189 million in 1974 to $2.7 billion in 1980. All of these massive increases made the last half of the 1970s one of the most prosperous on record for Egypt and would not have occurred had Egypt pursued a different foreign policy during these years.

Yet, despite these vital economic gains, Egypt's deep-seated economic problems remained. Although Sadat had promised a peace dividend resulting from the agreement with Israel, the military budget did not shrink. No less than 85 percent of American assistance was channeled to the Egyptian military—a payment designed to purchase the military establishment's support for

Sadat's policies. Egypt's expanding population, which was growing at a high rate of 2.5 percent per year, also was a drag on the economy. It meant that high economic growth rates, greater than Egypt had achieved thus far in the twentieth century, would have to be attained if people were to feel the effect of the peace dividend. In addition, the 1977 food riots had compelled the state to reinstitute commodity subsidies and to continue to cope with large budgetary deficits. Nor did the foreign trade imbalances become positive.

A development that Sadat was proud of and believed would benefit many in the population was an expansion of university education. In the 1970s, the state opened many regional universities and saw the number of students entering universities rise three-fold, but educational quality declined. Funds allocated for buildings, laboratories, and faculty and staff appointments did not keep pace with expanded enrollments. Classrooms could not accommodate the large numbers enrolled, and private education of many sorts revived after having declined in the 1950s and 1960s. Private, fee-paying schools like the American University in Cairo, which had seen its appeal to students diminish during the Nasser years, prospered. Not only did private institutions offer excellent training in English, a skill in high demand as tourism boomed, but class sizes were smaller and library, laboratory, social, and sporting facilities were superior to those available at many Egyptian state-run universities.

Even more disappointing than the overall performance of the Egyptian economy was the international response to the Egyptian-Israeli peace treaty. The Nobel Prize award notwithstanding, Sadat was dismayed at Ronald Reagan's assumption of the American presidency in 1980. Sadat had counted on Carter's reelection as a guarantee that the Americans would carry forward his own and Carter's vision for a comprehensive peace accord in the Middle East. Carter had secured Sadat's signature on the Camp David Framework for Peace by arguing that the accord would enable him to win a second term when he would work toward securing Palestinian rights. Sadat's meeting with Reagan shortly after the election did little to lift Sadat's spirits. He found the American president cold and concluded that Reagan, unlike Carter and his senior foreign policy officials, saw international politics entirely in the light of the cold war and was not interested in the Palestinian question. For Carter, Palestine was a burning issue.

Far more unsettling to Sadat, however, was the interpretation that Begin and the Israelis placed on the Camp David accords and the peace treaty. Their statements and actions dashed whatever hopes Sadat had of persuading moderate Arab leaders and the Egyptian people that his agreement with Israel held out promise for the Palestinians. The Arab League had warned Sadat not to sign a treaty with the Israelis. Statements made by top Israelis officials, with Begin usually in the lead, offered no grounds for Arab moderates to alter their attitude to Egypt. Under heavy attack from his own right wing in Israel, especially for agreeing to dismantle Israeli settlements in Sinai and return the Israeli airbases in Sinai to the Egyptians, Begin defended himself by arguing that he had secured a durable peace with Israel's most formidable military foe. He had done so without sacrificing Israel's strategic and geographical interests in the West Bank and Gaza. In particular, as a riposte to his critics, he claimed that the Israeli Defense Forces were not obligated to withdraw from the West Bank and Gaza, although the Camp David framework and the peace treaty stipulated that some of the Israeli Defense Forces would be withdrawn and others would be redeployed into a limited number of security locations. Nor did Begin's claim that the Palestinian self-governing authority would be only an administrative body conform to the understanding of these issues on the part of Egyptian and American diplomats. The latter officials pointed out that, according to the treaty, the final powers and responsibilities of the authority were to be determined in negotiations with the interested parties (Egypt, Israel, Jordan, and representatives of the Palestinian authority), not by the Israelis alone, after which they would be put to a vote by the Palestinian electorate.

Even more damaging to Sadat and a significant reason for the cabinet resignations of Ezer Weizman, the Israeli minister of defense, and Moshe Dayan, foreign affairs secretary, were a number of extraordinarily provocative actions that the Israeli prime minister took in 1980 and 1981. These acts made it difficult for Egyptians to form any other conclusion than that the Egyptian-Israeli peace treaty gave Israel more than it gave Egypt, especially allowing Israel a free hand to carry out aggressive military actions against its Arab neighbors. On July 30, 1980, the Knesset enacted into the fundamental law of Israel the statement that Jerusalem was the country's united and indivisible capital, an action provoked by the separate exchange of letters over Jerusalem at Camp David (see Chapter 6), but an action that offended the Egyptians. Another provocation took place after Mustafa Khalil, Egypt's prime minister, had tried to silence Egyptian and Arab critics by arguing that the treaty held out genuine prospects for a future Palestinian state. Begin took up this challenge by asserting that a state called Palestine would never come into existence in Judea, Samaria, and Gaza, using for effect the Biblical and Hebrew terms for the West Bank. An act that surely rubbed salt into the wounds of the Egyptian president was Israel's announcement of plans for establishing ten new settlements in the West Bank, made on the very eve of the signing of the peace agreement. The final acts, for which Sadat never forgave Begin, occurred in 1981: an Israeli air attack on the Iraqi Osirak nuclear reactor on June 7, 1981, and the bombing of the Palestine Liberation Organization offices in Beirut on July 17, 1981. Both occurred shortly after public meetings between the two men. Sadat knew nothing about these plans, though his critics attacked him, believing that the Israeli prime minister must surely have secured Sadat's agreement before unleashing his military.

The opposition to Sadat reached a crescendo in the last two years of his rule. The critics' attacks were so frequent and came from so many directions that his wife feared for his life and saw him retreat into a lonely and subdued existence. The press and the political parties led the assault on the president. On the left, Tagammu complained that the president failed to hold the line on the prices of essential commodities while Mustafa Amin, whom Sadat had placed in charge of the newspaper *al-Akbar al-Yawm* took up the Wafd Party's chief criticism that Sadat had been unable to bring real democracy and freedom of expression to Egypt.

A constant complaint, heard in the independent press but circulated even more broadly by word of mouth, was that power had gone to the head of the president and his wife and that they used the office of president to enrich themselves and their supporters and weaken their opponents. Here, their chief critic, former friend and supporter Mohamed Heikal, claimed that the Sadats occupied numerous residences and lived extravagantly, even though Heikal knew that the president was abstemious in diet and daily activities and that the residences that he most enjoyed at Ismailia, Alexandria, Aswan, and the barrages just north of Cairo were not his own but belonged to the state.

Heikal also accused Sadat of doling out expensive gifts, often antiquities, to influential foreigners and losing all sense of proportion and decorum when in the presence of international glitterati. Heikal cited the president's over-the-top welcome of Elizabeth Taylor for her starring role in the 1963 movie *Cleopatra* despite her well-known sympathies for the state of Israel, which had put her on the Arab blacklist. Sadat even went so far as to present her to Egyptian dignitaries as the queen of Egypt and to provide her entourage with many favors, including placing a government helicopter at her disposal. In Heikal's view, "not since the days of Khedive Ismail had Egypt been the scene of looting on such a massive and organized scale as it was during the last years of President Sadat."[1] The pleasure that Sadat took in wearing expensive, well-tailored clothes also grated with many, especially among those who had admired the austere lifestyle of his predecessor, and added to the suspicion that the Sadats lived far beyond their means. So sensitive were critics to these symbols of power and wealth that wits dubbed him "King Sadat," and one of his most savage critics claimed that the man was "all sashes, sequins, fancy breeches, and riding boots."[2]

In truth, it is difficult to determine how corrupt Sadat was. He did not indulge in many aspects of his life: he restricted his

Anwar al-Sadat and his wife, Jihan.

diet to healthy and simple foods; adhered to a strict regime of daily walks, regular naps, and fixed times for praying; and fasted during the month of Ramadan. He clearly took pride in his personal appearance and enjoyed wearing fashionable and expensive clothes and living comfortably in his own well-appointed residence. An Italian clothing organization once voted him one of the ten best-dressed men in the world, an award that would have pleased him but would not have pleased his critics. Nor did his extremely attractive wife, well dressed herself, highly sophisticated and cultured, and a strong feminist, win the hearts of conservative Egyptians, who held up the retiring wife of Nasser as the appropriate model for the president's spouse. Apparently, his younger brother, Esmat, born in 1925, took advantage of the president's position by obtaining work at the newspaper *al-Gumhuriya*, where Sadat had once been editor in chief, only to be dismissed from this position after being accused of embezzlement and check kiting.

Perhaps the most effective left-wing attack on the president came from the lawyers' syndicate. Although most of the professional syndicates, which included engineers, lawyers, journalists, students, and the like, were increasingly infiltrated by Islamic groups, syndicates like those that represented lawyers and journalists were acutely sensitive to restrictions placed on their freedom of expression. The lawyers' syndicate, which had grown rapidly in the 1970s as a result of the expansion of university education, led the dissent against Sadat's efforts to restrict freedom of expression. Although Sadat attempted to dominate this and other syndicates by running his own candidates, his effort to control the lawyers' syndicate failed. His candidate to head up the lawyers' syndicate, Abd al-Aziz al-Shurbagi, was, in fact, elected, but once in office he became an outspoken critic of the president, opposing Sadat on Camp David and using the weekly seminars that the syndicate organized and were attended by large numbers to attack any antiliberal legislation that the regime enacted. Sadat shut down the organization in late July 1981.

It was ultimately on the right, however, that Sadat faced his most determined and best organized resistance. Here, opposition drew strength from a resurgent Islamic movement, which traced its origins back to 1928 when Hassan al-Banna founded the Muslim Brotherhood. As we have seen (see Chapter 1), the Brotherhood arose alongside the Free Officers movement and held many of the same political views that propelled the young soldiers to seize power in 1952. Once in power, the military struggled to deal with the Muslim Brotherhood and offshoot Islamic groups, courting their favor at certain periods and endeavoring to repress them at other moments. Eventually radical Islamists would assassinate Sadat.

Perhaps the most influential voice after Banna's assassination, certainly the most radical voice, belonged to Sayyid Qutb, whose call for violence against godless regimes like the Nasser government in Egypt, led to his imprisonment and eventually his execution in 1966. Like Banna, he too had attended Dar al-Ulum, from which he graduated in 1933. Disillusioned by his experience in the United States, which he found to be a materialist and immoral country, he returned to Egypt as an apostle of Islam. He became editor in chief of the Muslim Brotherhood newspaper, *al-Ikhwan al-Muslimin*. At this stage, he did not propound violence but expected a reformist Islamic movement to enact legislation that would eradicate income inequalities and create a just and devout society. The secularism of the Nasser regime and its inability to empower the people radicalized him, as did the way in which the government handled his and others' dissent. He was one of the many Muslim Brothers rounded up and put in jail in 1954, and, although he was released briefly in 1964, the state rearrested him and had him executed in 1966. While in prison he wrote a pamphlet, *Milestones*, which was eventually smuggled out and distributed widely, and which contained a call for action from Muslim peoples. It stressed the need to oppose rulers who governed against Muslim principles. In his view, Islam's time had finally arrived. Western capitalism and godless Soviet communism had both failed, the first because of its exploitative imperialist actions, the second because of its atheism and repressive forms of government. "Any society that is not Muslim," he asserted, "is *jahiliyya* [functioning in ignorance of God's will] ... as is any society in which something other than God alone is worshipped. ... Thus, we must include in this category all the societies that now exist on earth."[3] Nor, in his opinion, could the Muslim community, the *ummah*, exist if any single part of the world was governed other than by the laws of God.

Given the fact that Sadat was entirely familiar with the reputation of the Muslim Brotherhood and their record of having mounted the strongest resistance to the government, his decision to free a large number of political prisoners, including many Muslim Brothers, upon becoming president appears puzzling on the surface. In fact, he had many reasons for doing so. Pragmatic considerations would have been paramount in his decision. In his view, much of the opposition to his presidency originated on the left, notably from Nasserites and pro-Soviet Communists and Socialists, against whom the Muslim Brothers could provide a counterweight. But personal religious and political beliefs were also involved in the decision to release political prisoners. To begin with, the president was committed to governing Egypt in a more open and accessible way than his predecessor had. When he burned the tapes that had alerted him to plots against his presidency (see Chapter 3), he also proclaimed that Egypt would benefit from freer, more transparent institutions and practices. His travels in the United States and Western Europe had persuaded him that democracy and free market capitalism offered more to Egypt than Soviet-style authoritarianism. Sadat took office believing that the radical departures that he contemplated, including aligning Egypt with the Americans, even signing a peace treaty with Israel, were also likely to compel him to move the country toward democracy.

But the decision to allow Muslim Brothers out of jail should not be seen purely in pragmatic and political terms. Sadat was an intensely religious person. Critics made fun of the blackened bump on his forehead, what in the Arab world is referred to as a *zabib*, the Arabic word for raisin, claiming that he used it for effect to win clerics and the religious element in Egypt and the Arab world to his side. Critics were also suspicious of his intentions when after the 1973 war Sadat proclaimed himself as "the believer president," or when he had the 1971 constitution state that Islam was the religion of the state, Arabic the official language, and "the principles of Islamic *sharia* . . . a principal source of legislation."[4] To be sure, Sadat used religion to enhance his image among the people and legitimize his presidency, but his personal religiosity is beyond question. If proof is required, one need only recall that one of the demands he made of the organizers of Camp David was that a private place be set aside for him to carry out his daily prayers.

Although the Muslim Brothers did not constitute the most radical and violent wing of Islam, they often raised their voices with the many other groups protesting Sadat's policies. The Supreme Guide of the Muslim Brotherhood, Umar Telmesany, whom Nasser had imprisoned in 1954 and who became editor of the Brotherhood's influential and widely disseminated journal, *The Call*, which Sadat hoped would serve as a Muslim mouthpiece supporting the regime's policies, vigorously criticized Sadat between 1977 and 1981 for being too accommodating toward the Americans and their Middle Eastern client state, Israel, and for enacting free market policies that heightened income inequalities and led to hostility between the rich and the poor. *The Call* urged Sadat to draw more closely to other Islamic states and to revive the military option in Egypt's relationship with Israel.

Another source of trenchant criticism of the president came from independent Islamic preachers, many of whom took over mosques not fully under the influence of the state and used their oratorical skills to pillory the country's leadership. Although Sadat had succeeded in gaining the approval of some influential clerics, fatwas from state-appointed officials like that issued by the shaykh of al-Azhar and the minister of religious endowments in support of the Camp David accords and the peace treaty did not carry much weight. Nor did they prevent clerics from writing and preaching against these agreements. In Cairo, Abd al-Hamid Kishk, preaching in the Kubba Mosque, and in Alexandria, shaykhs Mahalawi from the *minbar* mosque of Ibrahim and Eid from the *minbar* of the Hidaya mosque accused Sadat of violating Islam, being corrupt, and bringing to power even more corrupt ministers and businesspersons. Their taped sermons circulated widely among the believers and included attacks on the president's wife for her views on family life and women's rights and for accumulating wealth illegally. An even more radical message came from the lips of Shaykh Umar Abdal-Rahman, a teacher at al-Azhar and lecturer in theology at Asyut University, one of the most vigorous centers of dissent against the policies of the state. It was Shaykh Abdal-Rahman who issued the fatwa that provided religious sanction to the men who carried out the killing of Sadat. In it, he claimed that striking at godless rulers, even in this case the president of the republic of Egypt, did not violate Muslim law. Although Umar Abdal-Rahman was arrested and brought to trial following the assassination of Sadat, he was acquitted, exiled from Egypt, and eventually moved to the United States, where he was imprisoned for his alleged involvement in the 1993 bombing of the World Trade Center.

The clerics were the external face of a rising radical and secretive Islamist movement that Sadat had not foreseen when he released political prisoners and which was to prove his undoing. The first group to emerge and to engage in violent actions was known as the Fanniya Askariya society, whose members were students at the Military Technical College in Cairo. They attempted to overthrow the government and establish an Islamic state in an ineptly planned effort on April 18, 1974. Security forces easily brushed aside their effort to seize college buildings in Heliopolis. A more serious threat occurred three years later in 1977 when another of these secretive Islamic groups, known as

al-Takfir w-al-Hijra (the Excommunication and Withdrawal society), kidnapped the Egyptian minister of al-Azhar and religious
endowments, Shaykh Muhammad Hussein al-Dahabi, demanding that the government release its imprisoned members. The
state refused, and the group murdered the minister. The murder
led the state to a hunt for the perpetrators of the crime, which
resulted in the arrest of 620 men, 54 of whom were put on trial
and 5 of whom, including their leader, Shukri Mustafa, were
executed.

The leader of *al-Takfir w-al-Hijra*, Shukri Mustafa, provides
an example of the issues that were driving groups to promote
violence in opposing the Sadat regime and to find ideological
foundations for their resort to violence within the tenets of Islam.
A graduate of Asyut University in 1942 where he had studied
agronomy, his involvement in politics and his ties with the
Muslim Brotherhood led to his imprisonment from 1965 to 1971.
Released like so many other Muslim political prisoners in 1971,
he believed that the power of the state could only be challenged
by equally determined rival power groups, willing to embrace
violence. *Al-Takfir w-al-Hijra* looked back to the days of the
Prophet, preaching, as Muhammad did in that period a withdrawal (*hijra*) from a godless society, a renunciation of false ways
(*takfir*), and a willingness to embrace militant action to overthrow the government.

Although the state repressed these two groups (*Fanniyya
Askariyya* and *al-Takfir w-al-Hijra*), it did not succeed in damp-
ing down the flames of radical Islam. The writings of Sayyid
Qutb circulated among young militant Muslims as did the tenets
of the late thirteenth-century and early fourteenth-century
Muslim scholar, Ibn Taymiyya (1263–1328), who had lived in
Syria at a time when that area came under Mongol rule. He wrote
in favor of carrying out a holy war (*jihad*) and argued that not
only was it allowable but it was also mandatory against rulers
like the Mongols, who in his opinion were governing in violation
of Islamic norms. Two of the groups that embraced these ideas

and that the state was unable to suppress, *Jamaat al-Islamiyya* (the Islamic Groups) and *al-Jihad*, were later involved in Sadat's assassination.

Not only did Sadat encounter opposition from radical Muslim groups but he also felt stings of criticisms from the Coptic Christian community, which found an energetic and aggressive spokesman in the person of Shenouda III, selected to be the 117th Coptic Patriarch in November 1971. Educated at Cairo University, where he studied history, he was, in the opinion of Mohamed Heikal, "the outstanding representative of the new generation of militant monks, determined to change the church from an isolated and backward institution into something more in tune with the contemporary world."[5] It was inevitable that Sadat and Shenouda, both coming to power with radical agendas at roughly the same time, would clash; Sadat courting the favor of Muslim leaders, and Shenouda ambitious to expand the influence of Christianity within Egypt and beyond. They argued over many issues, but the focus of their differences involved the Coptic hierarchy's plans to construct new churches at a faster pace than the state was prepared to accept. According to law, Copts had to gain state authorization before any new churches could be erected, and inevitably, because of normal bureaucratic delays but also because of opposition from Muslim groups, Coptic dignitaries believed that authorizations were not forthcoming in a timely fashion.

Sadat was drawn into the middle of these clashes and deeply embarrassed when on several occasions the Coptic leadership placed advertisements in foreign newspapers protesting the rise of Muslim extremism in Egypt and the failure of the regime to protect their community. Eventually, the tension became so extreme that Sadat took the unprecedented action of exiling Shenouda to the Wadi Natron monastery in the Western desert, charging the patriarch with attempting to set up a separate Coptic state with Asyut as its capital.

Muslim-Coptic tension culminated in a violent conflict in June 1981 when clashes broke out between the two communities

in Zawiya al-Hamra, a suburb of Cairo. The incident began inno-
cently enough, a dispute between neighbors over the construction of a tiny mosque on land owned by Copts that had been set
aside for the construction of a church. The anger spread beyond
the neighborhood, attracting the attention of National Democratic Party members, who sought to block the erection of a
church on the land. The army and police had to be called in to
quell violence, which left seventy-seven people killed, fifty-four
injured, and thirty-four weapons discovered.

A final issue that aroused opposition to Sadat and particularly inflamed many Muslims was the personal status law, which
the president enacted as a presidential decree in 1979. Known as
Jihan's law, because of the efforts made on behalf of it by the president's wife, it endeavored to reform existing legal provisions on
divorce, marriage, and custody of children. Egypt's personal
status law had been little changed in the twentieth century and
was based mainly on *sharia* law. Although the military regime
when coming to power had proclaimed its commitment to promoting women's rights, it had backed off changing existing *sharia*
laws that dealt with the family. In her memoirs, Jihan Sadat states
that her frequent contacts with families in Sadat's village of Mit
Abul-Kum had awakened her to the plight of Egyptian women.
Here, she was struck at the level of subordination of Egyptian
wives to their husbands and women to men, and she determined
to lend her weight to Egypt's feminist movement.

While adhering to the Muslim tenet that men could take up
to four wives and repudiate their wives, Law No. 44 of 1979 stipulated that women could obtain the services of arbiters if a conflict should arise over a divorce, require husbands to inform their
wives that they were divorcing them or taking another wife,
permit wives to pursue divorces on their own if husbands took a
second wife, and give wives custody of children until sons reached
the age of ten and daughters the age of twelve. The law also
imposed alimony obligations on husbands who divorced their
wives and allowed women to retain the family home while raising

the children. It raised the legal age of marriage from sixteen to eighteen. At the same time that Sadat enacted the personal status law, he also issued a presidential decree that increased the representation of women in the People's Assembly.

The personal status law was highly controversial. Admired by many women, it also brought criticism. Muslims, even those sympathetic to many of its provisions, were offended by its seemingly anti-Islamic tone. The women's organization of the Tagammu political party, known for its leftist and secularist orientations, opposed the law because it had been enacted through a presidential decree rather than by the People's Assembly and represented further evidence of Sadat's autocracy. And, in fact, the law was quashed by the Egyptian Supreme Court in 1985 on the grounds that the country was not in a true state of emergency at the time that the decree was issued and hence the president had exceeded his authority. Shortly after being set aside, the law, in a diluted form, was passed by the People's Assembly.

A considerable part of the opposition to Jihan's Law, and to the president himself, stemmed from the ambivalent attitudes, at times bordering on outright hostility, to the president's wife. Beautiful, sophisticated, and ambitious for herself and her husband, Jihan had a penchant for alienating even those Egyptians who admired what she stood for. The contrast between Nasser's wife and her could not have been more striking. Tahia Kazim Nasser, daughter of a well-to-do Iranian father and an Egyptian mother, shunned the limelight. She believed that her main wifely duty was to provide a supportive home for a man of heavy responsibilities. She rarely appeared at public events. In contrast, Jihan was in front of the cameras and the press seemingly at every conceivable moment, visiting wounded soldiers in the military hospital during the 1967 and 1973 wars and championing the Egyptian nationalist cause whenever the opportunity presented itself. Sadat's decision in 1971 to confer on his wife the title of First Lady of Egypt was not well received in Egypt. It was viewed as an effort to exalt his wife's power and to make her over in the image of American presidential wives, even though no such tradition existed in Egyptian politics. Although she claims in her memoirs to have made her own clothes, few would have believed her, so elegant was her wardrobe. The couple, in their sartorial splendor, were seemingly unaware of how greatly their lifestyles separated them from the common people and grated on many Egyptians.

Sadat fought back as the groundswell of opposition became stronger, enlarging the powers of the government. Just as he had in 1973 in preparation for war with Israel, now again in 1980 he assumed the office of prime minister (May 15, 1980), reminding the population that he had become prime minister in 1973 in order to prosecute the war and now he was becoming prime minister to lead the country toward peace and prosperity. He also had the People's Assembly pass a law setting aside the requirement that a president seek office only two times and making him the president for life. Like much else at this time, he had this decree put before the population in the form of a referendum, which was overwhelmingly endorsed. Moreover, as Sadat's actions and decrees became increasingly controversial, he made more and more use of referendums, using them so that he could claim that the population did indeed endorse his policies.

As part of his campaign to reclaim control over the country Sadat enacted a highly controversial law, called the Law of Shameful Conduct. Debated in the People's Assembly on February 15, 1980, the law, though justified on the grounds that it would replace the state of emergency, in effect when Sadat became president, extended the powers that the state had possessed previously. Strong opposition to the law came from the Bar Association, which held a highly publicized meeting on February 15, 1980, attended by 2,000 individuals, including the country's foremost lawyers and judges. Mustafa Marei, one of the country's most highly respected jurists, an expert on constitutional law and a political activist whose career reached back into the pre-Nasser period, delivered a stinging rebuke of the law, which came into effect on April 29, 1980.

The Law of Shameful Conduct was a catch-all piece of legislation that criminalized a large number of activities and heightened the power of the state to regulate the behavior of its citizens.
The law prohibited such activities as advocating doctrines that
were in violation of divine teachings, opposing the state's political, social, or economic system, promoting class warfare, allowing children or youths to go astray, challenging popular religious,
moral, or national values, and broadcasting false or misleading
information that might inflame the public or threaten national
unity. It was to be administered by a special tribunal, placed outside the regular judicial system, called a court of values, on which
would sit seven members, of whom only four were professional
judges, the remaining three being government appointees. The
debate in the People's Assembly over the law was a spirited one
that ended in fist fights.

Even this draconian measure did not suffice, for on September
3, 1981, Sadat ordered the arrest and imprisonment of a large
number of persons whom he deemed a danger to the state. The
largest numbers arrested were radical Islamists, but many others,
who would hardly have qualified as radicals or enemies of the
state, felt the president's wrath. Among those trundled off to
prison was Mohamed Heikal, who was stunned when arrested,
even more so when he saw the heavily armed group of soldiers sent
to take him to jail. He was even more astonished to find himself
surrounded in prison by so many influential and sensible people,
including many ex-cabinet ministers, that he felt that he could
have constituted a highly qualified government from the prison
inmates. Sadat's actions convinced Heikal that he was seeing the
last act of a desperate ruler. Among those arrested were Fuad
Serag al-Din, the head of the New Wafd Party; Hilmi Murad and
Fathi Radwan, two highly respected intellectuals on the left; all of
the independent members of the People's Assembly; the leading
figures in the Lawyers' Syndicate and the Journalists' Syndicate;
and numerous Muslim preachers, including Kishk, Mahalawi,
and Eid, who had been so outspoken against the president.

Sadat took these extreme steps because he feared that the increased political instability and violence that Egypt was witnessing would provide the Israelis with an excuse to postpone or perhaps even to abrogate the terms of the Egyptian-Israeli peace, thus freeing Israel from returning all of Sinai to Egypt as it was obligated to in early 1982. Nonetheless, Sadat's actions also revealed the control he had lost over his country and for that matter over himself. He manifested his panic in a press conference that he held shortly after he had imprisoned his opponents. When questioned about his actions and asked whether in his meeting with President Reagan he had cleared these actions, he blurted out: "If this was not a free country, I would have you shot."[6]

Sadat's roundup of opponents was impressive, but not total. One of those whom Sadat said he was looking for was Abbud al-Zumur, a thirty-three-year-old lieutenant colonel in military intelligence and a known advocate of a religious revolution for Egypt like that carried out in Iran in 1979. He was high on the government's list of enemies because he was believed to be plotting against the president and the government. At the very moment that Sadat spoke, Zumur was, in fact, hatching plans to kill the president and topple the government. He found accomplices among younger, radicalized army officers, one of whom, Khalid al-Islambouli, a first lieutenant posted to Upper Egypt, had been selected to participate in the October 6 military parade celebrating the October War. Islambouli, a member of the radical al-Jihad group, had at first tried to beg off from the duty, but after his superior officer would not allow it, he recruited a small team of coconspirators and prepared them to carry out the assassination. A vital member of the group was Abdel Salam Farag, who became its spiritual and theological guide. Farag, who had studied the writings of fundamentalists and had himself written a number of small books that contained citations to the writings of Ibn Taimiyya and the Pakistani Islamist and proponent of jihad, Abul Ala Mawdudi (1903–1979), offered religious sanctions for the group's violent undertaking. In a tract, written in 1979 and entitled *The Neglected Duty*, he implored Muslims to engage in jihad against impious regimes. "The rulers of this age," he asserted, "are in apostasy from Islam. They were raised at the tables of imperialism, be it Crusaderism, or Communism, or Zionism."[7] Although a professional engineer rather than a military man, Farag elected to join the assassination team on the fateful day.

On the morning of October 6, 1981, the eighth anniversary of the October War, the Egyptian sun rose into a cloudless sky, holding forth the promise of a glorious day. Jihan Sadat recalls waking that morning refreshed, spared her usual feelings of dread for her husband's life, certain that he would be safe, surrounded by the Egyptian army, "his army," as he led his countrymen and women in a celebration of one of Egypt's proudest moments. She watched her husband dress, understanding the delight that he took in donning military uniforms. On this important day, Sadat chose to wear a specially designed tight-fitting German uniform, which he always finished off by carrying a field marshal's baton. Inadvertently, he left it behind, an oversight that did not displease his wife, who considered carrying the baton an unappealing and militaristic affectation. Even so, when the president first appeared at the viewing grandstand, wearing the blue and gold uniform, the star of Sinai emblazoned on his chest, with a broad green sash stretching from shoulder to waist, and knee-high brown leather boots, the audience, always accustomed to seeing their ruler well turned out, "gasped audibly."[8] The parade, which was 10 miles long, began at 11:00 a.m. Already by 1:00 p.m., the crowd was growing restless but was awakened and applauded joyfully as American Phantom jets and French Mirages F-1s roared overhead, ejecting colorful plumes of smoke. At that very instant, a military vehicle carrying the assassins stopped within 40 yards of the president's stand. Attackers tossed grenades to create confusion, and one of the group, an expert marksman, fired the first shot at Sadat, who had risen to greet the soldiers. This shot probably killed the president. But, because there was no response from the police, security guards, and body guards for

another thirty seconds, Islambouli was able to reach the edge
of the grandstand, where he continued to fire at the president
whose body had been belatedly protected by chairs hastily and
desperately thrown over it. Sadat was flown by helicopter to the
military hospital at Maadi, but efforts to revive him were unavailing. In all, Sadat and seven others were killed. An additional
twenty-seven were wounded, including Vice-President Husni
Mubarak.

In his trial, Islambouli, after boasting that he had killed the
pharaoh, said that the president had brought on his own death.
He had governed Egypt irreligiously, made peace with Israel, and
imprisoned Muslim dignitaries. Sadat's severest critics would
have agreed, arguing that although the assassins constituted only
a small group; they were not like the loners and deranged individuals who took the life of President John F. Kennedy and attempted
to kill President Ronald Reagan and Pope John Paul II. Quite the
contrary, their action, they claimed, sprang from the boiling resentment against Sadat and drew from a wellspring of hatred of
oppressive rulers that had led to the overthrow of the Shah of

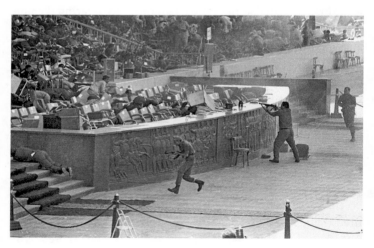

Sadat's assassination.

Iran. Resentment was, in fact, widespread, for the euphoria that had accompanied the October War had given way to complaints about the inability of the government's new free market, *infitah* policies to generate significant economic progress and about a separate peace with Israel, which had not produced as its peace dividend rising standards of living and economic prosperity, nor damped down the feelings of guilt and distress that Egypt's peace had come at a huge expense—Palestinian rights.

Yet, while Heikal and others were correct in stressing the hostility toward Sadat, undoubtedly major security failures lay behind Sadat's assassination and raised questions about whether anyone in power had colluded in the killing. Some of the failures are easily attributable to Sadat himself, the consequence of his egoism. He refused to wear body armor for reasons of personal appearance. He asked security forces and bodyguards to stay out of sight, and snipers, who usually stood on nearby tall structures to protect the president, were instructed not to be visible lest the presence of these groups reveal how disliked the president knew he was and how unstable his regime seemed. Flaws of overconfidence and hubris, which had manifested themselves repeatedly during Sadat's career, finally proved his undoing. But the president was not responsible for other failures on that day, the most obvious of which was the fact that the assassins' unit was not checked for live ammunition. Nor is Heikal's implication that Egypt was on the verge of a regime change correct. The assassins hoped that slaying the president would lead to an uprising, hopes that were quickly dashed. Fellow conspirators attempted to seize power in Asyut but failed utterly. Power passed to Sadat's vice president, Husni Mubarak, who continued his predecessor's policies, including the peace agreement with Israel, the free market orientation of the economy, and the reliance on the United States in economic and foreign policy matters.

CHAPTER 8

| SADAT ON THE WORLD STAGE |

AT THE SADAT AND BEGIN presentation ceremonies for the Nobel Peace Prize for 1978, Aase Lionaes, chairman of the Norwegian Nobel Committee, commended the two recipients "for their contribution to the two-frame agreements on peace in the Middle East and on peace between Egypt and Israel, which were signed at Camp David on September 17, 1978," adding that "never has the Peace Prize expressed a greater or more audacious hope—a hope for peace for the people of Egypt, for the people of Israel, and for all the peoples of the strife-torn and war-ravaged Middle East." Sadat's and Begin's acceptance speeches were entirely predictable, yet also highly revealing of what each individual believed that he and his country had achieved in the Camp David accords. Sadat's speech, read by his friend and government colleague Sayyid Marei, praised Jimmy Carter for "his signal efforts to overcome obstacles in the way of peace" and returned to the themes of peace and the horrors of warfare that Sadat had emphasized in his remarks to the Israeli Knesset in 1977. Again, he spoke passionately about how wars destroyed lives, left wives as widows, and deprived innocent children of their parents. He made no mention of his corecipient, in marked contrast to Begin, who spoke generously of Sadat and congratulated the Egyptian president on receiving the award, surely an indication of Sadat's distaste for the Israeli president. As expected, Begin, who delivered his own remarks, gave a capsule account of Zionism and the creation of the state of Israel, presenting himself as "one of the generation of the Holocaust and Redemption."[1]

The announcement of the prize received mixed reviews. In applauding the choices, Henry Kissinger stated that Sadat and Begin had "demonstrated the moral fact that the greatest triumph lies not in their victories over other nations but in their reconciliations." Others were offended. The left-wing activist Noam Chomsky, professor of linguistics at the Massachusetts Institute of Technology, said that awarding the prize to individuals who had sacrificed the rights of Palestinians was "farcical," while the Palestine Liberation Organization observer at the United Nations declared that the award "is against the concept of peace and justice."[2]

The peace treaty between Egypt and Israel, prefigured in the Nobel Peace Prize and realized one year later, was indeed a singular moment in Sadat's presidency. Not only did it underline his importance as an international leader, it reshaped Egyptian foreign policy just as the *infitah* policies that he had introduced in 1974 reshaped the Egyptian economy, directing it toward free markets and private-sector initiatives. While Sadat's assassination could have led to a repudiation of his policies, his successor as president, Husni Mubarak, drew even more closely to the Americans in foreign policy and strengthened the country's economic ties to Western economies—directions that he steadfastly maintained for the next thirty years until Egyptian protestors forced him from office in February 2011.

Although Nasser's legacy, notably his commitment to pan-Arabism, his strident anticolonial nationalism, and his faith in the power of the state to improve the lives of common people, retains a hold on the minds of many in Egypt and elsewhere, it was Sadat's vision of a more open, more American-centered Egypt at peace with its major adversary, Israel, that dominated Egyptian developments for three decades after Sadat's death.

Sadat's ascent onto the world stage was neither predictable nor easily achieved. Whether Nasser ever regarded Sadat as a worthy successor remains unclear. What is not in dispute, however, is that those officials who had expected to remain powerful after Nasser's death and had agreed to elevate Sadat to the presidency, only after having been assured by Sadat and his supporters that he would build consensus as president, turned against him within the first year of his presidency. They botched their plans to limit his powers, even perhaps to remove him from office, in May 1971, a failure that gave Sadat opportunities to act even more decisively than he had to that point. After replacing those individuals who had aspired to power with persons committed to him, Sadat was ready to pursue radical new directions in Egypt's domestic affairs and foreign policies, even to challenge the main tenets of his predecessor. He turned first of all to Egypt's most compelling issue, the retaking of the Sinai Peninsula. The October War, with its spectacular early Egyptian military successes, accomplished Sadat's original goals, even though it ended in a military defeat. The war reinvigorated involvement of the great powers in Middle Eastern affairs and ultimately, after many twists and turns, led to the restoration of Egyptian sovereignty over Sinai. Next for Sadat was Egypt's beleaguered economy, where he sought to promote private-sector development and foreign investment. The *infitah* project, however, did not achieve traction. It did not attract the foreign investment of those countries that Sadat and his advisers had targeted—especially Middle Eastern oil-exporting countries that had expanding dollar reserves as a result of the sharp rise in the world price of oil in 1973. Nor did Egypt's massive bureaucracy ever embrace Sadat's *infitah* vision. Its officials used their offices to delay the applications of potential foreign investors and to protect the position of public-sector enterprises. Neither did foreign investors respond enthusiastically to the Egyptian opening. Foreign capital hesitated to place its funds in a country still at war; investors remembered the expropriation of non-Egyptian assets that had marked the Nasser policies of the 1950s and 1960s. Moreover, the *infitah* policies, which had the endorsement of the International Monetary Fund, the World Bank, and the American Embassy in Egypt, came under a withering attack during the January 1977 food riots, which erupted as a protest against the lifting of price controls on commodities that Egyptians regarded as essential to their existence, and that, to the rioters, reflected a level of foreign interference in domestic affairs reminiscent of the British period.

Still, the food riots did not deter Sadat from embarking on further radical policies. Indeed, they were a factor, though not the most important one, underlying his decision to go to Jerusalem in 1977 and to follow that stunning departure from longstanding Egyptian diplomacy by concluding the Egyptian-Israeli peace treaty of 1979. If they did nothing else, the riots persuaded the president that the country could not achieve economic progress without first ending its state of belligerency with Israel and strengthening its relationship with the United States. Although signing a peace accord with Israel ran the risk of alienating the rest of the Arab world, especially if the interests of the Palestinians were seen as being sacrificed, Sadat had confidence that his negotiating skills and the importance that other Arab leaders attached to Egypt would serve him well. His confidence was to be proved misplaced.

As a major figure in international affairs, Sadat represented a new generation of leaders in the decolonized world. In many respects, he showed the way to this new group of national leaders, the successors to the original architects of national independence: the Nassers, Nkrumahs, Nehrus, and Sukarnos, who had led their countries out of colonial rule and promoted pan-Arab, pan-African, pan-Asian, and pan-Muslim goals, and who sought to achieve Third World solidarity through neutralism in foreign affairs, playing off the superpowers against each other and believing that economic planning and a state-led economic development would generate prosperity. Sadat concluded that these policies had failed Egypt and were failing elsewhere, and, in

searching for new directions, he saw only a single way forward—
that of opening the economy to outside investment, stimulating
the private sector, and taking Egypt off its war footing. All of
these departures meant coming to terms with the Americans, the
stronghold of free-market capitalism and the staunch champion
of Israel. No doubt, a crucial part of this decision was Sadat's real-
ization, already prefigured in Nasser's last dealings with the Soviets, that the Soviets were not prepared to challenge America's
commitment to Israel and would not support their Arab allies to
the same extent that the Americans aided Israel. As he so frequently and colorfully, yet accurately, put it, America held 99 percent of the cards in the Middle East.

Sadat's ascent to power and the policies that he championed
contrasted sharply with the actions of his contemporaries in the
Arab world. Most of the men who ruled the Arab states in the
decade of the 1970s and beyond came to power through coups,
ruled ruthlessly, and clamped down heavily on freedom of expression. Rulers like Saddam Hussein in Iraq (r. c.1968–2003),
Muammar Qaddafi in Libya (r. 1969–2011), Gaafar al-Nimeiry in
Sudan (r. 1969–1985), Ali Abdullah Saleh in Yemen (r. 1978–
2012), and Hafez al-Assad (r. 1970–2000) and his son and designated successor, Bashar al-Assad (r. 2000–) yielded power only
after American intervention (Iraq), countercoups (Sudan), and
popular uprising associated with the Arab Spring (Tunisia,
Mubarak's Egypt, and Yemen).

Sadat's great strength as a global leader stemmed from his uncanny grasp of the new trends in international affairs. While his
left-wing critics believed that Egypt should strengthen its public
sector, arguing that state-promoted economic development had
failed in Egypt not for intrinsic reasons but because of easily cor-
rectable management flaws and an unsteady belief in state-led
approaches, he concluded that the future lay with an American
form of capitalism and that Egypt needed to reform its economic
institutions and practices in light of the impending global surge
of free market economics. Similarly, in international politics, the

Egyptian president also understood that, given America's dominance in international politics, Egypt and the rest of the Arab world could only aspire to gain back the territories lost in the Six-Day War with American support.

However pragmatic and realistic Sadat's policy departures are judged, they were not without gross miscalculations. He was carried away by the early successes in the October War and exposed his army to heavy, even catastrophic, losses when he ordered the rush to the passes on October 14, 1973. He allowed the International Monetary Fund and the World Bank to bully his government into removing the subsidies from many essential commodities in January 1977. Perhaps his most serious failure, however, was his inability to persuade his countrymen or even a single leader of the other Arab countries that his peace accord with Israel was in the best interests of the Arab world. The irony of his life was that while he gloried in his village and peasant roots, he fell increasingly out of touch with the ordinary Egyptians even as he became exalted as a leader of stature in the West. Exactly how he could have conveyed his message to Egyptians and the rest of the Arab world, a message that diverged radically from the bedrock of Egyptian and Arab foreign policy, is hard to imagine. Yet his failure to do so was palpable to the whole world. The resignations of three foreign ministers and his most highly respected military leader in protests over his journey to Jerusalem and his peace treaty with Israel provided irrefutable evidence that his policies, though in many ways essential to Egypt's future, failed to strike a responsive chord among the Egyptian people.

Sadat watchers characterized the man as a romantic, a mystic, and a visionary. Putting aside the pan-Arab dreams that had driven his predecessor, he embraced Egypt's separate, virtually unique historical identity. He was more Egypt-centered than Nasser, in many ways a true Egyptian patriot. But in moving Egypt away from the failed policies of the 1960s, his inability to bring his country along with him cost him his life.

The question of whether Sadat would have pursued the policies that his successor, Husni Mubarak, did had he not been struck down by assassins' bullets has rarely been raised. Mubarak has been portrayed as a more pragmatic, less confrontational version of Sadat, as the man who fully implemented Sadat's vision for Egypt's future without antagonizing the rest of the Arab community. But are these suppositions valid? Would Sadat have been as accommodating to the Israelis as Mubarak was? Would he have devoted so high a proportion of American aid to the Egyptian military, allowing it to become a state within the state and a powerful economic and financial force? Although he had the People's

SADAT AND VICE-PRESIDENT HUSNI MUBARAK REVIEWING THE TROOPS AT THE OCTOBER 6, 1981, MILITARY PARADE. *Mubarak was slightly wounded in the attack on Sadat. Mubarak became Egypt's President following the assassination and remained in office from 1981 until he was ousted in 2011.*

Assembly designate him as president for life, would he, in fact, have clung to power as zealously and eventually as desperately as his successor did? Early in his presidency he had argued that open, democratic governments were the wave of the future and required legislatures and presidents to be responsive to the wishes of the electorate and prepared to step aside to allow for new leadership. He justified being president for life because of the internal turmoil in Egypt and the possibility that the Israelis would use Egypt's political instability to refuse to return Sinai. Would he have stepped down after the return of Sinai? Begin's interpretations of the Camp David Accords and the Peace Treaty of 1979 outraged the president. Would Sadat have been less accommodating to the Israelis when the Israeli Defense Force intervened in Lebanon in 1982? Having argued that the treaty with Israel brought a peace dividend, would Sadat have allowed Egypt's military to siphon off the lion's share of American economic and financial support?

Many of these questions have come to the fore again as a result of the Arab Spring uprising of 2011 that removed Husni Mubarak and most of his political allies from office. In 2012, a new, democratically elected president took office. The government of Mohamed Morsi endorsed a great deal of the Sadat legacy. Morsi's successor and opponent, Abdel Fattah al-Sisi, seems even more committed to honoring the Egyptian-Israeli peace treaty and maintaining good relations with the United States. For the moment, at least, Sadat's radical departures from the stances of Gamal Abdel Nasser remain foundations for the Egyptian state.

PRIMARY SOURCE EXCERPTS AND STUDY QUESTIONS

THIS BOOK HAS SHOWN Sadat to be a highly controversial figure in Middle Eastern and cold war diplomacy. He appears not to have played a central role in the July 1952 overthrow of the civilian regime and King Faruq and the military regime led by Nasser that replaced the previous government. Yet he became Nasser's vice president just before Nasser's death and succeeded him as president of Egypt.

I.
SADAT ON NASSER

The two excerpts, one taken from the period when Nasser was in power (Revolt on the Nile) *and the other from Sadat's memoir* (In Search of Identity), *published in 1978 when Sadat was president and just before he negotiated his peace deal with Israel, reveal quite different views that Sadat had of the Nasser years. In the first excerpt, he was "all in" with Nasser, praising him as the indispensable leader of a transforming Egypt. In the later memoir, he was quite critical of his predecessor. Critics have seen sycophancy and bluster in these two views. But it is possible to believe that the years changed Sadat's attitude toward a man whom he had greatly admired at first but whose policies he concluded had increasingly led Egypt in wrong directions.*

(excerpt from al-Sadat, *Revolt on the Nile*, pp. 13–15)

In the year 1938, chance, or perhaps it was the providential scheme of things, brought together in the garrison of Mankabad, in the province of Said, a group of young officers who had recently graduated from the Military Academy at Abbasieh. We spent all day on manoeuvres, returning dog-tired in the evening to our tents. We sat around a camp-fire at the foot of Mount El Cherif and talked into the night.

We were young men full of hope. We were brothers-in-arms, united in friendship and in a common detestation of the existing order of things. Egypt was a sick country. The social and political unrest in Egypt was the theme of our debates.

Our days were sad, but the nights made up for it. One of our company was a manly and straight-backed young officer, nearly six feet tall, who was reserved and serious in manner. If we started a light-hearted conversation, it was invariably Gamal Abdul Nasser who interrupted to bring us back to graver topics. He had lost his mother early in life, and he bore the marks of that grief. . . .

What did Gamal Abdul Nasser say to us as we sat around the camp-fire on Mount El Cherif? His message to us was this: "We must fight imperialism, monarchy and feudalism, because we are opposed to injustice, oppression and slavery. Every patriot wants to establish a strong and free democracy. This aim will be achieved, by force of arms if need be. The task is urgent because the country has fallen into chaos. Freedom is our natural right. The way lies before us—revolution."

So, at the beginning of 1939, the officers of Mankabad founded a secret revolutionary society dedicated to the task of liberation. In 1942, the society was organised in sections, each composed of separate cells. The supreme command was invested in a Central Committee with a dozen members. All the revolutionary forces were controlled by this committee. The Committee made the plans. It was a secret assembly in the fullest sense of the word. It was the embryo of the Council of the Revolution which assumed power after the *coup d'état* of July 23rd, 1952.

The aim of the Committee was to establish by force a democratic and republican government, which implied the expulsion of the British from Egyptian soil and the destruction of the feudalist oligarchy which ruled our country. From the beginning, our movement attracted many adherents in the Army and in civil life, and it grew rapidly in influence and numbers. . . .

It need scarcely be stated that our organisation was illegal. We worked in darkness, awaiting the dawn. It was a long-term plan, and Gamal Abdul Nasser was to be the architect and the strategist. His energy, his clear thinking, his balanced judgment equipped him, more than anyone else, for this task. Gamal's wisdom preserved us from premature action and from many dangerous adventures. Revolutionary tactics demand patience and lucid thought. We proceeded cautiously. It was useless and dangerous to make ambitious claims if we had not the means to translate them into reality.

We swore an oath to remain faithful to our country and to work with all our strength for its regeneration. The Army had a right to intervene, since both the government and the opposition parties were incapable of ending oppression.[1]

(excerpt from al-Sadat, *In Search of Identity*, pp. 19 and 20, 77 and 78, and 123 and 124)

The circle of friends meeting in my room in the mess widened every day and the sessions expanded. I saw Gamal Abdel Nasser for the first time at one of those sessions, when his battalion moved to Manqabad. My impression was that he was a serious-minded youth, who did not share his fellows' interest in jesting; nor would he allow anyone to be frivolous with him as this, he felt, would be an affront to his dignity. Most of my colleagues therefore kept

1. Colonel Anwar al-Sadat, *Revolt on the Nile*. Translated by Thomas Graham. London: Allan Wingate, 1957, p. 13–15.

their distance and even refrained from talking to him for fear of being misunderstood. He listened to our conversations with interest but rarely opened his mouth. I immediately realized how serious he was and wanted to know him better. However, he had obviously erected an almost insuperable barrier between himself and other people. He kept to himself so conspicuously, in fact, that our relationship at the time never went beyond mutual respect, and even that was still from a distance. . . .

Some people have wondered how I managed to spend such a long time by Nasser's side. Having avoided ever clashing with him, and having been the only man among the 1952 Revolution leaders not to be harmed by him (I was the only vice-president at the time of his death), I must have been, they concluded, either too insignificant or too cunning. Such a naïve conclusion reveals ignorance of my nature. I was not a nonentity during Nasser's lifetime, nor was I ever cunning. All there was to it was that Nasser and I had been friends since we were nineteen. When he assumed the presidency after the revolution, I welcomed it. It made me happy to see my colleague and friend become president of Egypt. I experienced the same feeling when he became the leader of the Arab world and surrounded himself with an aura of glory. . . .

Nasser's blinkers were not easily removed when he suffered from such intractable inner "conflicts." As I was his friend, I am bound in duty not to reveal them; all I can say is that they existed. Nasser died without ever experiencing *joie de vivre*. He was always alert.

I hadn't as yet realized all the facets of Nasser's character. My love for him blinded me to the truth. Besides, one tends to judge others in terms of one's own character. I naturally trust everybody until some definite fact warrants a change of heart. Nasser (I later came to realize) suspected everybody and everything until there were facts to warrant the contrary; although in the circumstances of the complex life we lead, the contrary is rarely proved. . . .

I have said that Nasser was known to be suspicious by nature, especially when it came to his personal security. His pathological view of personal security was perhaps responsible for all the emergency measures taken at that time on an interim basis but later established and magnified into the rule rather than the exception. They came to constitute a nightmarish burden for the people.[2]

II.
SADAT'S TWO MOST SIGNIFICANT SPEECHES

Sadat gave numerous speeches and interviews, many of which have been collected and published. Without doubt, the two most important were the one that he gave to the People's Assembly on November 9, 1977, in which he said that he would go to Israel if it would bring peace to the region, and his speech to the Israeli Knesset on November 20, 1977. The most significant portions from these two speeches are excerpted here. Bear in mind that in his speech to the People's Assembly Sadat was laying out the year's work for the Assembly and only toward the end did he turn his attention to foreign policy.

SPEECH OF PRESIDENT ANWAR EL SADAT
at the inaugural session of the People's Assembly
November 9, 1977

In the name of God,
Brothers and Sisters,
Members of the People's Assembly,

2. Anwar el-Sadat, *In Search of Identity, An Autobiography.* New York: Harper & Row, 1977, p. 19–20, 77–78, 123.

Today, we inaugurate, with God's blessing, the second session of the legislative part of your august assembly. This year coincides with the 25th anniversary of the Revolution, which transferred the people from revolutionary law to constitutional law.

Since your first session, you have faithfully expressed the will of the people who chose you to be their honest representatives in the People's Assembly. Much has been accomplished by you in the past 94 morning and evening meetings that have stretched until they have almost merged in this new session. It is an event which highlights the experience the democratic framework of which is defined in the Constitution . . . represented in a totally responsible government answering to the People's Assembly, that has full rights of complete supervision. I attest that I followed the events that occurred under this dome and the dynamic endeavours of the Assembly's committees with great satisfaction and profound confidence that our democratic aims have found the right course for a healthy interaction between the various viewpoints. It has made me very happy, having been placed in the seat of responsibility as head of the united Egyptian family, to see that the Assembly's leaderships has been given the opposition the opportunity to express itself freely.

Brothers and sisters, Members of the People's Assembly,

Let us stop for a while and search our souls. Where do we stand today with regard to our experiment?

Here, in this hall, you have issued the party law, which is a legislative announcement of a new step on the road to a sound democratic life, a looking forward to a free interaction among views, as well as a sincere confidence in the need of the one family to listen to the views of everyone they choose, without fanaticism or prejudice, and what is better for the group and in the interest of the majority.

From these premises also you issued the law organising the relation between landlord and tenant, after long well-briefed

debates; you also amended the law of foreign and Arab investments and Free Zones in consolidation of the open-door policy;
then social insurances were extended to cover any deficiency in
employment or resources; you raised the minimum limit for
pensions.

Yours was not just slogans but practical accomplishments for
the sake of political and economic democracy in our land. I will
not try to review now what you have discussed and accomplished, because in your report for the last session there is ample
proof for all that the national action is on its true constitutional
course, adhering with great honesty to all the constituent elements of the concept of popular representation; from the view-
point of legislation and supervision and speaking out freely on
all events or challenges facing us.

There remains for me to lay before you and, through you, to
the people the whole picture of the external situation. As you
must be aware, since the people entrusted me with this responsibility, I pledged myself, feeling confident in Almighty God, in
myself and hopeful for the future, to devote all my thoughts and
actions to the national, patriotic cause. Nothing is closer to the
heart than liberating the soil of the homeland and restoring the
legitimate right of brothers of a sister country with whom fate
placed us in an indivisible unit showing a common destiny.

Egypt's destiny was and still is to bear the greatest burden in
any confrontation between the Arab nation and its enemies or
those coveting it. This is a tax that the Egyptian people accept will-
ingly out of conviction, and not surrendering to fate. It is a deliber-
ate choice as they are convinced of the need for struggle, while
fully aware of its serious consequences, unlimited dangers and the
sacrifices involved, whether material or on the battlefield.

You know well the successive efforts exerted in the last few
months with a view to holding the Geneva. Conference as soon
as possible and specially before the end of this year, provided
that prior to the conference the appropriate preparations are
made to ensure that the objective of the conference is attained.

Such preparations should lead us to achieve a peaceful, just and overall settlement within a reasonable time and prevent the conference from becoming an oratory platform or an arena for exchanging accusations and putting on record positions for propaganda purposes.

It is only fair to say that the United States played a major role in this respect, and that President Carter had devoted much of his time and attention to the problem, and given it priority over many other problems he faces at home and abroad. We shall always remember his attitude with appreciation because it reflects a deep and accurate vision of the nature of the conflict, its regional and international dimensions, and its possible repercussions throughout the world, should it remain unsolved. Moreover, the United States has a special responsibility with regard to this conflict, in view of the diplomatic, economic, political and military aid it gave and is still giving Israel. The most outstanding achievement of President Carter in this context might well be his grasping of the cause of the Palestinian people and his well-known influence within the U.S. society, had succeeded to obliterate the distort of over 25 years. President Carter was able, within a few months, to remove the blindfold from the eyes of the American people, and to place the Palestinian question within its true perspective, whether with regard to its political dimension, that is, the Palestinians' right to self-determination, and to their own homeland, or its humane dimension, namely the need to eradicate the oppression and injustice which befell more than one million Palestinians who were forcibly expelled from their homes and land and compelled to live in painful conditions.

As we approach this delicate stage, I must lay before you and before the Arab nation the broad lines which guide us in the liberation process. First, we do not fear any form of confrontation with Israel because we have given it its true size without any exaggeration; neither a ruthless all-powerful force commanding events at will, nor a weak entity with no will of its own. Israel has been restored to its normal size after the glorious October War. We have come to see it as an entity that can be taught to mind its limits and whose aggression can be repelled. However powerful and influential Israel is, and whatever the networks that operate on its behalf and heed its orders on the international arena, we do have elements of power that exceed by far any forces that Israel can mobilize against us.

You heard me say that we care little about procedural methods. Let me state clearly before our people, the Arab nation and the world at large that we are ready to go to Geneva and to sit for the peace talks, despite all the procedural impediments raised by Israel to deprive us of the opportunity by irritating us so that we will say «No», as we used to do in the past. To say «no, we will not go, » so that it can appear as the advocate of peace before the world.

I am ready to go to Geneva. You must have heard me say that I would go to the end of the world to spare an injury to one of our men, much more the death of one. Israel must be greatly surprised to hear me say that I am even ready to go to the Knesset and discuss with them.[3]

PRESIDENT ANWAR SADAT'S ADDRESS TO THE ISRAELI KNESSET
(November 20, 1977)

In the name of God, the Gracious and Merciful.
Mr. Speaker, Ladies and Gentlemen:

Peace and the mercy of God Almighty be upon you and may peace be for us all, God willing. Peace for us all on the Arab land, and in Israel as well, as in every part of this big world,

3. *Speeches and Interviews of President Anwar El Sadat, July-December 1977 vol 7, pt 2*. Cairo: Arab Republic of Egypt State Information Service. P. 367–369, 389–401.

which is so complexed by its sanguinary conflicts, disturbed by its sharp contradictions, menaced now and then by destructive wars launched by man to annihilate his fellow man. Finally, amidst the ruins of what man has built and the remains of the victims of Mankind, there emerges neither victor nor vanquished. The only vanquished remains man, God's most sublime creation,

I come to you today on solid ground, to shape a new life, to establish peace. We all, on this land, the land of God; we all, Muslims, Christians and Jews, worship God and no one but God. God's teachings and commandments are love, sincerity, purity and peace.

As I have already declared, I have not consulted, as far as this decision is concerned, with any of my colleagues and brothers, the Arab Heads of State or the confrontation States. Those of them who contacted me, following the declaration of this decision, expressed their objection, because the feeling of utter suspicion and absolute lack of confidence between the Arab States and the Palestinian People on the one hand, and Israel on the other, still surges in us all.

After long thinking, I was convinced that the obligation of responsibility before God, and before the people, make it incumbent on me that I should go to the farthest corner of the world, even to Jerusalem, to address Members of the Knesset, the representatives of the People of Israel, and acquaint them with all the facts surging in me. Then, I would leave you to decide for yourselves. Following this, may God Almighty determine our fate.

First: I have not come here for a separate agreement between Egypt and Israel. This is not part of the policy of Egypt. The problem is not that of Egypt and Israel. Any separate peace between Egypt and Israel, or between any Arab confrontation State and Israel, will not bring permanent peace based on justice in the entire region. Rather, even if peace between all the confrontation States and Israel were achieved, in the absence of a just solution to the Palestinian problem, never will there be that durable and just peace upon which the entire world insists today.

Here, I would go back to the answer to the big question: how can we achieve a durable peace based on justice?

In my opinion, and I declare it to the whole world from this forum, the answer is neither difficult nor impossible, despite long years of feud, blood vengeance, spite and hatred, and breeding generations on concepts of total rift and deep-rooted animosity. The answer is not difficult, nor is it impossible, if we sincerely and faithfully follow a straight line.

You want to live with us in this part of the world. In all sincerity, I tell you, we welcome you among us, with full security and safety. This, in itself, is a tremendous turning point; one of the landmarks of a decisive historical change.

We used to reject you. We had our reasons and our claims, yes. We used to brand you as "so-called" Israel, yes. We were together in international conferences and organizations and our representatives did not, and still do not, exchange greetings, yes. This has happened and is still happening.

Yet, today I tell you, and declare it to the whole world, that we accept to live with you in permanent peace based on justice. We do not want to encircle you or be encircled ourselves by destructive missiles ready for launching, nor by the shells of grudges and hatred. I have announced on more than one occasion that Israel has become a fait accompli, recognized by the world, and that the two super powers have undertaken the responsibility of its security and the defence of its existence.

Yet, there remained another wall. This wall constitutes a psychological barrier between us. A barrier of suspicion. A barrier of rejection. A barrier of fear of deception. A barrier of hallucinations around any action, deed or decision. A barrier of cautious and erroneous interpretations of all and every event or statement. It is this psychological barrier which I described in official statements as representing 70 percent of the whole problem.

Today, through my visit to you, I ask you: why don't we stretch our hands with faith and sincerity so that, together, we might destroy this barrier?

To tell you the truth, peace cannot be worth its name unless it is based on justice, and not on the occupation of the land of others. It would not be appropriate for you to demand for yourselves what you deny others. With all frankness, and with the spirit that has prompted me to come to you today, I tell you: you have to give up, once and for all, the dreams of conquest, and give up the belief that force is the best method for dealing with the Arabs. You should clearly understand and assimilate the lesson of confrontation between you and us.

There are facts that should be faced with all courage and clarity. There are Arab territories which Israel has occupied by armed force. We insist on complete withdrawal from these territories, including Arab Jerusalem.

Let me tell you, without the slightest hesitation, that I did not come to you under this dome to make a request that your troops evacuate the occupied territories. Complete withdrawal from the Arab territories occupied in 1967 is a logical and undisputed fact. Nobody should plead for that. Any talk about permanent peace based on justice, and any move to ensure our coexistence in peace and security in this part of the world, would become meaningless, while you occupy Arab territories by force of arms. For there is no peace that could be in consonance with, or be built on, the occupation of the land of others. Otherwise, it would not be a serious peace.

As for the Palestinians cause, nobody could deny that it is the crux of the entire problem. Nobody in the world could accept, today, slogans propagated here in Israel, ignoring the existence of the Palestinian People, and questioning their whereabouts. The cause of the Palestinian People and their legitimate rights are no longer ignored or denied today by anybody. Rather, nobody who has the ability of judgement can deny or ignore it.

Even the United States, your first ally which is absolutely committed to safeguard Israel's security and existence, and which offered and still offers Israel every moral, material and military support - I say - even the United States has opted to face up to reality and facts, and admit that the Palestinian People are entitled to legitimate rights and that the Palestinian problem is the core and essence of the conflict and that, so long as it continues to be unresolved, the conflict will continue to aggravate, reaching new dimensions. In all sincerity, I tell you that there can be no peace without the Palestinians. It is a grave error of unpredictable consequences to overlook or brush aside this cause.[4]

III.
FOUR CONTRASTING VIEWS OF SADAT AS A POLITICAL LEADER AND STATESMAN

Not surprisingly, Sadat aroused strong emotions in the individuals with whom he worked closely on domestic and foreign affairs. The American leadership, as revealed in the excerpts from Henry Kissinger and Jimmy Carter, held him in the highest regard. They considered him a shrewd, intuitive statesman, seeking to overcome Nasser's misjudgments and create a safer and more prosperous Middle East. His Egyptian opponents, as represented here by Mohamed Heikal, who helped Sadat succeed Nasser but eventually fell out with the president, David Hirst and Irene Beeson, journalists based in the Middle East, and Ismail Fahmy, a talented minister of foreign affairs, who resigned over Sadat's decision to travel to Jerusalem, thought that he sacrificed larger

4. "President Anwar Sadat's Address to the Israeli Knesset, November 20, 1977." Jewish Virtual Library http://www.jewishvirtuallibrary.org/jsource/Peace/sadat_speech.html. From Israel Ministry of Foreign Affairs, "73 Statement to the Knesset by President Sadat-20 November 1977," *MFA*, November 20, 1977.

*interests, especially those of the Palestinians, to Egypt's desire to
gain back Sinai and win the approval of the Americans. Heikal
also condemned Sadat for using his office to enrich himself and
his family members.*

(excerpt from Kissinger, *Years of Upheaval,* pp. 646–648)

In the years following that first meeting with Anwar Sadat in
1973, he became a world figure. At the time he was little known in
the United States, at best considered one of the many volatile
leaders in the Arab world whose posturing, internecine quarrels,
and flowery eloquence were as fascinating to contemplate as they
were difficult to fathom. But from that meeting onward, I knew
I was dealing with a great man.

I had the honor of working in tandem with Anwar Sadat for
the first few steps of his journey to peace. Then I left office and he
went on within a year to new, bold strides that I had thought
might take decades. When within sight of his dream, he was
murdered. Prophets perform their service by inspiring ordinary
men and women with their vision, but they pay the price of being
consumed by it. So the reader will forgive a brief diversion as
an appreciation of my fallen friend.

Isaiah Berlin once wrote that greatness is the ability to transform paradox into platitude.

When Anwar Sadat appeared on the scene, the Arab countries
had too little confidence in their arms and too much faith in their
rhetoric. The majority of them relied on the Soviet Union, which
could supply weapons for futile wars but no programs for progress
in diplomacy. Negotiations consisted of exalted slogans incapable
of achievement; the Arab countries seemed to want the fruits of
peace without daring to pronounce the word. The nations of the
West stood on the sidelines, observers at a drama that affected
their destiny but seemingly without the capacity to influence it.

Within a few years, Sadat overcame these riddles. When
he died, the peace process was a commonplace; Egypt's friendship with America was a cornerstone of Mideast stability.

By his journey to Jerusalem in 1977 he had demonstrated to all those obsessed with the tangible the transcendence of the visionary. He understood that a heroic gesture can create a new reality.

The difference between great and ordinary leaders is less formal intellect than insight and courage. The great man understands the essence of a problem; the ordinary leader grasps only the symptoms. The great man focuses on the relationship of events to each other; the ordinary leader sees only a series of seemingly disconnected events. The great man has a vision of the future that enables him to put obstacles in perspective; the ordinary leader turns pebbles in the road into boulders.

Sadat bore with fortitude the loneliness inseparable from moving the world from familiar categories toward where it has never been. He had the patience and serenity of the Egyptian masses from which he came. I visited him once in the simple house to which he regularly returned in his native village of Mit Abul-Kum in the Nile delta. For someone used to conventional topography, the unequivocal flatness of the countryside came almost as a shock. There was no geographical reference point, nothing to mediate between the individual and the infinite; one's relation with the universe was established through the medium of a pervasive, enduring mass of humanity. The population pressure in the village is a standard feature of the literature on the country. In Sadat's village, as I suppose in all villages of Lower Egypt, one sensed it almost palpably though one saw it only in the smoke rising from innumerable chimneys over the trees and hedges that screened Sadat's small property from his neighbors. A pensive stillness cloaked the activity one knew all around one; the rhythm of a civilization was intuited but neither seen nor heard. One felt strangely sheltered, as if in a womb. Sadat said to me once, seemingly enigmatically, that he felt most relaxed at dusk when he knew all the villagers were preparing their meals at home. Sadat's inner security and instinctive sense of his people's yearning for peace were periodically renewed at their source.

But there was also another Sadat not content with resting with his origin: a man on a restless peregrination around his beloved country. Mrs. Sadat once told me it was a legacy of his time in prison; he felt confined if he stayed so long in one place. Sadat's dread of confinement was not only physical; he felt psychologically ill at ease with anything that limited the meaning of life to the status quo. He raised his people's gaze toward heretofore unimagined horizons. In the process he accomplished more for the Arab cause than those of his Arab brethren whose specialty was belligerent rhetoric. He recovered more territory, obtained more help from the West, and did more to make the Arab case reputable internationally than any of the leaders who regularly abused him at meetings of the so-called rejectionist front. He moved his people toward a partnership with the West, knowing that a sense of shared values was a more certain spur to support than a defiance based on striking poses. And when he had thus transformed the paradox and solved the riddle, he was killed by the apostles of the ordinary, the fearful, the merchants of the ritualistic whom he shamed by being at once out of scale and impervious to their meanness of spirit.

Sadat's passion for peace grew in intensity and profundity as his mission proceeded. When I first met him, peace had been a tactic in the pursuit of Egypt's interests. By the time he died it had become a vocation in the service of humanity.

Early in our acquaintance, in a military hospital he was inspecting he spoke movingly to me of how much Egypt had suffered, how an end had to be put to pointless conflict, how he did not want to send any more men to die. Egypt needed no more heroes, he said. The last time I saw him was on a plane from Washington to New York in 1981, during what turned out to be his final visit to our country. He had begun his cooperation with us. He seemed a little tired and perhaps the slightest bit discouraged that our political process forced him at such short intervals to start over building confidence and explaining his vision. But then his old buoyancy returned. He was planning a week's celebration on the occasion of the return of the Sinai to Egypt, he said, at the end of April 1982. Perhaps I could join him for at least part of it, considering that we had started the journey together. And on the day afterward we might go to Mount Sinai; there he planned to consecrate the peace by building three chapels—Moslem, Jewish, and Christian—side by side. And then he and I could meditate there for a while.

But a statesman must never be judged simply as philosopher or dreamer. At some point he must translate his intuition into reality against sometimes resistant material. Sadat was neither starry-eyed nor soft. He was not a pacifist. He did not believe in peace at any price. He was conciliatory but not compliant. I never doubted that in the end he would create heroes if no other course he considered honorable was left to him.

Any simple assessment of Sadat is therefore likely to be mistaken. Dozens of visiting Americans were charmed by him. But he was also aloof and reflective and withdrawn. Like many men of power, he had an almost carnal relationship with authority. He could hold his own with small talk, but on deeper acquaintance it became clear it bored him. He much preferred to spend idle time in solitary reflection. Most of his bold initiatives were conceived in such periods of seclusion and meditation, often in his native village. I know no other leader who understood so well the virtue of solitude and used it so rigorously.[5]

(excerpt from Carter, *Keeping Faith*, p. 282)

Then, on April 4, 1977, a shining light burst on the Middle East scene for me. I had my first meetings with President Anwar Sadat of Egypt, a man who would change history and whom I would come to admire more than any other leader.

In preparation for his visit, I had been studying about him and his country for several weeks, reviewing the long record of our nation's involvement in Northern Africa and the Sinai region,

5. Henry Kissinger, *Years of Upheaval*. Boston: Little, Brown and Company, 1982, p. 646–648.

learning about the level of economic aid to Egypt from the United States and other countries, trying to understand Sadat's relationship to his neighbors in Africa as well as to Israel, and the potential that existed for improving Egypt's lot in the future—if peace and security could be brought to that war-torn country.

At the beginning of Sadat's visit to Washington I thought he was a bit shy, or ill at ease, because he was sweating profusely as we exchanged our first words together. But he told me he had been unwell, with chills in Paris and a high fever since he'd arrived in our country. Sadat's complexion was much darker than I had expected, and I noticed immediately a callused spot at the center of his forehead, apparently caused by a lifetime of touching his head to the ground in prayer. He didn't smoke very much, but he always wanted his pipe nearby, and was irritated when his aide was slow in delivering it to him.

It soon became apparent that he was charming and frank, and also a very strong and courageous leader who would not shrink from making difficult political decisions. He was extraordinarily inclined toward boldness and seemed impatient with those who were more timid or cautious. I formed an immediate impression that if he should become a personal ally, our friendship could be very significant for both of us, and that the prospects for peace in his troubled region might not be dead.[6]

(excerpt from Hirst and Beeson, *Sadat*, pp. xi–xii)

My purpose in writing this book will be served if people in the West start asking themselves questions—and if it helps them to find answers to their questions. They must ask why it was that a man so much admired in the West was so isolated in his own world; why the man whom Henry Kissinger had dismissed as a "bombastic clown" before the 1973 war should in the space of a few years become in the opinion of the same judge "the greatest since Bismarck"; why a man who was mourned as a heroic and

6. Jimmy Carter, *Keeping Faith: Memoirs of a President*. New York: Bantam Books, 1982, p. 282.

far-seeing statesman in the West found hardly any mourners among his fellow-countrymen; why a man who had for so long filled the television screens and captured the headlines should, so soon after his death, be almost completely forgotten. The West must finally ask why it is that foreign leaders whom it has taken so fervently to its bosom because they seemed to speak its language— Chiang, Suharto, the Shah, Marcos, Sadat, and many others— have so significantly failed to win the affection of their own people.

I know that what I have written will cause offence to some people in Egypt. Sadat's policies did benefit a small, privileged circle, and their fortunes must inevitably fluctuate with his reputation. But Egypt, like the West, needs to take a long hard look at what happened. La commedia é finita. The play is over. The stage is in darkness. The day of the superstar has passed, and ordinary mortals must learn to recognize and to live with each other.[7]

(excerpt from Heikal, *Autumn of Fury*, p. 183)

Not since the days of Khedive Ismail had Egypt been the scene of looting on such a massive and organized scale as it was during the last years of President Sadat. Corruption spread from the top of the pyramid of Egyptian society to the bottom.

At the beginning of his presidency Sadat had assembled all the close members of his family—brothers, sisters, nephews, nieces—and told them that he had no objection to their engaging in business, but if the slightest whiff of impropriety reached him he would deal ruthlessly with the guilty ones. If in the end this threat was never implemented, that is in part at least due to the president's own failure to distinguish between his public and private capacities. His generosity towards foreign politicians and others has been noted, and it must be assumed that this was not all a one-way traffic; Sadat was a receiver as well as a giver of gifts, but there is no trace of any of these gifts or record of them in any government

---

7. David Hirst and Irene Beeson, *Sadat* (London, 1981), pp. xi–xii.

department. What went out of the country was public property; what came in remained private property. It is therefore not surprising that others should have made the same confusion between public and private. Thus one of the president's brothers was able to tell journalists, while on a visit to Salonika in 1980, that he was proposing to invest $7 million in a textile factory in that town. He was not rebuked, nor were questions asked how someone who not long before had been an employee in a small concern came to have millions of dollars to invest abroad.

Cairo became a city of middlemen and commission agents, men from Europe and America and Japan in their neatly pressed suits and Gucci shoes shuttling between the luxury hotels and government ministries, wheeling and dealing on an ever-increasing scale. Now there were not only the importers of luxury goods but agencies in the public sector, including arms. No longer was the supply of arms a government-to-government matter; "diversification" opened the door to arms dealers of all nationalities. And now not only was there a proliferation of agencies but a new breed of "consultants," to be found in every sort of business enterprise, public or private. If Beirut in its boom years had been a caricature of Cairo in the final hectic days of the monarchy, Cairo had now become a caricature of Beirut before it was crippled by civil war.[8]

(Fahmy, *Negotiating for Peace in the Middle East*, pp. 12 and 13 and 274–275)

However, Sadat unexpectedly decided to receive me. I went to see him at the residence near the Barrage outside Cairo, where he often stayed, and spent with him not the customary few minutes but two and a half hours.

This was my first meeting with Sadat, and it was marked by extreme frankness on both sides. I was astonished by the

---

8. Mohamed Heikal, *Autumn of Fury: The Assassination of Sadat.* New York: Random House, 1983, p. xi–xii, 182–184.

openness with which he talked to me, expounding his views and asking for my opinion on a very wide range of topics. . . .

The most important part of our discussion centred on the possibility of a new war with Israel. Sadat told me that he saw no way out of the impasse with Israel other than by initiating a war. Strangely, he justified his decision to go to war by declaring, 'I want to awaken the Egyptian people.' I have to admit that I was rather shocked by this statement, not because I was against military action, but because I thought it too drastic a step merely to awaken Egypt. Furthermore, Sadat did not have any convincing answers when I asked him whether politically Egypt was ready for war. On the contrary, he was very critical of the internal situation. . . .

I left Sadat with rather mixed and confused impressions. He seemed to be a natural and sincere man, somewhat complex but not sophisticated, willing to say what he thought. But he also seemed to be very isolated, with no special relationship with anybody, in fact distrustful and contemptuous of those around him. He did not appear to have any clear ideas about long-term policies, but rather to be inclined to live from one day to the next, in fact from moment to moment, dealing piecemeal with problems as they arose. I was much more impressed by his human qualities than by his genius, and was rather apprehensive about what might happen to Egypt with Sadat at the helm. . . .

To my complete surprise, however, the moment I finished talking Sadat suddenly shifted back to his idea to go to Jerusalem and deliver a speech in the Knesset. It was inconceivable to me that he could revert to Jerusalem after talking about Geneva, a new Arab strategy and a new Arab summit, and after all the praise he lavished on me for my achievements in Tunisia. My shock became more profound when Sadat informed me that he had already instructed his press counselor, Saad Zaglool Nassar, to announce on radio and television at 8.30 p.m. that the president intended to go to Jerusalem and deliver a speech in the Knesset. For a moment I hoped that Sadat might be joking, so incredible did this entire story appear, particularly as he was going to pay a formal visit to Damascus on the next day, 16 November.

I reacted sharply to Sadat's words, and a very heated discussion ensued. We argued on the phone for over an hour. I again strongly objected to his decision to go to the Knesset after all that had been agreed and accomplished in Tunisia. I specifically reminded him of his anger at Begin's address to the Egyptian people and of his own request that I prepare a very strong rebuttal to what Begin had said. Then, I inquired of President Sadat whether, during my stay in Tunisia, he had received any new concrete proposals justifying the revival of the idea to go to Jerusalem. He informed me that there was nothing new whatsoever. Then I inquired of him: 'What new extraordinary development took place which induced you to think once again to go to Jerusalem in spite of the fact that you still have nothing concrete on the basis of which you can justify our trip?' President Sadat had no answer.

I decided to try a different tactic 'Mr. President', I asked, 'is this a dictatorship or a democracy?' 'What do you mean?' he asked in surprise. I merely repeated my question: 'Is this a dictatorship or a democracy?' 'A democracy, of course,' he answered. 'Then I propose that you convene a small group of top officials, tell them of your plan and seek their reaction.' I went on to say: 'I promise that I will not say anything. If they agree with you, or even if half of them agree, I will go along with you irrespective of my personal objection. But if there is massive opposition to your plan, you should reconsider your decision.' Sadat became furious: 'Whom do you want me to consult?' 'Just the top people, the members of the National Security Council,' I answered. He almost lost control of himself, screaming, 'I will not discuss it with anybody, I don't care for anybody's opinion, I will not do it.'[9]

9. Ismail Fahmy, *Negotiating for Peace in the Middle East*. London & Canberra: Croom Helm, 1983, p. 12–13, 274–275.

STUDY QUESTIONS

1. Do you see Sadat as a transformative political figure in Egypt, Middle Eastern, and cold war diplomacy, and what is it that enabled Sadat to become such a transformative figure?

2. What is your view of Sadat's radically different attitudes on Nasser as a political leader?

3. What made these speeches so important in the framework of Middle Eastern and cold war politics? Do the speeches presage Sadat's willingness to sign a peace agreement with the Israelis, which he did only two years later?

4. Why were the Americans so infatuated with Sadat as a political leader and so deeply shocked at his assassination? Why did his peace agreement with Israel arouse so much opposition in Egypt, leading ultimately to his assassination?

FURTHER READING

Although Anwar al-Sadat was president of Egypt for only eleven years and died at the age of sixty-two, the amount of material on him is immense. Among the most important archival sources that cast light on his life are the records of the United States Department of State, to be found at the National Records and at the National Archives and Records Administration in Washington, D.C., and the archives of the International Monetary Fund and the International Bank for Reconstruction and Development (the World Bank), also based in Washington, D.C. Fortunately, some of the most important parts of these materials have been made available online or in published collections. In particular, the United States Department of State's *Foreign Relations of the United States* published a number of volumes that covered Sadat's presidential years (1970–1981), the most important of which, volume XXV in the series, contains 425 documents mainly from the American State Department archives that deal with the October War of 1973. The title of that volume is *Arab-Israeli Crisis and War, 1973*. Another valuable source is a digitized collection of important documents from various American government agencies, entitled the Digital National Security Archive, accessible at http://nsarchive.chadwyck.com/home.do. Professor Shibley Telhami, the Anwar Sadat Professor for Peace and Development at the University of Maryland, has made available at http://sadat.umd.edu/archives/introduction.htm a great deal of unpublished correspondence involving the Egyptian president and American government officials. The archive also contains copies of Sadat's most important speeches, video clips from his life, and an indispensable bibliographical guide to works written by and about Sadat. Compiled by Saliba Sarsar, it covered works written up to June 2003.

Sadat was a prolific writer, and though his books must be read with caution, they are invaluable for information on the events of his life and insights into his personality. The most important of them is his autobiography, *In Search of Identity: An Autobiography*, which since it was published in 1978 covers in detail the October War and the trip to Jerusalem but has no information on Camp David or the Egyptian-Israeli peace treaty of 1979. In it, Sadat is highly critical of his friend and predecessor as president, Gamal Abdel Nasser, and therefore must be read alongside Sadat's earlier writings that sing the praises of Nasser. His book, *Revolt on the Nile* (London, 1957), which also appeared in a slightly different form in Arabic (*Qissa al-Thawrah Kamila*) (Cairo, 1965), championed the early achievements of the military and extolled its ideology. Even more effusive in their praise of *al-Rais* (the boss in Arabic, in other words, Nasser) are two polemics that he wrote—*Ya Waladi, Hadha 'Ammuk Jamal* (*O, My Son, Here Is Your Uncle, Gamal*) (Cairo, 1957) and *Asrar al-Thawra al-Misriya* (*Secrets of the Egyptian Revolution*) (Cairo, 1965). Raphael Israeli, a professor of Islamic, Middle Eastern, and Chinese History at Hebrew University, brought together the texts of speeches, press conferences, and interviews that Sadat gave between 1970 and 1976 in three volumes: *The Public Diary of President Sadat: Part One: The Road to War, October 1970–October 1973* (Leiden, 1978); *Part Two: The Road of Diplomacy: The Continuation of War by Other Means, November 1973–May 1975* (Leiden, 1979); and *Part Three: The Road of Pragmatism, June 1975 to October 1976* (Leiden, 1979). Professor Israeli also published a laudatory biography of Sadat, *Man of Defiance: A Political Biography of Anwar Sadat* (London, 1985). The Egyptian Ministry of Information issued a multivolume collection of the speeches and interviews that President Sadat gave from September 1970 when he became president through 1978.

A list of publications by members of the Sadat family would not be complete if it did not include the radically different views of the man by two of the women in his life, in the first instance his wife Jehan Sadat, *A Woman of Egypt* (New York, 1987) and, second, his daughter by his first wife, Camelia Sadat, *My Father and I* (New York, 1985).

Oddly enough, no one has attempted a full-scale biography of Sadat, though there have been many detailed portraits of the man and his political career that for the moment stand in for the larger study. These works tend to present Sadat either as a heroic figure who defied all odds or a villain who sold out his countrymen and the Arab world. The extollers include the previously mentioned Raphael Israeli along with Joseph Finklestone, *Anwar Sadat: Visionary Who Dared* (London, 1996). His detractors are David Hirst and Irene Beeson, *Sadat* (London, 1981) and Mohamed Heikal, *Autumn of Fury: The Assassination of Sadat* (New York, 1983). Of course, Sadat is dealt with in many studies, two of which, written by individuals who knew him well and were sympathetic to his political leadership, at least at first, are worth noting: Muhammad 'Abd al-Salam al-Zayyat, *Al-Sadat: Mudhakkirat* (*Sadat: Memoirs*) (Cairo, 1989) and Musa Sabri, *Al-Sadat* (Cairo, 1985). One should also consult the memoirs of Sayyid Mar'i, *Awraq Siyasiya* (*Political Pages*), volume three, *Ma'a al Rais Anwar al-Sadat* (*With President Anwar al-Sadat*) (Cairo, 1979).

Many scholars have catalogued the rise of the Egyptian military to power. The first on the scene and still one of the best was P. J. Vatikiotis, *The Egyptian Army in Politics* (Bloomington, IN, 1961), a work that he followed with an equally compelling study of the ideological commitments and formative influences on the young officers who seized power in 1952—*Nasser and his Generation* (London, 1978). Many scholars delved into the life of Nasser, and I will cite only the two most recent works: Joel Gordon, *Nasser: Hero of the Arab Nation* (Oxford, 2006) and Said K. Aburish, *Nasser: The Last Arab* (New York, 2004). These works contain up-to-date bibliographies on this period and much information on Sadat's role in Egyptian politics in this era. The military rulers themselves, including, as we have seen, Sadat, eager to promote their reputations, wrote extensively about their coming to power and their exercise of power when in office. In particular, the following studies contain a great deal of information on the Nasser years and have many references to Sadat: 'Abd al-Latif al-Baghdadi, *Mudhakkirat 'Abd al-Latif al-Baghdadi* (*Memoirs*) (Cairo, 1977), 2 volumes; Ahmad Hamrush, *Qissa Thawra 23 Julio* (*The Story of the Twenty-Third of July Revolution*) (Cairo, 1974), 5 volumes; Khalid Muhyi al-Din, *W-al-An Atakallam* (*And Now I speak*) (Cairo, 1992); and Mohamed Naguib, *Egypt's Destiny: A Personal Statement* (New York, 1955).

Of the works that deal with the Nasser years, I limit myself to only a few, each of which contains bibliographies that lead to the voluminous scholarly literature on this period: Joel Gordon, *Nasser's Blessed Movement: Egypt's Free Officers and the July Revolution* (Oxford, 1992); Kirk J. Beattie, *Egypt During the Nasser Years: Ideology, Politics, and Civil Society* (San Francisco, 1994); and Robert L. Tignor, *Capitalism and Nationalism at the End of Empire: State and Business in Decolonizing Egypt, Nigeria, and Kenya, 1945–1963* (Princeton, 1998).

The Sadat era likewise has a plethora of scholarly studies, which I can only touch upon lightly. I begin with the political overviews, singling out Kirk J. Beattie, *Egypt During the Sadat Years* (New York, 2000); Raymond William Baker, *Egypt's Uncertain Revolution Under Nasser and Sadat* (Cambridge, MA, 1978) and *Sadat and After: Struggles for Egypt's Political Soul* (Cambridge, MA, 1990); Mark N. Cooper, *The Transformation of Egypt* (London, 1982); Raymond A. Hinnebusch Jr., *Egyptian Politics Under Sadat: The Post-Populist Development of an Authoritarian-Modernizing State* (Cambridge, 1985); and John Waterbury, *The Egypt of Nasser and Sadat: The Political Economy of Two Regimes* (Princeton, 1983). An Egyptian insider's view of these years comes from Mohamed Heikal in *The Road to Ramadan* (New York, 1975); *The Sphinx and the Commissar: The Rise and Fall of Soviet Influence in the Middle East* (New York, 1978); and *Secret Channels: The Inside Story of the Arab-Israeli Peace Negotiations* (London, 1996). Heikal was editor in chief of the semiofficial Egyptian daily, *al-Ahram*, as well as one of Nasser's closest confidants. He was influential in effecting the transition from Nasser to Sadat but had a falling out with Sadat and became one of his most outspoken critics.

The October War of 1973 has an enormous primary source literature. The place to begin is the two accounts written by leading Egyptian generals—Lt. General Saad el Shazli, *The Crossing of the Suez* (San Francisco, 1980) and Mohamed Abdel Ghani El-Gamasy, *The October War: Memoirs of Field Marshall El-Gamasy of Egypt*, translated by Gillian Potter, Nadra Marcos, and Rosette Frances (Cairo, 1995). Other accounts from the Egyptian side are Musa Sabri, *Watha'iq Harb Uktubir* (*Documents from the October War*) (Cairo, 1974), written by a man close to the Egyptian president, and Muhammad Hassanayn Haykal (Mohamed Heikal in English), *Harb Uktubir: 'Ind Muftaraq al-Turuq* (*The October War: The Crossroad*) (Beirut, 1990), a collection of talks and conversations that the author had between October 1973 and February 1974 at the height of the October War when Heikal fell out with Sadat. Egyptian diplomacy was in the hands of two individuals from 1964 to 1977, Mahmoud Riad, who was foreign minister from 1964 to 1972 and wrote *The Struggle for Peace in the Middle East* (New York, 1982), and Ismail Fahmy, foreign minister from 1973 until 1977, when he resigned in protest over Sadat's decision to go to Jerusalem. Fahmy wrote *Negotiating for Peace in the Middle East* (London, 1983). There are many accounts of the war from the Israeli side. Uri Dan's *Sharon's Bridgehead* (Tel Aviv, 1975) is a memoir written by a man who was with Sharon's division during the October War; also see Avraham (Bren) Adan, *The Banks of the Suez: An Israeli General's Personal Account of the Yom Kippur War* (Jerusalem, 1979). General Adan was in command of a northern division of Israeli forces in Sinai when the war began and was also involved in the crossing. The memoirs of Israeli military leaders and politicians are valuable for the war and also for the Sadat's visit to Jerusalem, the Camp David accords, and the Egyptian-Israeli peace treaty: Ariel Sharon, with David Chanoff, *Warrior: The Autobiography of Ariel Sharon* (New York, 2001); Moshe Dayan, *Moshe Dayan: Story of My Life* (New York,

1976); Golda Meir, *My Life* (New York, 1975); Abba Eban, *An Autobiography* (New York, 1972); and Yitzhak Rabin, *The Rabin Memoirs* (Boston, 1979). A crucial study of the war, based on captured Egyptian military documents and the most recent and in many ways comprehensive treatment of this conflict, is a work by Dani Asher, *The Egyptian Strategy for the Yom Kippur War: An Analysis*, translated by Moshe Tlamin (London, 2009).

The Americans and the Soviets became deeply involved in the war, even to the point of an American nuclear alert. Their principal actors have left records. The most valuable are the works of Henry Kissinger not merely because of Kissinger's crucial role in the war but because of his careful and copious use of American documents in these studies: *Years of Upheaval* (Boston, 1982); *Years of Renewal* (New York, 2000); and Matt Golan, *The Secret Conversations of Henry Kissinger: Step-by-Step Diplomacy in the Middle East*, translated by Ruth Geyra Stern and Sol Stern (New York, 1976). Also important are the memoirs of Richard Nixon, *The Memoirs of Richard Nixon* (New York, 1978) and Alexander M. Haig, Jr., written with Charles McCarry, *Inner Circles: How America Changed the World: A Memoir* (New York, 1972). The Soviet side is also represented in English-language works, notably in Andrei Gromyko, *Memories*, translated by Harold Shukman (London, 1989); Anatoly Dobrynin, *In Confidence: Moscow's Ambassador to America's Six Cold War Presidents (1962–1981)* (New York, 1995; and Victor Israelyan, *Inside the Kremlin during the Yom Kippur War* (University Park, PA, 1995), the last account written by a Soviet scholar brought into the Politburo just before this crisis erupted. Many of the American, Egyptian, Syrian, and Soviet principals reassembled for a review of these events, the results of which were published in Richard B. Parker (ed.), *The October War: A Retrospective* (Gainesville, FL, 2001).

Most of the information on Sadat's *infitah* policies comes from secondary studies but three works deserve mentioning. Fu'ad Mursi, an important left-wing Egyptian intellectual and commentator on political and economic matters, sums up the worries of many relating to the move away from a state-controlled economy in the direction of free markets and foreign investment in *Hadha al-Infitah al-Iqtisadi (This Is the Economic Opening)* (Cairo, 1976). The book by the economist, Khalid Ikram, *The Egyptian Economy, 1952–2000: Performance, Policies, and Issues* (London, 2006) is more than an overview since it was written by an individual involved with the World Bank in assessing the Egyptian economy during the Sadat years. Ikram was the coordinating author of a 1980 World Bank publication, *Egypt: Economic Management in a Time of Transition: The Report of a Mission sent to the Arab Republic of Egypt by the World Bank*. Much the same can be said of Galal Amin's book, *Egypt's Economic Predicament: A Study in the Interaction of External Pressure, Political Folly, and Social Tension in Egypt, 1960–1990* (Leiden, 1995), valuable because it represents the thinking of one of Egypt's outstanding commentators on politics and economics. Finally, Uthman Ahmad Uthman (Osman Ahmed Osman in English) became the face of the *infitah* as well as a close friend to the Sadat family. His memoirs, *Safahat min Tajrabati (Pages from My Experiences)* (Cairo, 1981) contains much information on the Nasser and Sadat eras from the perspective of a dynamic businessman.

The journey to Jerusalem, the Camp David meetings and accords, and the Egyptian-Israeli peace treaty produced an explosion of writing by the principals. On the Egyptian side, one should consult the accounts of two members of the Egyptian team, the two ranking officers in Egypt's foreign ministry, Mohamed Ibrahim Kamel, the foreign minister, *The Camp David Accords: A Testimony by Sadat's Foreign Minister* (London, 1986) and Boutros Boutros-Ghali, the Egyptian minister of state for foreign affairs and later secretary general of the United Nations, *A Personal Account of the Egypt-Israel Peace Negotiations* (New York, 1981). The Israeli accounts include those by Moshe Dayan, a member of the delegation at Camp David and Menachem Begin's foreign minister, *Breakthrough: A Personal Account of the Egypt-Israel Peace Negotiations* (New York, 1981); Ezer Weizman, also part of the Israeli delegation, minister of defense at the time, and the member of the delegation whose friendship with Sadat was invaluable in overcoming difficulties in the lead-up to Camp David, *The Battle for Peace* (New York, 1981). Moshe Fuksman Shaal's *The Camp David Accords: A Collection of Articles and Lectures* (Jerusalem, 2010) contains several accounts, written thirty years later, by members of the Israeli delegation. Nor were the Americans restrained in writing about their role in Camp David and the Egyptian-Israeli peace treaty of 1979. See, in particular, Jimmy Carter, *Keeping Faith: Memoirs of a President* (New York, 1982); William B. Quandt, a Middle East specialist, member of the National Security Council, and part of the American delegation, *Peace Process: American Diplomacy and the Arab-Israeli Conflict Since 1967* (Berkeley, 1993) and also his *Camp David: Peace Making and Politics* Washington, D.C., 1986); Cyrus Vance, the American secretary of state and member of the American team at Camp David, *Hard Choices: Critical Years in America's Foreign Policy* (New York, 1983); Zbigneiw Brzezinski, National Security Council director and member of the American team at Camp David, *Peace and Principle: Memoirs of the National Security Adviser, 1977–1981* (New York, 1983). The recent study of Camp David by Lawrence Wright, *Thirteen Days in September: Carter, Begin, and Sadat at Camp David* (New York, 2014) explores the intense and stressful negotiations that ultimately resulted in the Egyptian-Israeli peace accord. It also contains considerable background material on the personalities of the chief negotiators and the relations between Egypt and Israel leading up to the accord.

NOTES

INTRODUCTION

1. Henry Kissinger, *Years of Renewal* (Little Brown, Boston, 1982), pp. 648 and 649.
2. Jimmy Carter, *Keeping Faith: Memoirs of a President* (Bantam Books, New York, 1982), p. 282.
3. Andrei Gromyko, *Memories*, translated by Harold Shukman (Hutchison, London, 1989), p. 270.
4. David Hirst and Irene Beeson, *Sadat* (Faber and Faber, London, 1981), p. 355.
5. Mohamed Heikal, *Autumn of Fury: The Assassination of Sadat* (Random House, New York, 1983), p. 183.

CHAPTER 1

1. Anwar el-Sadat, *In Search of Identity: An Autobiography* (New York: Harper & Row, 1978), p. 5.
2. Mohamed Heikal, *Autumn of Fury: The Assassination of Sadat* (New York: Random House, 1983), p. 11.
3. Sadat, *In Search of Identity*, p. 15.
4. Anwar al-Sadat, *Revolt on the Nile* (London, A. Wingate, 1957), p. 13. One should also consult another of Sadat's early books, *Asrar al-Thawra al-Misriya* (Secrets of the Egyptian Revolution) (Cairo, Al-Dar al Qawmiyah lil-Tiba'ah wa-al-Nashr, 1965).
5. Sadat, *In Search of Identity*, p. 20.
6. Ibid., p. 22.
7. Ibid., p. 73.

CHAPTER 2

1. Sadat, *Revolt on the Nile*, p. 116.
2. Sadat, *In Search of Identity*, p. 119.
3. Raphael Israeli, *The Public Diary of President Sadat: Part One: The Road to War, October 1970–October 1973* (Leiden, Brill, 1978), p. 114.
4. Sadat, *In Search of Identity*, p. 138.
5. Ibid., p. 121.
6. Naguib, *Egypt's Destiny*, p. 208.
7. Ibid., p. 209.
8. Hirst and Beeson, *Sadat*, p. 93, as quoted in Ali Saber, *Nasser en Proces: Face a la nation Arabe* (Paris, Nouvelles Editions Latines, 1968), p. 108.

9. Michael Oren, *Six Days of War: June 1967 and the Making of the Modern Middle East* (Oxford: Oxford University Press, 2002), p. 47.
10. Guy Laron, "Stepping Back from the Third World: Soviet Policy toward the United Arab Republic, 1965-1967," *Journal of Cold War Studies* 12, no. 4 (Fall 2010), p. 101.
11. Sadat, *In Search of Identity*, p. 173.
12. Ibid., p. 172.
13. Ibid., p. 184.

CHAPTER 3

1. Matt Golan, *The Secret Conversations of Henry Kissinger: Step-by-Step Diplomacy in the Middle East*, translated by Ruth Geyra Stein and Sol Stein (New York, Quadrangle/New York Times Book Company, 1976), p. 36.
2. Mohamed Heikal, *The Road to Ramadan* (New York, 1975), p. 51.
3. Heikal, *The Road to Ramadan*, p. 87.
4. Sadat, *In Search of Identity*, p. 199.
5. Robert Springborg, *Family, Power, and Politics in Egypt: Sayed Bey Marei—His Clan, Clients, and Cohorts* (Philadelphia, University of Pennsylvania Press, 1982), p. 187.
6. Mark N. Cooper, *The Transformation of Egypt* (London, Croom Helm, 1982), p. 67.
7. Beattie, *Egypt During the Sadat Years*, p. 55.
8. Jehan Sadat, *A Woman of Egypt* (New York, Simon and Schuster, 1987), p. 253.
9. Israeli, *The Public Diary: Part One*, pp. 107–109.
10. Ibid., p. 253.
11. The full text of the note can be found in appendix I in Sadat, *In Search of Identity* and also in Mohamed Heikal, *The Sphinx and the Commissar: The Rise and Fall of Soviet Influence in the Middle East* (New York, Harper and Row, 1978), pp. 247–252. The texts are slightly different, and I have drawn from Heikal's text.

CHAPTER 4

1. Dani Asher, *The Egyptian Strategy for the Yom Kippur War: An Analysis*, translated by Moshe Tlamin (London, McFarland, 2009), p. 23.
2. Sadat, *In Search of Identity*, p. 244.
3. Yitzhak Rabin, *The Rabin Memoirs* (Boston, Little, Brown, 1979), p. 190.
4. No. 55, Memorandum of a conversation, May 12, 1973, *Foreign Relations of the United States 1969–1976: Arab Israeli Crisis and War* (hereafter *FRUS*), volume 25, p. 157.
5. Lt. General Saad el-Shazly, *The Crossing of the Suez* (San Francisco, American Middle East Research Center, 1980), p. 186.
6. Ibid., pp. 101 and 164.
7. Ibid., pp. 24–25.

8. Ibid., p. 234.

9. Ibid., p. 7.

10. *Speeches and Interviews of President Mohamed Anwar el-Sadat, January–December, 1973* (Cairo, 1974), pp. 363–369.

11. Ariel Sharon with David Chanoff, *Warrior: The Autobiography of Ariel Sharon* (New York, Simon and Schuster, 1999), p. 316.

12. Sadat provided many accounts of these events. A number of them were brought together by Raphael Israel, *The Public Diary of President Sadat, Part Two*, notably on pages 473, 475, 511, and 682. Musa Sabri, who was close to Sadat and an advocate for his policies, also has information on this matter in *Al-Sadat* (Cairo, al-Maktab al Misri al-Hadith, 1985), p. 350. Sadat offered the most extreme version of his position in his memoirs (*In Search of Identity*, p. 268), where he claimed that he was ready to "liquidate" the Israeli forces on the west bank by bringing the Second and Third Armies together, but he feared American intervention and decided instead to seek peace. He also mentions that later he had a conversation with Henry Kissinger, who agreed with Sadat that the Egyptians could have destroyed the Israeli army. But Kissinger added that had the Egyptians attempted to do so, "the Pentagon will strike you." There are no references to this conversation in the American diplomatic records.

13. Sadat, *In Search of Identity*, p. 263.

14. Musa Sabri, *Al-Sadat*, p. 360.

15. Alexander M. Haig Jr. with Charles McCarry, *Inner Circles: How America Changed the World: A Memoir* (New York, Warner Books, 1992), p. 412.

16. Sadat, *In Search of Identity*, p. 261.

17. No. 304, Memorandum from Secretary of Defense, Schlesinger, to President Nixon, November 1, 1973, *Foreign Relations of the United States* (hereafter *FRUS*), vol. 25, p. 804.

18. This important document is missing from *FRUS*, vol. 25, but exists in the National Security Archive, No. 51, Telegram from Kissinger to Scowcroft, October 21, 1973. In No. 225, Telegram from Kissinger to the US Mission to the United Nations, Kissinger did indicate that while the Americans did not want to delay discussions at the United Nations, "we do not have the same interest [as the Soviets] in . . . speed." *FRUS*, vol. 25, p. 646. In his memoirs, *Years of Upheaval*, p. 569, Kissinger mentions that he had "a sinking feeling that I might have emboldened them, in Israel, to gain their support, I had indicated that I would understand if there was a few hours' 'slippage' in the cease-fire deadline while I was flying home."

19. No. 241, Message from Brezhnev to Kissinger, October 23, 1973, and No. 246, Hotline Message from Brezhnev to Nixon, October 23, 1973, *FRUS*, vol. 25, pp. 676 and 684.

20. No. 262, Message from Brezhnev to Nixon, October 24, 1973, *FRUS*, vol. 25, p. 727.

21. No 267, Message from Brezhnev to Nixon, *FRUS*, vol. 25, p. 735.

22. No 268, Transcript of Telephone Conversation Between Kissinger and Haig, *FRUS*, vol. 25, p. 736.
23. Haig, *Inner Circles*, p. 416.
24. No. 269, Memorandum for the Record, *FRUS*, vol. 25, pp. 737–742.
25. Ray S. Cline, "Policy Without Intelligence," *Foreign Policy*, vol. 17, Winter, 1974–75, pp. 121–135.
26. Victor Israelyan, *Inside the Kremlin During the Yom Kippur War* (University Park, PA, Pennsylvania State University Press, 1995), p. 180.
27. Richard Ned Lebow and Janice Gross Stein, *We All Lost the Cold War* (Princeton, NJ: Princeton University Press, 1994), p. 266.
28. Raymond L. Garthoff, *Détente and Confrontation: American-Soviet Relations from Nixon to Reagan* (Washington, D.C., Brookings Institution, 1994), p. 435.
29. Ibid., pp. 251ff.
30. No. 284, Transcript of Telephone Conversation Between Kissinger and Dinitz, October 26, 1973, *FRUS*, vol. 25, p. 762.
31. No. 289, Transcript of Telephone Conversation between Kissinger and Dinitz, October 26, 1973, *FRUS*, vol. 25, p. 772.
32. Kissinger, *Years of Upheaval*, p. 647.
33. Richard B. Parker, *The October War: A Retrospective* (Washington, D.C., University Press of Florida, 2001), p. 129.

CHAPTER 5

1. Sadat, *In Search of Identity*, p. 245.
2. Hirst and Beeson, *Sadat*, p. 202, quoting Sadat's speech as reported in *al-Ahram*, August 27, 1974.
3. Galal A. Amin, *Egypt's Economic Predicament: A Study in the Interaction of External Pressure, Political Folly, and Social Tension in Egypt, 1960–1990* (Leiden, E. J. Brill, 1995), p. 6.
4. Israel, *The Public Diary of President Sadat*, Part Two, p. 1056.
5. Baker, *Sadat and After*, p. 23.
6. Ibid., p. 26.
7. Cooper, *The Transformation of Egypt*, p. 106.
8. Heikal, *Autumn of Fury*, p. 90.

CHAPTER 6

1. Ismail Fahmy, *Negotiating for Peace in the Middle East* (London, Croom Helm, 1983), pp. 74–75.
2. Jimmy Carter, *Keeping Faith: Memoirs of a President* (New York, Bantam Books, 1982), p. 282.
3. Cyrus Vance, *Hard Choices: Critical Years in America's Foreign Policy* (New York, Simon and Schuster, 1983), p. 174.
4. See the excerpted speech in the reading section of this volume.
5. Fahmy, *Negotiating for Peace*, p. 275.
6. Ibid., p. 13.

7. Boutros Boutros Ghali, *Egypt's Road to Jerusalem: A Diplomat's Story of the Struggle for Peace in the Middle East* (New York, Random House, 1997), pp. 13–14.
8. Moshe Dayan, *Breakthrough: A Personal Account of the Egypt-Israel Peace Negotiations* (New York, Knopf, 1981), p, 82.
9. Ezer Weizman, *The Battle for Peace* (New York, Bantam Books, 1981), p. 33.
10. Ibid., pp. 17–18.
11. Mohamed Ibrahim Kamel, *The Camp David Accords: A Testimony by Sadat's Foreign Minister* (London, KPI, 1986), p. 271.
12. Elyakim Rubinstein, "Thirty Years Since the Camp David Accords," *The Camp David Accords: A Collection of Articles and Lectures* (Jerusalem, Merkaz Moreshet Menachem Begin, 2011), p. 24. Justice Rubinstein was a member of the Israeli delegation to Camp David.
13. Carter, *Keeping Faith*, p. 322.
14. Kamil, *The Camp David Accords*, pp. 356–358.
15. Betty Glad, *An Outsider in the White House: Jimmy Carter, His Advisers, and the Making of American Foreign Policy* (Ithaca, NY, Cornell University Press, 2009), p. 150. The second part of that quotation comes from Rosalynn Carter, *First Lady from Plains* (Boston, Houghton Miflin, 1984), p. 263.
16. Vance, *Hard Choices*, p. 228.
17. William B. Quandt, *Peace Process: American Diplomacy and the Arab-Israeli Conflict Since 1967* (Berkeley, University of California Press, 1993), p. 446.

CHAPTER 7

1. Heikal, *Autumn of Fury*, p. 183.
2. Hirst and Beeson, *Sadat*, p. 211.
3. Gilles Kepel, *The Prophet and the Pharaoh: Muslim Extremism in Egypt* (London, Al-Saqi Books, 1985), p. 47.
4. Hesham al-Awadi, *In Pursuit of Legitimacy: The Muslim Brothers and Mubarak* (London, Taurus, 2004), pp. 36–37.
5. Heikal, *Autumn of Fury*, p. 162.
6. Ibid., p. 20.
7. As quoted in John Calvert, *Sayyid Qutb and the Origins of Radical Islam* (New York, Columbia University Press, 2010), p. 283.
8. Hirst and Beeson, *Sadat*, p. 11.

CHAPTER 8

1. The quotations from the Nobel Peace Prize award ceremony come from http://www.nobelprize.org/nobel_prizes/peace/laureates/1978.html.
2. These remarks were reported in the *Harvard Crimson*, October 28, 1978.

CREDITS

INDEX

al-Assad, Hafez; October War (1973)
  acts of, 93, 94, 95*f*, 101, 107–8;
  as Syrian president, 69
assassination; of al-Banna, 24, 26; as
  Muslim Brotherhood tool, 27, 42;
  Nasser escaping, 42; Reagan
  escaping, 196; of Sadat, 1, 2, 187,
  189, 194–97, *196*, 199, 223–24
Aswan dam; America against, 45–46;
  electricity from, 58; financing for,
  45–46, 58, 61; for industrialization, 123; Osman for, 135–36
*Autumn of Fury: The Assassination of
  Sadat* (Heikal), 3, 223–24

al-Banna, Hassan, 23, *24*; assassination of, 24, 26; capitalism wrong
  to, 21, 184; founding Muslim
  Brotherhood, 20, 21, 22; Free
  Officers with, 24; *al-Manar*
  inspiring, 20; missionaries wrong
  to, 21
Barak, Aharon, 162–72
Beeson, Irene, 218, 223–24
Begin, Menachem, *158*; at Camp
  David talks, 162–72; as detail
  oriented, 166; at Ismailia negotiations, 160–61; Knesset speech of,
  158; as Likud Party leader, 118,
  173–74; Nobel Prize of, 2, 175,
  198–99; Palestine undermined
  by, 179–80; as prime minister,
  149–50, 152; Sinai ceded for
  peace by, 168–69
boyhood; angry and poor in, 13, 14;
  idolizing military in, 15; Mit
  Abul-Kum in, 11
Brezhnev, Leonid; arms from, 63–64,
  80–81; détente of, 85; Nixon
  ceasefire dialog with, 108–9,
  111–13, 116, 118–19; October
  War (1973) ceasefire through,
  86–87, 107–12, 118–19
Britain; British-French-Israeli invasion (1956) of, 46, 55, 58, 70–71,

  132; Cromer of, 7–8; Disraeli of,
  9; Egypt colony of, 6–8; Egypt
  industry opposed by, 8–9; Egypt
  military under, 15; Nasser ousting, 46, 207; as oppressors, 8–9,
  12; revolution (1919–1922)
  against, 7, 12, 130; Suez Canal
  base of, 35–37
Brotherhood. *See* Muslim
  Brotherhood

Cairo, *145*; captured and imprisoned
  in, 25, 26–27; training in, 23
Camp David; Accord framework
  from, 1, 2, 4, 162–72, 172–73;
  Arab states repudiating, 175–76,
  179; Begin at, 162–72; Carter
  success formula at, 167, 174, 198;
  Egypt land issue key at, 78–79,
  99, 100, 145, 174–75, 200;
  opposition to, 3, 144, 175–76,
  179, 189–90, 223
capitalism; economic growth from,
  130–31; seductions of, 21, 184;
  Suez Canal symbol of, 20,
  35–36
capture and imprisonment, 25,
  26–27
Carter, Jimmy, 2, 147, 151, *158*, 218; at
  Camp David talks, 162–72; *Keeping Faith* by, 222–23; Palestinians
  key to peace for, 148; success
  formula of, 167, 174, 198
ceasefire, October War (1973), 86–87,
  107, 120, 143; Brezhnev and
  Nixon for, 108–9, 111–13, 116,
  118–19; détente undercut in, 117;
  Watergate crisis complicating,
  112–13
children, 26, 27, 30–31, 72, 135
Christianity; criticism from, 189–90;
  missionaries from, 21
client state war, 84–85
colonization, 6–8. *See also*
  anticolonialism

Free Officers; al-Banna with, 24; on
central committee of, 32; coup of,
1, 38–39, 42, 207–8; Nasser leading, 4, 16; reforms supporting,
34–35; vision lacking from,
57–58, 59
funeral; of Nasser, 3, 72; of Sadat, 2, 3

al-Gamasi, Muhammad Abdal-
Ghani; in October War (1973),
92, 100, 103, 144; shakeup
advancing, 90–91
geopolitics, 5, 6–7, 36
Germany, 2, 18, 19, 20, 25
Ghali, Boutros Boutros; at Camp
David talks, 162–72; in Knesset
delegation, 156, 158
government; America diplomatic
relations with, 138; Arab Socialist
Union and, 73–74, 129; Brotherhood prisoner release by, 185–86,
187; in Camp David Accord, 1, 2,
4, 162–72, 172–73; critics of, 3,
13–14, 68, 73–74, 181–82,
184–87, 189–90, 197, 218;
domestic reforms of, 64–65,
126–27; education reforms of,
46, 58, 178; Egypt-Israel Peace
Treaty (1979) for, 1, 3, 4–5, 86,
142, 161–62, 170, 172–73, 175,
176–77, 178–80, 185, 187, 199,
201, 203, 205; Fahmy in, 144–45,
151, 152–53, 218, 225–27; Fawzi
defense minister in, 67, 77;
foreign policy reforms of, 64,
126–27, 210–17; geopolitics in, 5,
6–7, 36; "go to the Knesset," 151,
152, 155–56, 157–59, 210–14;
al-Gumhuriya newspaper of, 45,
47, 50–51; infighting hindering,
48, 54–55; infighting in UAR, 52;
Ismail (khedive) as, 3, 9, 123, 181,
223; Israel diplomatic relations
with, 175; as largest employer,
131; left, center and right plat-

forms in, 127, 128–30; as loser
in Israel peace, 180; Marei in, 74,
77, 128, 192–94, 198; military
doubted in, 88–89; military for
future of, 35–37, 50; Mubarak
vice president in, 125, 156;
National Assembly speaker in, 51;
nationalism in, 7, 12, 16, 18, 22;
opponents arrested by, 193; overtures to America by, 72, 81–82;
overtures to Israel by, 72–73, 149;
as parliamentary, 19, 20, 50; president of, 1, 2, 3, 4, 45, 67–70,
192, 204, 205; reforming, 77–78,
126–27; as republican, 42, 207;
revolution in, 57–59; Sabri in, 68,
73–74; secret Israeli talks with,
149; sequestration by, 70–71, 132,
133, 136; Sinai I & II with, 120,
143–44; single-party state of,
124–25; solidified power over,
74–75, 77, 78; Soviet treaty with,
79; subsidies from, 138–42, 178;
successes of, 58; in United Arab
Republic, 51; vice president of,
4, 59, 66–67; war losses for, 56,
60, 133, 154
Gromyko, Andrei, 2, 116
al-Gumhuriya; as government newspaper, 45, 47; Naguib undermined by, 50–51

Heikal, Mohamed; as al-Ahram
editor, 47, 77, 125–26; as arrested
and jailed, 193; Autumn of Fury:
The Assassination of Sadat, 3,
223–24; as confidant/critic, 3,
13–14, 68, 181–82, 197, 218; as
IMF and World Bank critic, 140;
as Nasser confidant, 47; sidelining,
77, 126
Hirst, David, 2–3, 218

IMF. See International Monetary
Fund